Moments that Changed Us

Moments that Changed Us

Colum Kenny

Gill & Macmillan

Gill & Macmillan Ltd
Hume Avenue, Park West, Dublin 12
with associated companies throughout the world
www.gillmacmillan.ie

0 7171 3770 8

Index compiled by Cover To Cover
Typography design by Make Communication
Print origination by O'K Graphic Design, Dublin
Printed in Malaysia

This book is typeset in 10.5/13pt Minion.

The paper used in this book comes from the wood pulp of managed forests. For every tree felled, at least one tree is planted, thereby renewing natural resources.

A CIP catalogue record for this book is available from the British Library.

5 4 3 2 1

In memory of
Jimmy Curran

There is nothing I treasure more than a present of an artistic work, from the simplest piece of pottery to filling an empty space on my wall with a Jack Yeats.

TÁNAISTE MARY HARNEY, 3 NOVEMBER 1998

Ireland is a peculiar society in the sense that it was a nineteenth-century society up to about 1970 and then it almost bypassed the twentieth century.

JOHN MCGAHERN, THE OBSERVER, 6 JANUARY 2002

CONTENTS

RITUALS

PREFACE

'Ireland has changed so much in the last thirty years.' That is the kind of comment that is overheard, frequently, today. The words are spoken with a mixture of pride and anxiety, but mostly with relief.

In 1957, Hubert Butler of Co. Kilkenny complained that, 'Our island is dangerously tilted towards England and towards Rome, good places in themselves, but best seen on the level.'* Today, the influences of both England and Rome are much reduced, especially in respect of economic matters and personal behaviour. Our membership of the European Union and our generation of greater national wealth have facilitated the development of new perspectives. We may not know where exactly we are heading, or even where we wish to go, but we have a fair idea of the places to which we do not want to return.

If Ireland entered the modern world in the 1960s, as many of its inhabitants appear to believe, during the subsequent decades of the twentieth century we gradually matured as a country. From Ballilogue to Ballina, and from Derry to Dingle, Ireland was transformed and grew confident. It has been an exciting and disturbing period.

Particular moments marked our progress, either because the action of an individual burst upon our consciousness or because a moment somehow encapsulated underlying trends that were themselves the result of various cultural, social, political or economic shifts. In this book, I shall reflect on some of those moments and on what they have meant for Ireland. Have we really changed as much as we might like to believe, or is it at times a case of 'the more things change, the more they stay the same'? Certainly, some events that might have been expected to herald a fundamental restructuring of the political and moral order have yet to be seen to result in much more than a rise in the level of scepticism about public life.

When Gill & Macmillan invited me to write this book, they asked if I would be sure to include moments that have mattered to the

* In a draft section of his uncompleted autobiography, later published as 'The auction' at H. Butler, *Grandmother and Wolfe Tone* (Lilliput Press: Dublin, 1990), p. 19.

peoples of Northern Ireland. This I have gladly done, believing that what is significant on one side of the Irish border is likely to be significant also on the other.

The moments considered below have occurred during a period of remarkable growth in the population of the Republic of Ireland. This growth has been due partly to the fact that, given virtually full employment in recent years, people are now immigrating to the State rather than emigrating from it. Following the Great Famine, the number of people living in what is now the Republic of Ireland steadily declined from its pre-famine total of 6.5 million in 1841, until it reached a recorded low of 2.8 million in 1961. However, as the State's economy then began to expand, the number of people living here increased. From 1961, the population has risen by at least 43.5 per cent, although severe recession in the 1980s briefly interrupted that trend. In 2004, the Central Statistics Office estimated that (for the first time since 1871) more than four million people reside in the counties of the Republic of Ireland. One EU agency (Eurostat) predicts a continuing rise, to 4.9 million by 2025 and 5.5 million by 2050, in marked contrast to an anticipated decline or levelling off in the populations of most other European countries.

Very many people have helped me by providing relevant information for this book — far too many to thank individually. However, special words of gratitude are due to my wife Catherine, and to our sons, for enduring the author's moods as he grappled with Ireland in its contemporary guises and for lending support in various other ways. This book is dedicated to the memory of Catherine's late father, Jimmy Curran, who died in 1993 and who would have welcomed many of the more recent changes and revelations had he lived longer. At the same time, he would have maintained his sceptical attitude towards those in positions of power and influence, knowing that the human condition tends to give rise to new forms of old problems no matter how much we pride ourselves on our ability to change and make progress.

Bray, Co. Wicklow
1 May 2005

Sexual relations

Everything came at my beck and call
Till a woman appeared and destroyed it all.
A beautiful girl with ripening bosom,
Cheeks as bright as apple blossom,
Hair that glimmered and foamed in the wind
And a face that blazed with the light behind,
A tinkling laugh and a modest carriage
And a twinkling eye that was ripe for marriage.

BRIAN MERRIMAN, *The Midnight Court*, c.1780
TRANSLATED BY FRANK O'CONNOR, 1945

AN IRISH SOLUTION

Naas, Co. Kildare, 28 February 1979

He was sentenced to jail, and lost his pensionable job as a railway worker in Naas, Co. Kildare, because he sold a few condoms. This was Ireland in December 1957, when providing contraceptives was condemned as both a crime and a sin, rather than being regarded as a social service. To import or to sell condoms in the Republic of Ireland was a breach of section 17 of the Criminal Law Amendment Act 1935. Before sentencing him to two months' imprisonment and a fine of £20, Justice P. D. O'Grady said: 'I have given this case careful consideration and I look upon it as a very serious matter.' (*Leinster Leader*, 14 Dec. 1957) One month later, a senior counsel persuaded the Circuit Court to remit his prison sentence and reduce the fine to £10. However, not only did he not get his job back at Naas Station, but the local parish priest took steps to ensure that he would not receive the State pension for which he had worked for years.

No doubt some people genuinely believed that condoms were wicked in themselves, that their availability encouraged infidelity and undermined the stability of marriage, encouraged premature sexual activity among the young and increased the amount of unhappiness in the world. But the persecution of a railway worker was first and foremost a demonstration of the power of the Catholic Church, which had long wielded its influence in Irish bedrooms and which had used its ability to do so as a test of its continuing dominance. For too long in Ireland, sexual relations among the laity loomed large as the activity requiring the closest moral scrutiny by a celibate clergy. The faithful lived in fear of damnation for minor sexual acts, with even masturbation or the use of a condom thought to involve one's permanent separation from God and eternal punishment in the fires of Hell (unless absolved in the confessional).

The availability of the pill as a 'cycle regulator' helped greatly to change attitudes. It was an effective new form of contraception, but it could also be used simply to regulate a woman's menstrual cycle where that was deemed, for any reason, to be medically appropriate. This allowed doctors to connive with their patients by prescribing the pill while not needing to specify that it was being prescribed principally as a contraceptive. Many got around the law in this way. As a student at University College Dublin in the early 1970s, I recall female students making use of the professional services of two particular male doctors, who significantly enhanced their incomes by prescribing the pill, knowing well that it was required in fact solely for contraceptive purposes.

The Vatican and the Irish bishops attempted to make a theoretical distinction between what they called 'natural' family planning and other methods of contraception. The natural methods relied predominantly on gauging the time of the month or taking body temperatures. The artificial methods were ruled out, notably in 1968 by means of the papal letter, *Humanae vitae* (Of Human Life). The public did not accept that distinction. In growing numbers, couples used various forms of contraception to limit the size of the family or to delay having children until they felt that the time was right.

This use of artificial contraception was a remarkable phenomenon in that it indicated that Irish Catholics were consciously rejecting the official teaching of their own Church and deliberately engaging in behaviour which they were told was wrong. At the same time, thanks partly to statements by a minority of nuns and priests who disagreed with the Pope and the bishops, many such Catholics continued to participate in church ceremonies and even to share in communion. They could not, in conscience, hold that the use of science to control fertility was a sin when the deliberate use of various natural methods was not. One priest who paid the price for breaking ranks was Fr James Good, then professor of theology at University College Cork. When he questioned aspects of *Humanae vitae* in 1968, he was banned from preaching and hearing confessions in the diocese of Cork. He subsequently stepped down from the chair of theology.

As growing numbers began to use the pill, it became clear that there were political issues relating to its availability. The law looked increasingly sectarian in a country beginning to come to terms with diversity. Even those who were not Roman Catholics were effectively prevented from using contraception. Condoms were already on sale in Northern Ireland, a fact highlighted by a celebrated protest in 1970, when some women travelled the short journey by train from Dublin to Belfast and purchased contraceptives. On returning to Dublin they challenged customs officers at Connolly Station to arrest them for the illegal importation of contraceptives. The customs officers allowed the women to pass. This protest took place against the background of a growing feminist movement in Ireland, and in the context of the foundation of various family planning centres which steered a careful course around the provisions of the criminal law. In 1969, the Irish Family Planning Association had been founded (known until 1973 as the Fertility Guidance Company).

The pretence of treating the pill solely as a cycle regulator was inefficient, cumbersome and ridiculous. And the pill did not suit everyone: it had certain dangers. Condoms were more appropriate as a form of birth control for some couples. There was a growing demand that members of the public should have access to the contraceptive of their choice. However, politicians were extremely nervous about the possibility of a direct confrontation with the Catholic Church, and many themselves still held (or purported to hold) very conservative views in the matter. During the early 1970s, attempts to liberalise the law on contraception failed.

It took a legal challenge to begin to move matters along. In 1973, in the McGee case, the Supreme Court declared that the existing ban on the importation of contraceptives was unconstitutional because it interfered with the right to privacy of married couples. Subsequently, the coalition government led by Liam Cosgrave introduced in the Dáil a Bill that proposed to allow pharmacists to sell contraceptives, but only to married couples! However, in a bizarre and surprising twist,

Taoiseach Liam Cosgrave helped to defeat his government's own proposal when he and some other particularly conservative members of Fine Gael voted against it.

The next government succeeded in implementing the Supreme Court's judgment. By 1977, Fianna Fáil was in power and Charles J. Haughey was Minister for Health and Social Welfare. A married man, involved in a long-running extra-marital affair, Haughey set about finding a way around the bishops' outright opposition to legislation. He introduced the Health (Family Planning) Act 1979, which legalised the sale of condoms by pharmacists to people who had a doctor's prescription. Its full title gives one a taste of the tortuous thinking behind it: 'An Act to make provision for family planning services and, with a view to ensuring that contraceptives are available only for the purpose, bona fide, of family planning or for adequate medical reasons, to regulate and control the sale, importation, manufacture, advertisement and display of contraceptives and to provide for certain other matters.' On 28 February 1979, Haughey coined his infamous 'Irish solution to an Irish problem' phrase as he moved the second stage of his Bill in Dáil Éireann. He said:

> This legislation opens no floodgates, but it seeks to meet the requirements of those who either have no objection to the use of artificial contraceptives or who, having found other methods unsatisfactory, wish to utilise means other than natural family planning methods. It invokes the co-operation of the medical profession whose involvement in the provision of family planning services is the best guarantee of their availability and their successful implementation.
>
> It provides that those who find the provisions unacceptable need not involve themselves in any way. This Bill seeks to provide an Irish solution to an Irish problem. I have not regarded it as necessary that we should conform to the position obtaining in any other country.
>
> I commend the Bill to deputies on the basis that it will be found acceptable by and meet the wishes of the great majority of sensible, responsible citizens.

Haughey made a passing reference to 'commercial interests seeking their own ends', by which he may have meant investors in family planning clinics and the manufacturers of condoms. His Act was passed by the Oireachtas. People in Naas and elsewhere could now be legally provided with contraceptives. Yet, still, in 1983 a doctor was prosecuted under Haughey's Family Planning Act for supplying ten condoms directly to a patient outside the terms of the legislation. He was fined £500, although the fine was later lifted. Finally, in 1985, facing down his opponents, Minister for Health Barry Desmond, of the Labour Party, introduced the (Health) Family Planning Amendment Bill. This Bill, proposing to make contraceptives available without a doctor's prescription to anyone over the age of 18, was narrowly passed.

Today there are machines dispensing condoms in nearly every pub in Ireland. They are also now widely sold in chemists' shops without a prescription, as well as being openly traded at counters in record shops and elsewhere. Their availability was accelerated by the arrival of the AIDS virus, because condoms not only prevent conception but also act as a barrier against disease. Other forms of contraception are also now freely available.

Since 1979, Charles Haughey has defended his conception of an Irish solution to an Irish problem as being in line with political thinking in other states, which also adapt legislation to their peculiar circumstances. Yet many have mockingly deployed the phrase to refer to what is perceived within Ireland as a particular Irish propensity to address the need for social or political change indirectly, and to avoid openly confronting powerful interests. Such an approach simultaneously appeals to the vanity of those who believe that 'we do things differently here', defuses the anger of opponents by 'saving face', avoids the impression that we are simply following foreign trends, and allows us to square our consciences with our inclinations by not entirely and overtly adopting measures that the biggest Church in Ireland says are wrong. This last consideration has become far less compelling in recent years, not least because of various sexual scandals, and it is easy for younger people to underestimate the extent of the changes that have taken place in respect of both the provision of contraception and the authority of the Irish Catholic Church in sexual matters.

THE GRAVEL PIT

Galway City, 7 May 1992

In May 1992, Eamonn Casey resigned suddenly as Bishop of Galway and fled from Shannon on board an Aer Lingus 747, bound for New York. He left in a manner that was both quick and startling, and his departure was a catalyst for change. Following his hasty departure, it transpired that Eamonn Casey had made his bed (with a young Irish-American as it happened), but had not been prepared to lie on it. For years, single Irish mothers and couples who slept together outside marriage had been castigated or punished by some priests and nuns for their pregnancies and relationships.

Casey resigned on 6 May 1992. It was only when *The Irish Times* appeared the next day that the public began to understand what was really going on. That paper's reference to the bishop paying a woman in Connecticut made it clear, on 7 May 1992, that Casey had a past that was not entirely behind him. To the amazement of the public, it emerged that he was the father of Peter Murphy, and Peter was angry at Casey's failure to keep in touch.

In April 1973, Annie Murphy had come to Ireland as a guest of Eamonn Casey. She was recovering from the emotional consequences of the stillbirth of her first baby and the failure of her marriage, among other misfortunes. Casey, an old friend and distant relative of Annie Murphy's father, was already Bishop of Kerry. He met her at the airport, he in his mid-forties and she aged 24. He had last seen her when she was a child during a visit to his widowed sister in

Manhattan. Annie's parents had helped to care for Eamonn's sister and her children. Now Eamonn took Annie under the roof of his private residence at Inch, Co. Kerry. What followed in 1973 was the development of an intense relationship lasting many months and involving frequent trysts at a number of venues in Kerry and Dublin. Murphy has published a detailed account of their relationship.

As a priest, Casey had worked for years with Irish emigrants in Britain, building up a good reputation, especially for his efforts in helping people to get housed. Returning to Ireland, he crusaded about injustice in other countries but was not regarded as a threat to the Irish social order. He was Bishop of Kerry from 1969 to 1976, and of Galway from 1976 until 1992. He devoted much of his time and energy as bishop to campaigning for justice for the peoples of Latin America. He was chairman of Trócaire, the Irish Catholic agency for world development, and even managed to persuade his hierarchical colleagues to express displeasure at American foreign policy during President Ronald Reagan's visit to Ireland in 1984. The fact that Casey was able to persuade his colleagues to take such an unprecedented position on an international issue is evidence of the esteem, or even awe, with which they regarded him. Members of the hierarchy were struggling to find a way of relating to the concerns of modern Ireland in the aftermath of the Second Vatican Council and in the light of other changing circumstances. Popular, not to say populist, prelates such as Eamonn Casey seemed to provide a possible means of appearing 'relevant' while not having to change Church structures significantly or to engage in any radical thinking. It was an era of trendy and singing priests, whose desperate attempts to curry favour with the public would later be parodied by Dermot Morgan and his fellow comedians in *Father Ted*, the popular TV programme. The clergy had little space within their Church to be other than silently obedient or awkwardly populist.

Bishop Casey benefited from the wealth of the Irish Catholic Church, driving fast and expensive cars while hosting sumptuous dinners. He was also fond of consuming large quantities of alcohol, being arrested in London on one occasion for drunken driving. His taste for liquor was shared by another 'media-friendly' bishop, who also resigned later. In Brendan Comiskey's case, it was his handling of complaints of clerical sexual abuse rather than his fathering a child that prompted the fall. Their passing was not entirely lamented by some of their colleagues, who continued to cling vainly to the hope that life for the hierarchy might somehow return to an earlier era of staid normality.

My own contacts with Casey had not led me to regard him as a saint. He had rebuffed me twice as a journalist when I requested interviews, and on each occasion had done so on grounds that I felt were unreasonable. On the first occasion, I was attempting with an RTÉ camera crew to reach a Traveller family that was under siege from local people in their new home on a Galway housing estate. Having been personally assaulted by a mob, who set upon my car and punched my passenger in the face, I was astonished to hear on RTÉ a local parish priest giving an account of events which I considered to be both inaccurate and unfair to the Travellers. I contacted the then Bishop of Galway, Eamonn Casey, and explained to him what was happening, asking him to come down and see for himself. He accused me of trying to get him 'to make the news', which did not seem to me to be such a bad thing for a prelate who was considered a social radical in other contexts. He informed me sharply that he would depend for his information on his local priests.

On another occasion, Casey told me that he would not talk to someone who had 'treated my good friend Dermot Clifford' in the manner that he felt I had treated Clifford on national television. Clifford, who is today Archbishop of Cashel and Emly, was diocesan secretary when Casey was Bishop of Kerry. According to Annie Murphy, Clifford accompanied Casey when the bishop came to see Annie and Peter on their first return to Ireland. When Casey became Bishop of Galway, Clifford stayed in Kerry. Clifford later agreed to be interviewed by me for an RTÉ report about a controversy relating to the Kerry diocese's disposal of church property. The diocese subsequently made vigorous complaints about my report. My interview with Clifford was held to be fair by the independent Broadcasting Complaints Commission, but not by Eamonn Casey who refused to talk to me because of it.

Annie Murphy's account of her relationship with Casey is, clearly, just one side of the couple's story. What is certain is that their child, Peter, was not conceived during a one-night stand, as some may have assumed when they first learnt about the bishop's son. Theirs was no brief liaison. Ferrying her around in his official Mercedes, or his brand new Lancia imported directly from Italy, he had sex with her frequently and in a variety of places. These included his house at Inch where she lived for a while, and his apartment in Dublin where she also stayed. They also included the bishop's palace and a gravel pit outside Dublin. Her description of their heated coupling in the confined space of a fancy sports car on wet nights at a quarry remind us that they were passionately involved. Murphy believes that it was at the gravel pit that their son was conceived.

Her account of Casey's behaviour when Peter was born, and of the aggressive efforts that Casey and others made to convince her to have the child adopted, is very disturbing. Annie Murphy also suggests that the bishop may have had an earlier child by another woman and had that child adopted. She herself insisted on keeping Peter, although she claims that her health was nearly destroyed by the struggle to do so. Yet, even after all that, she was later to continue meeting the bishop and to have intercourse with him again when she returned to Dublin, as well as in New York.

Reading her *Forbidden Fruit*, which was written with the assistance of author Peter de Rosa and published in 1993, is a somewhat unsavoury and voyeuristic experience. However, it humanises the couple's story and prevents her being retrospectively cast as a 'temptress'. There were those who condemned Annie Murphy, despite the fact that Eamonn Casey issued a statement a few days after his resignation acknowledging Peter as his son. In 1993, she returned to Ireland to promote her book and appeared on Ireland's leading television programme, *The Late Late Show*. Its respected host, Gay Byrne, seemed uncharacteristically ill at ease, and even hostile.

In his statement of May 1992, after he fled Ireland, Casey confessed: 'I have grievously wronged Peter and his mother Annie Murphy.' He confirmed that for some years he had been sending regular if modest payments to the United States for Peter. He stated that in 1990 he had paid a lump sum of IR£70,669.20 from diocesan funds to Annie Murphy. He claimed that he had always intended to repay this. The lump sum was repaid 'by several donors' between the dates of his resignation and of his statement. Casey was spared the further indignity of a criminal investigation into the use of his church's funds.

Casey spent the first few months after leaving Ireland at a location in Hartford, Connecticut, just a short drive from where Annie and their son lived. They did not know this. Later, he went on to work in a parish in Ecuador, South America, before returning to Europe in 1998 to live in England.

DIVORCE

Co. Limerick, 24 November 1995

The result was close but decisive. On 24 November 1995, a majority of Irish voters decided that the ban on divorce should be removed from the Constitution of Ireland. There were fewer than 10,000 votes separating both sides.

In Britain and Ireland in the nineteenth century, divorce had been uncommon and required a personal petition to the parliament of the United Kingdom. Following the foundation of the Free State with its powerful Catholic hierarchy, the chances of legislation being introduced to allow divorce in an independent Ireland were nil. Article 41 of the Constitution of 1937 included the specific provision: 'No law shall be enacted providing for the grant of a dissolution of marriage.' Thereafter, for decades there was no practical possibility of the ban on divorce being challenged. Many Irish Catholics especially prided themselves on living in a country where there was no divorce.

A ban on divorce did not mean that all Irish marriages were happy. There were women who felt trapped in violent and abusive relationships. There were men and women who continued to live together but who no longer enjoyed any emotional or physical intimacy. There were couples who agreed to separate, some of whom travelled to other states for a divorce. The status of such divorces, if the couple were not actually domiciled in that other jurisdiction, was and remains even now legally weak in Ireland. As an increasing number of stories were published in the media about the failure of some Irish marriages, and about the problems of those who wished to form a second and more stable relationship, the demand for divorce grew. One reaction of the Catholic hierarchy to this development was to stretch the concept of nullity of marriage to breaking point, allowing a growing number of Catholics to be judged to have never really consented to their Church marriages. However, such decrees of nullity had no status in civil law and tempted citizens into relationships which were acceptable to their Church but bigamous or void in law. The psychological impact of such decrees of nullity on the children of couples who were granted them, and the consequences for offspring of any subsequent union, do not appear to have been matters of much concern to the hierarchy and others.

In 1967, a Dáil committee chaired by George Colley suggested that divorce might be made available for those whose Church allowed it. It was a well-intended if sectarian proposal, but it was not acted upon once it became clear that the Catholic hierarchy opposed it.

As arguments in favour of introducing divorce were heard with growing frequency, the Catholic bishops fought to counter them. In 1983, an anti-abortion amendment had been inserted in the Constitution. Recalling this on 1 September 1984, Bishop Kevin McNamara issued a pastoral letter in which he took the opportunity to rally those who were opposed to the introduction of divorce. He wrote in terms that were quite 'typical' of the hierarchy's position at that time:

> I want to refer briefly, however, to a danger that seriously threatens the family in our country at this time. It is the proposal, increasingly heard today, that steps be taken to introduce legislation permitting divorce and remarriage. Such a move would cause untold damage to the family and society. It is an inescapable fact that divorce breeds divorce. For this reason the Second Vatican Council has rightly described divorce as 'a plague'. As Pope John Paul II said in Limerick: 'Divorce, for whatever reason it is introduced, inevitably becomes easier and easier to obtain and it gradually comes to be accepted as a normal part of life. The very possibility of divorce in the sphere of civil law makes stable and permanent marriages more difficult for everyone. . . . May the Irish always support marriage, through personal commitment and through positive social and legal action.'

Do not listen, my dear people, to those who tell you that divorce in Ireland will be carefully limited to a small number of cases; that somehow or other, things will be different here from all the other countries where divorce has come in.

Once introduced into Ireland, divorce will lead to the same tragic consequences as elsewhere. It will lead to an increasing number of children who, because of the divorce of their parents and the remarriage of one parent or of both, will suffer greatly and may well be emotionally scarred for the remainder of their lives. It will lead to insecurity among those who are married and will make marital fidelity more difficult. It will lead sooner or later to an entirely new idea of marriage in our society, the idea of marriage not as a lifelong, unbreakable union, but as a provisional arrangement that may be terminated as required.

Nowadays divorce and remarriage is granted in many countries not only where one of the partners is seriously at fault, as earlier divorce laws provided, but simply on evidence of what is called irretrievable marital breakdown. This type of divorce, which is obviously easier to obtain and accordingly spreads more rapidly, has also had the effect of reducing maintenance allowances for divorced wives and their children, since the husband is not seen as being at fault and the courts, therefore, are reluctant to burden him with the costs of maintenance. Wives and children, therefore, suffer more than ever under this form of divorce, which has today become common. It is precisely this 'no fault divorce', or divorce based on 'irretrievable marital breakdown', we are now being told, which should be introduced into Ireland.

Let us be under no illusion about the devastating blow that a law permitting divorce and remarriage would inflict on the Irish family and on our whole society. God has made known to us his plan for marriage and the family and we disregard it at our cost. The State which prohibits divorce, therefore, is acting for the good of society. On a matter such as this the law of the land cannot be neutral; the State must either support marriage by forbidding divorce, or undermine marriage by allowing it.

The Pope's visit to Limerick, which Bishop McNamara recalled, had taken place on 1 October 1979. It has been described as 'the greatest gathering in the history of the city with an estimated 300,000 packing Greenpark Racecourse' (*Limerick Leader*, 1 January 2000). People came from all over the country and one banner bore the legend, 'Arise Knocknagoshel and take your place amongst the nations of the earth' (words which the *Limerick Leader* reported had first been used at a Parnell rally in Newcastle West a century before). Many people were in tears when the Pope eventually emerged from his helicopter. In the presence of the Bishop of Limerick, Jeremiah Newman, and leading clergy, he spoke of the value of the family and used the occasion to warn against abortion, divorce and contraception.

In the short term, Bishop McNamara and those who agreed with him succeeded. On 26 June 1986, a proposed amendment to remove the ban on divorce from the Constitution was put to the electorate by a Fine Gael/Labour coalition led by Garret FitzGerald. FitzGerald was widely respected as a socially liberal conservative, but his proposal was heavily defeated, not least because Fianna Fáil undermined the campaign for divorce in an effort to gain short-term political advantage. A total of 538,279 voted to introduce divorce, while 935,843 were against. Locally, for example, voters in Limerick East rejected the proposal by 27,440 to 14,879, and in Limerick West by 20,530 to 6,812.

In 1986, the anti-divorce lobby argued that divorce impoverishes women and children. However, research on the working of Irish maintenance law under the Family Law (Maintenance of Spouses and Children) Act 1976, published in 1990, revealed that Irish women after separation experienced identical problems to those experienced in other countries after divorce: low rates of maintenance combined with high rates of default. This showed that it was not divorce itself that left the women and children impoverished.

More difficult to assess were and are the emotional and psychological effects of divorce on children. Many children do not wish to see their parents divorced, even when there are continuing arguments and strains. However, their wishes and opinions tend to take third place after the wishes and opinions of their two parents.

Before a government again proposed deleting the divorce ban from the Constitution in 1995, a comprehensive package of legislation dealing with a broad range of family law matters was passed or published in draft form so that the public could fully inform itself of what was intended and be assured that the economically vulnerable might be protected. On the day of the second Irish divorce referendum, 24 November 1995, a total of 818,842 voted in favour of the proposed amendment to the Constitution, while 809,728 voted against it. Comparing the result of 1995 with that of 1986, the swing in favour of an amendment was greater than 13 per cent. One constituency that reflected both the narrowness of the result and its momentous nature was Limerick East. Here in the city of Limerick, the Catholic bishops had long wielded great influence and the local confraternity was known throughout Ireland for the uncompromising fierceness of its Redemptorist preachers. We have seen already that it was in Limerick, during his Irish visit, that the Pope cautioned against 'the very possibility of divorce in the sphere of civil law'. In 1986, Limerick rejected divorce. However, in 1995 the city voted in favour. Limerick East carried the amendment by 23,184 votes to 23,140, a margin of 44. The rural Limerick West still held the line with only 10,617 in favour, while 18,159 voted against, although even that was closer than nine years earlier.

As a consequence of the 1995 referendum, the ban on any law providing for a dissolution of marriage was replaced by a new provision in Article 41 of the Constitution, which states now that a court may grant a dissolution of marriage where, but only where, it is satisfied that 'at the date of the institution of the proceedings, the spouses have lived apart from one another for a period of, or periods amounting to, at least four years during the five years' and that 'there is no reasonable prospect of a reconciliation between the spouses'.

Opponents of divorce mounted a legal challenge to the result of the referendum, arguing that an advertising campaign funded by the government in support of divorce had improperly and materially affected the close outcome. They lost. Later, Dr Michael J. Breen of Mary Immaculate College at the University of Limerick studied the influence of the media on the two divorce campaigns and stated: 'Media coverage of the divorce issue in both referenda is insufficient to explain the disparate outcomes. Media coverage tended to be similar in both campaigns'. He believes there was 'an overall balance of content during the campaigns'.

On 18 January 1997, the first divorce under the new Family Law (Divorce) Act 1996 was granted to a middle-aged man who was said to be terminally ill and who had been separated from his wife for a number of years. Within five years, more than 11,000 marriages had been dissolved by divorce, and since then the number has grown steadily.

The campaigns for and against changing the Constitution to allow divorce were at times bitter. Yet, since the law was changed there has been very little public debate or discussion about Irish divorce or its consequences. It will require a number of sociological studies to determine what the children of divorced parents think about its impact on them, although it is difficult to know if they would have been emotionally better off had their estranged parents stayed together 'for the sake of the children'.

FROM CONFRATERNITY TO CELTIC BABES

Limerick City, 26 July 2000

Today, Ireland seems almost indifferent to sexual explicitness. We have lap-dancing clubs, sex shops, phone sex lines and racks of pornographic magazines of a type once banned. It would have been unthinkable not long ago. The authorities would have put a stop to women slithering up and down greasy poles. No Ann Summers outlet would have been permitted on our main streets.

What changed us? Until 1995, even *Playboy* magazine was regarded as too shocking and unacceptable to be allowed on sale in this State. Seán O'Faoláin, one of Ireland's most respected authors, regularly wrote for *Playboy*, but Irish customs officers seized copies of the magazine that were sent to him. Today, there are condom machines in local pubs and a pile of male fantasy magazines in most newsagents. Internet pornography defeats national regulators and censors. Liberalisation sometimes looks like confusion when we fail to distinguish between the erotic and the pornographic, and when women's bodies are treated as commodities.

On 26 July 2003, a newspaper profile of Dublin's lord mayor captured the strange way in which we now square our Irish Christian heritage with forms of sexual activity that were once anathema. At the time, Royston Brady was one of the rising stars of Fianna Fáil and would, in 2004, become a candidate for membership of the European

Parliament. With his clean-cut, shining visage, he could have slotted easily into the ranks of a pin-up boy band. Róisín Ingle of *The Irish Times* visited him at home, where she found a Sacred Heart picture and a St Brigid's Cross above his sitting room door. The lord mayor told her: 'I enjoy getting a good Mass.' However, the presence of traditional symbols of Irish Catholicism did not deter him from criticising the Gardaí for 'going over the top' in clamping down on Ireland's new lap-dancing clubs. He told Ingle: 'If they are a front for crime then deal with it. If it is legitimate then they are doing nobody any harm — let them off.' He said that he himself had sometimes socialised in lap-dancing clubs when he lived in America, and proclaimed: 'There are bigger issues to worry about.'

In the Ireland of Boyzone and naughty underwear, Royston was not afraid to nail his colours to the mast, even if an almost naked woman was writhing around it. His reluctance to be worried about the growth of lap-dancing venues seemed fairly representative of public opinion.

Lap-dancing clubs had already spread beyond Dublin. On 26 July 2000, even Limerick learnt that it was to become home to such a venue. According to a report that day in the *Limerick Leader:*

> The news was revealed as three girls revealed all this Wednesday night when the Celtic Babes took to the stage in front of hundreds of Limerick lads.
>
> Ashling and Lorraine from Dublin, and Cheyenne from France, performed their routine the night before an all-male strip troupe, the Celtic Knights, performed for hundreds of Limerick girls at the same venue.

Referring to Limerick in 1945, Frank O'Connor had said: 'Nowhere else in Ireland has Irish Puritanism such power.' The city of a most Catholic confraternity, once widely associated with priests preaching fire and brimstone, was now hosting a new kind of devotion. The promoter of the venture, who already owned one of three lap-dancing clubs in Dublin, told the local paper: 'Clubs in Dublin are taking in around £4,000 a week on the door and the Limerick operation will cover the Munster area, being the first of its kind.' He added:

> The girls travel from England and perform in lap-dancing clubs in

> Dublin, so they will travel down here during their visits to do the lap-dancing circuit. The club will be run responsibly, with no touching or no propositioning of the girls. There will be a certain slickness to it and it will be very professionally run, not seedy at all. The girls will be in town solely to do their job and will not socialise in Limerick.

However, on 28 October 2001, one English lap-dancer did socialise in Limerick with a young Irishman. Coming to perform in Limerick, pop-star Bryan McFadden and other members of Westlife had been entertained on their private bus from Dublin by Amy Barker and another English lap-dancer. Later, in Limerick, McFadden attended a private performance by Amy in a hotel bedroom. McFadden and Barker became briefly but sexually intimate.

A few weeks after that incident, McFadden's 'fairytale' wedding to Kerry Katona of Atomic Kitten was splashed across the pages of *Hello* magazine and widely reported elsewhere. Unfortunately for McFadden, within a few months details of his lap-dancing liaison were also spread across the British tabloids. Echoing Bill Clinton's infamous denial of 1999 that such a form of contact constituted 'sexual relations', McFadden at first implicitly accused Barker of lying. However, he later admitted that there was 'a sexual encounter' and reportedly reached an out-of-court settlement with her. The Limerick of *Angela's Ashes* was now also the Limerick of Amy Barker and her trade.

Lap-dancing clubs gradually became quite a socially acceptable form of business venture. For example, on 12 December 2001, Judge Katherine Delahunt of the Circuit Court dismissed Garda objections that Club Lapello's basement premises was in fact unsuitable for public dancing. Lapello had been the first Irish lap-dancing club. One Garda inspector informed the court that Club Lapello already had a 'respectable clientele', which he said was mainly an upmarket one, and the judge commented that there was no evidence that anything illegal was occurring there.

Some argued that the new attitudes towards sexual expression were healthier than those of an earlier Ireland. Few wished to return to the days of hysterical censorship, or to the sort of sexually repressed atmosphere that bred and then facilitated the denial of various sex abuse scandals. Many were inclined to laugh off lap-dancing clubs and the like as a relatively harmless expression of human nature. Some took full advantage of financial opportunities offered by the sex industry, with former IRA men reportedly running a protection racket for clubs and *In Dublin* magazine being prosecuted for advertising brothels.

Those who denounced the sex industry as a front for prostitution and for the exploitation of women were not reassured when it emerged that many of those employed in lap-dancing clubs were immigrants without permission to work in Ireland. During the summer of 2004, a woman was found decapitated in a Kilkenny field. The daughter of the chief justice of Malawi, she was said to have become involved in lap-dancing and prostitution while living in Ireland. Few if any Irish women join in the celebration of sexual liberation by securing employment in lap-dancing venues.

Surfing the web during 2004, a woman seeking work in Ireland could have read the following invitation. It described the Lapello as 'Ireland's first famous strip club' and 'the most professional and well-run club in Ireland.' It offered employment to UK and EEC [*sic*] dancers who were looking for a one-month contract, and promised to supply an elegant shared house with a gym:

> Top girls can earn very good money here if they know how to hustle for dances. Some girls can make up to $10,000 usd per month. We do not pay airfare, but we do supply accommodation and a clean, safe, no contact work environment. Lapello requires Artists with EU Citizenship, as we do not process visas for foreigners.
>
> Artists work 6 days a week (or 7 days), but this is up to the Artist. Our hours are 8 p.m.–3 a.m. Artist will perform 3 promotional stage shows per night — no nudity. Topless lap dances are 15 euro for one song. Artist can dance on the lap of the customer, but are not permitted to touch the customer in any other way, nor is the Artist permitted to let the customer touch her breasts or body with his hands. Artist brings elegant evening gowns, cocktail dresses, costumes and shoes, and her own music (if preferred). The contract is 30 days.

Although Lapello was said to be recruiting EU dancers, and there is no suggestion here that it has broken the law or that its staff have been involved in prostitution, some clubs were said to be less particular about the origins of their workers. In June 2003, more than one hundred people were arrested in overnight raids on a total of ten lap-dancing clubs in Dublin, Cork, Limerick, Galway and Dundalk. Operation Quest targeted clubs believed to be employing immigrants without proper working permits.

Lap-dancing clubs are big business, and those who own them take them very seriously. Our communities are touched as never before by the sex industry. It is in our face. Some of the women who work in it claim to be proud of what they do. Some can make big money, but many are poor and nearly all are foreign. That adds to the thrill for customers. One club that was refused a licence had not employed any Irish women dancers. Its operations manager told the court: 'It was policy to accept only foreign girls as most customers wanted the fantasy of seeing exotic dancers from abroad.' Fantasies about 'exotic dancers from abroad' are quite possibly racist and sentimental. They may be as much about power and domination as about sex. The dancers are not regarded as women who are equal in status to our mothers, wives or sisters. It is easier to imagine that these are just foreign sluts, perhaps already prostitutes, who will ultimately do anything for money and for the benefit of living in Ireland.

Lap-dancers play with fire by making money out of men's lust. The word 'lust' is unfashionable and can sound ridiculous. But lust is a reality that leaves men frustrated. Stoked up by graphic pornography and by acts of sexual simulation, men can become less psychologically stable and more liable to engage in violence against women. One organisation that opposes lap-dancing clubs and offers help to people in the sex industry is the Ruhama Women's Project.

Ironically, although lap-dancing clubs are now operating openly in Ireland, the European Parliament's Dublin office decided in May 2004 that it ought not to broadcast in Ireland a certain public service announcement that included the image of a nursing mother baring her nipple. This suggests that our attitudes to the depiction of nudity and sexuality may not be entirely rational yet.

BERTIE AND CELIA

Dublin Castle, 14 May 2001

It used to be known as 'living in sin'. Today, people just talk about 'living together'. There has been a sea change in Irish attitudes towards cohabitation outside marriage. As much as anything else, the way in which Bertie Ahern and Celia Larkin conducted their personal relationship gave citizens a chance to express tolerant attitudes towards such couples.

In August 1982, the Holy Faith nuns in New Ross, Co. Wexford, sacked a teacher who became pregnant by a man with whom she was living and whose marriage had earlier broken down. Eileen Flynn had caused scandal locally by moving in with her partner. Her pregnancy was the last straw for those who believed that the ethos of a Catholic school could not be reconciled with her continued employment in such circumstances. It is difficult for younger generations to appreciate the level of disapproval of couples living together in Ireland not long ago.

If there was a single event that marked the change in public attitudes towards cohabitation, it occurred on 14 May 2001. That evening, Bertie Ahern and Celia Larkin jointly hosted an official reception at the State Apartments in Dublin Castle, in honour of Archbishop Desmond Connell's elevation to the rank of cardinal. The Dublin archdiocese later claimed that Ahern had told Connell in Rome the previous February, that the reception for him would be hosted by 'the Government and Cabinet'. It was a symptom of the declining power of the Catholic Church in Ireland, as much as it was a sign of Connell's wish to avoid direct confrontation, that the Cardinal proceeded to attend once it became clear who was actually hosting the event. Other bishops stayed away.

During the last two decades of the twentieth century, the number of people cohabiting in Ireland had steadily risen. Many partners in such relationships had never married. Others, like Bertie Ahern, had.

The story of Bertie and Celia, of a Taoiseach and his personal assistant who fell in love, is a tale of simple fact rather than startling romance. They conducted themselves with as much dignity as might any two lovers who find themselves in the public eye. They did not deny that they were partners; nor did they reveal the kind of personal intimate details that could have satisfied the idly curious. Theirs was the story of an ambitious man whose existing marriage had broken down, and of a younger woman who worked for him and who thought that he would eventually wed her.

However, if their involvement was normal, their circumstances were not. They made their first official overseas visit together to Washington, where they met President Bill Clinton and his wife Hillary. On an official trip to Mexico in January 2003, one translator repeatedly elevated Celia to the status of 'wife' of the Irish prime minister (although diplomats suggested that *signora* might signify any woman aged over 30). Bertie went alone to the Vatican for Desmond Connell's installation as cardinal and it was denied that Celia had been snubbed by being left off the Church's invitation.

In the summer of 2003, Celia was also not invited to the wedding in France of one of Bertie and Miriam Ahern's two daughters. By the time it became known publicly that Bertie and his wife were going to attend the wedding together, and that they would participate willingly in the exclusive photographing of festivities for *Hello* magazine, the relationship between Bertie and Celia was in deep trouble. It is an old story: a married man experiences difficulties with his wife and turns to another woman. That other woman believes he will formalise the break-up of his marriage, perhaps by getting a divorce. He promises that he is committed to his new partner, giving her a ring and other tokens of his affection. But years pass and there is still no divorce. By 2004 it was clear that Bertie and Celia had separated.

Some were disgusted that the private life of a politician was subjected to public scrutiny by the media. Others discerned an element of personal hypocrisy in the whole affair. Here was a Taoiseach parading Celia as his official partner at home and abroad, at some expense to the taxpayer, while remaining married to another woman. Some suspected that the Taoiseach would never seek a divorce, as much for political reasons as for personal ones. They believed that he feared a backlash from conservatives and fumed that he was courting the support of traditional Catholics on the matter of restricting abortion, and was receiving communion as a Catholic himself, while at the same time making a daily mockery of his own Church's teaching on cohabitation and divorce. Catholic bishops stayed silent, but the editor of the Church of Ireland *Gazette* wrote:

> It is remarkable that the leader of the government should feel no need to make an apology for this situation. It is even more remarkable that the Roman Catholic Church, until recently the staunch defender of public morality in this country, has been so silent in this instance.

The editor, like many others, wondered if continuing scandals about sex abuse and other matters were inhibiting the Catholic bishops. He thought that the British would not stand for such behaviour and warned that Ahern 'is not just an individual':

> He is the leader of the government. He is a role model. He represents our nation abroad. Ireland is changing fast. No longer are the old certainties so certain in politics or morals. It is an exciting time, a time of wonderful opportunities. But it would be a great pity if, in embracing the new, we were to lose some of the values of decency and responsibility which have served us well in the past.

At their reception for Cardinal Connell at Dublin Castle, the Cardinal was spared the humiliation of being greeted publicly by Celia, although diocesan sources later said that he shook hands with her that evening when they met in a private room at Dublin Castle.

It was by no means the first time that Celia's name had appeared on an invitation. There was no reason to believe that Bertie and Celia had deliberately taken revenge for his being stuck on his own in hot sunshine at the Vatican during the two hours it took Desmond

Connell and others to don their new red hats as cardinals.

The staterooms at Dublin Castle are sumptuous. They are also stuffy. Thick carpeting makes for a hot and heavy atmosphere at the best of times. And that Monday was not the best of times. Almost the entire Cabinet wandered around, looking shell-shocked after a special government meeting convened in Ballymascanlon, Co. Louth, to discuss current economic pressures. Just like Paul on the road to Damascus, some of them had had a conversion on the road to Dublin. Paul's was to Christianity, but theirs was to liberalism. Here were the soldiers of the legion of the rearguard, including some of the last politicians in Ireland to support the liberalising of Irish laws on contraception and divorce. But, just like Celia, they were determined to stand by their man that evening.

It was hard to move around, with 700 people in the crowded staterooms. I found myself chatting with a priest, a former classmate of the cardinal. He lectured me on the Reformation and Henry VIII, and on how Roman priests are basically superior to the Anglican variety because Roman ones are the direct successors of Christ. He did not agree that corrupt medieval popes might have complicated the notion of a direct line of descent.

Bertie got into the ecclesiastical mood. He quoted a theologian, Avery Dulles. For good measure he threw in a line by William Wordsworth. Not even the unusual sound of a Fianna Fáil Taoiseach quoting both theology and poetry inspired Bertie's co-host Celia to say anything. Connell also reached for the words of a theologian, Carlo-Maria Martini of Milan. Cardinal Martini's radical vision of Catholicism is not of a kind that was usually associated with that of Cardinal Connell, but perhaps Connell wished to show that he was not a complete fuddy-duddy. In fact, at the start of his speech the Cardinal even managed to get a polite laugh from guests. Turning to Bertie, that other resident of Drumcondra, a suburb on the north side of the Liffey, he confirmed that his new titular parish in Rome is also on the north side of the Tiber. It seemed a genuine effort by Connell to defuse tension. A single sentence about the home and marriage, well into his speech, sounded far less reproachful than was subsequently suggested by some commentators. It was sandwiched between an ecclesiastical sideswipe at abortion and an expression of concern about the growing disparity between rich and poor.

But what did seem significant on the night was the tone of the Taoiseach's whole address. His references to 'the Holy Father' (i.e.

Pope John Paul II) may have struck a note of deference, but overall the thrust of his speech was an assertion of secular power. Bertie thanked the Cardinal for what was in the past. He gave credit to 'the Church' for initiating for Ireland 'the opening to the world'. It sounded like he thought that St Patrick unlocked the door, Seán Lemass stepped through it, and now we can all walk free. The work of our Christian missions, said Bertie, has been noted 'wherever Irish representatives travel, whether in the context of the campaign for a seat on the UN Security Council, or in pursuit of trade and investment opportunities' and so on. The missionaries, said Bertie, 'have created a powerfully positive image for our country'. Now, where could you buy such branding for the new Celtic Tiger? That old religious groundwork was bound to come in handy one day.

Connell is a conservative who has every right as a leader of his Church to claim that all sex must allow for procreation and that the sexual act must take place exclusively within marriage. However, unlike Connell, most Catholics seem to feel today that there are exceptions to the rule — a lot of exceptions.

Those who believe that cohabitation of sexual partners is generally a bad thing may feel that the subsequent and highly publicised break-up of Bertie and Celia simply reinforces the fact that unions outside marriage are intrinsically unstable. There was a time when some such people saw to it that anyone entering into an irregular union was shunned and might even be sacked.

—

Today, it is not just straight couples who can live together with fewer fears of recrimination or victimisation than in earlier generations. Another Fianna Fáil member of the Cabinet was responsible for repealing the old criminal law relating to homosexuals. In June 1993, Minister for Justice Máire Geoghegan-Quinn successfully steered the Criminal Law (Sexual Offences) Act through the Oireachtas. Her government was responding to a 1988 decision of the European Court of Human Rights in a case taken by David Norris. The court had held Ireland to be in breach of the European Convention on Human Rights in so far as it discriminated against men in respect of their private sexual relationships. However, the new Irish law was less restrictive than it might have been, and more liberal than the provisions of comparable British legislation.

Mother and child

You never claimed to be someone special;
Sometimes you said you had no special talent;
Yet I have seen you rear two dancing daughters
With care and patience and love unstinted;
Reading or telling stories, knitting gansies
And all the while holding down a job
In the teeming city, morning until dusk.
And in the house when anything went wrong
You were the one who fixed it without fuss;

PAUL DURCAN, 'She Mends an Ancient Wireless'
FROM *Teresa's Bar*, 1976

WORKING MOTHERS

'Dunkellin', Munster, 31 July 1973

In March 1951, Minister for Health Noel Browne caused a furore when he moved to implement proposals known as 'the mother and child scheme'. A clash between Church and State led directly to the resignation from government of the gently spoken Browne, himself a medical doctor. The Catholic Church objected to what it regarded as his undue interference in family matters, and bishops feared that non-Roman Catholic health professionals might be allowed to give advice to Catholic mothers in public hospitals or clinics. The medical profession was unenthusiastic about changes that some thought might reduce the private income of its members. Browne's plan was suspended.

In 1951, a woman's place was definitely in the home. Few worked outside it. Women married younger and had more children than women today, and they were not welcome in the workplace once they were married. Gradually, however, Irish women chose to reduce the size of the average Irish family. On 25 July 1968, in his papal encyclical, *Humanae vitae*, Pope Paul VI rejected 'artificial' methods of contraception, but his teaching was widely disregarded by Irish lay Catholics. If most mothers today have fewer children than mothers used to have, they also have greater civil and social rights.

Until the passing of the Guardianship of Infants Act 1964, mothers did not even have guardianship rights equal to those of fathers. Moreover, until the passing of the Civil Service (Employment of

Married Women) Act 1973, a woman could neither be recruited nor continue in employment in the public service once she married. Subsequently, the Anti-Discrimination (Pay) Act 1974, the Employment Equality Act 1977 and other new legislation helped women to remain in the workforce and prohibited discrimination against them. Change had been fostered by the research and report of the Commission on the Status of Women, chaired between 1970 and 1973 by Dr Thekla Beere. Ireland's entry into the EEC in 1973 became a reason and an excuse for introducing social reforms.

Not every girl or woman was in a position immediately to enjoy the fruits of EEC membership. While some were preparing to join the civil service and some were planning fruitful careers or satisfying relationships for themselves, others were still mired in the ways of the past. One was 'Nuala', whose story of being forced into marriage with an elderly farmer in Munster in the 1970s has been told by Sean Boyne (*Sold Into Marriage: One Girl's Living Nightmare*, O'Brien Press: Dublin, 1998). Boyne has changed the names of people and places in his account, in deference to her wishes, but it is sobering to learn that some women were still contending with arranged marriages even as their fellow female citizens were being allowed back into the Irish civil service. Working for RTÉ in the mid-1970s, I met very old women around Gougane Barra in west Cork, whose marriages had been arranged much earlier, and one of whom insisted that such marriages turned out no more or less happy than regular unions. However, the story of Nuala and of her life in 'Dunkellin' and 'Knockslattery' is a sobering reminder of just how powerless women had been.

Even women in far more fortunate circumstances than Nuala did not find it easy to 'have it all' after the Bill to allow married women to work in the public service was passed on 31 July 1973. In practice, many continued to find it difficult to keep paid jobs outside the home once they became pregnant. The Maternity (Protection of Employees) Act 1981 assisted them by providing for fourteen weeks of paid maternity, and an optional four weeks unpaid. In 2001, the periods were increased to eighteen and eight weeks respectively. All female employees in Ireland are now entitled to maternity leave, including casual workers, no matter how long they have been working for the organisation or no matter the number of hours worked per week. Adopting parents may take fourteen weeks' paid leave at the time of adoption.

Marking his department's contribution to the celebration of 'Family Friendly Workplace Day', 1 March 2001, the Minister for Justice, Equality and Law Reform, John O'Donoghue, said:

> There have been major changes in Irish society and in the make-up of the labour force, due to Ireland's unprecedented rate of economic growth. The model of the man as sole bread-winner no longer applies. With the growth in the economy, more and more young mothers are staying in the workforce. In 1994, the female labour force participation rate was 35.7%. According to the latest CSO [Central Statistics Office] figures, it is now 49.4%. However, the participation rate for women aged between 15 and 45 roughly corresponding to child-bearing years is over 61%.

The choice that many women have made to work outside the home has resulted in a mushrooming of day-care facilities. Some of these are of a far higher quality than others, and the State has been criticised for failing to regulate adequately those who provide such services. The impact of long-term day-care on children is a matter of some concern.

Even apart from anxieties about the quality and expense of their children's day-care, many couples have found it very difficult to cope with maintaining a satisfactory family life while both partners work. The introduction of job-sharing has helped some parents to pursue a career while freeing them to spend more time with their children. However, the great majority of working women are employed full-time. The high cost of housing and other economic pressures can make it very difficult for one party in a relationship to give up working, even if that person wishes to do so.

Yet, some fathers believe that mothers are now so well protected and so well regarded in law that the courts tend to discriminate against men in family law cases. No matter how sceptical one may be about this viewpoint, it is the case that some men who have been involved in legal separations or in custody battles for their children are very bitter about their experiences.

For their part, women who are abused by men continue to have special needs. During the 1970s, a number of organisations were founded to assist them and to fight for changes in the legal system. The Women's Aid organisation runs more than a dozen refuges for battered women and their children. The Rape Crisis Centre network has also helped to heighten awareness of the vulnerability of women and of the need for the State to protect them. Both organisations have had to struggle to do a job for which insufficient funding and services were provided by the State.

According to a report by the Crisis Pregnancy Agency in 2004, one in every three Irish pregnancies is unplanned, and 15 per cent of these are terminated by abortion. The number of married and unmarried women giving Irish addresses when having abortions in Britain has risen steadily from 3,673 in 1987 to 6,673 in 2004.

The problem of balancing commitments to family and work are particularly acute for that growing number of mothers and fathers who now find themselves, by choice or circumstance, bringing up children on their own. It is no longer nearly as socially unacceptable as it once was for a single Irish woman to get pregnant or to keep her baby outside of wedlock, and many first pregnancies occur outside of wedlock.

The difficulties of balancing the demands of a full-time job with the everyday needs of one's family, as well as the wish of many women not to become tied down too soon by the requirements involved in raising children, have all contributed to the phenomenon of Irish men and women getting married later than did earlier generations. Later marriage, in turn, is a reason why families tend to be smaller than they used to be.

Because families are smaller today, the average child has fewer siblings. Where daughters and sons once competed with a larger number of brothers and sisters, today they fight for attention not only with daddy's but also with mammy's work outside the home. However, most also enjoy a far greater range of toys and other possessions than their ancestors possessed when they were young. In general, they travel more, are more electronically stimulated, and are fed a greater variety of foods. From the moment of birth they are subjected to parents who believe that, as parents, they are better informed than their own parents were about the psychological and emotional needs of offspring. Children are, on the other hand, targeted aggressively by marketing personnel, who recognise the compelling power of 'kids' to pester mum and dad to purchase advertised products, and who know that children and teenagers themselves have a considerable disposable income of their own. With increased wealth in Ireland has come increasing levels of obesity, partly caused by children eating too much fast-food and consuming sweets and fizzy drinks in unprecedented quantities. Teenagers are bombarded by promotions for alcohol. Television is referred to, only half jokingly, as 'the electronic babysitter'. The Broadcasting Commission of Ireland, and other organisations, study ways of protecting children from powerful commercial pressures.

—

Whether or not the average child today is happier than a child born in March 1951, when Noel Browne so ardently attempted to improve the health services available to mothers and children, is impossible to ascertain with certainty. But the greater freedom now enjoyed by women, including those who are parents, and the stimulation surrounding childhood, makes it seem unlikely that many mothers would wish to turn the clock back fifty years. Their liberation has been one of the greatest changes in Irish society in the recent past.

SCHOOL BEATINGS

Ballyhooley, Co. Cork, 1 February 1982

Since 1982, Irish children may no longer be subjected to corporal punishment at school. Previously, this had been meted out very aggressively by cane, leather and limb to many pupils. It is difficult for young people today to grasp what school was like in the days when teachers had wide powers to deliver humiliating and painful beatings.

The following regulation was circulated by John Boland, Fine Gael Minister for Education, to all schools on 26 January 1982, and took effect on 1 February 1982. It is simple, eloquent and almost poetic in its nature:

1. Teachers should have a lively regard for the improvement and general welfare of their pupils, treat them with kindness combined with firmness and should aim at governing them through their affections and reason and not by harshness and severity. Ridicule, sarcasm or remarks likely to undermine a pupil's self-confidence should not be used in any circumstances.
2. The use of corporal punishment is forbidden.
3. Any teacher who contravenes sections (1) or (2) of this rule will be regarded as guilty of conduct unbefitting a teacher and will be subject to severe disciplinary action.

Corporal punishment in schools severely scarred generations of Irish people. For some, it is difficult to distinguish the way in which corporal punishment was administered from darker and more serious forms of abuse that were sexual. One teacher affectionately called her leather 'Johnny'; another frequently insisted that his boys drop their pants and bend over. At the same time, it must be said that not all teachers used corporal punishment, and some only resorted to it occasionally or mildly. For many years, parents themselves beat their children in a way that is no longer socially acceptable.

Excessively violent beatings are perhaps most generally associated with the Christian Brothers, but even members of a religious order as supposedly sophisticated as the Jesuits engaged wholeheartedly in administering corporal punishment. Broadcaster Terry Wogan has written of his time at Crescent College, Limerick, and even this often good-humoured man uses the word 'torture' to describe his experiences of being repeatedly beaten there.

A few reformers long considered the punishment regime to be unacceptable. Most vocal among them was Noel Browne, the former government minister who had resigned in 1951 when his proposals to improve the welfare services for mothers and children were defeated. On 2 May 1957, rising in the Dáil to address the new Minister for Education, Jack Lynch, he admitted:

> I am probably in a considerable minority in my attitude to this question for I hold the view very strongly that corporal punishment is an utterly medieval and barbarous practice. . . . In most books now, educational authorities sum the whole thing up by calling it a barbarous practice. The difficulty, indeed, when reading into the question of corporal punishment, is to find an average modern book on child education which recommends the beating of a child as an aid to education. To me, it is so clearly absurd that I cannot understand why it is still retained. I know that most of us were beaten at one time or another. I do not think that justified the retention of the evil from one generation to the next. I have been told, 'I was beaten and look at me' by people who believe in the thing. I do look at them and I wonder are they the same people they think they are. Is this anxiety on their part to beat a child not one of the consequences of vindictive retention of hostility to an adult which they are now trying to pass on to the child?

Subsequently, on 5 June 1957, Browne revealed that there was actually no statutory basis for the use of the leather strap in Irish schools. Lynch blithely admitted that Rule 96 (3) of the Rules and Regulations for National Schools laid down that 'only a light cane or rod may be used for the purpose of corporal punishment, which should be inflicted only on the open hand'. The fact that leathers were being widely wielded in contravention of that regulation did not seem to disturb the minister. He simply proposed to amend the rule 'so as to delete such references to the means and methods to be used, but to emphasise that any improper or unreasonable punishment will be regarded as conduct unbefitting a teacher and will be visited with very severe sanctions'. The influence of the Catholic Church, and its determination to maintain control of education, was reflected in the following reference by Lynch to 'natural' law as the foundation of school management:

> I told the Deputy that it is not proper for the Minister to indicate or to authorise or to prohibit the means or methods. It is a matter entirely for the school manager and, subject to him and his authority, for the teachers in the school to correct children and to decide what means of correction are necessary. That is primarily a natural right of the parent and the teacher or manager in *loco parentis* has, naturally, that responsibility and the corresponding authority from the parent.

Browne complained: 'Instead of restricting this flagellating, adults beating children, he [the minister] is extending it.' He found that he was being disowned politely even by those who might have been expected to back reform. Brendan Corish, a future leader of the Labour Party, was one of them. On 4 June 1958, Corish told the Dáil: 'I am afraid I could not agree with Deputy Dr Browne about corporal punishment.'

> Corish: I do not want to be taken as one who supports or condones the idea that children should be beaten about the head or humiliated by being beaten in the face or that they should be beaten excessively. For the life of me, however, I cannot see what harm it does to slap a child on the hand. For the life of me, I cannot see why a child cannot be slapped on the rear end when he

will not do what he is told.

Dillon: More power to your elbow!

For his part, Jack Lynch is remembered fondly today as a gentle Taoiseach, and his views on corporal punishment were certainly not extreme when he was minister for education. Nevertheless, he consistently supported the practice and even invoked papal teaching in its defence. On 11 June 1958, he rose to reply again to Browne.

Lynch: I am glad to note that not one deputy agreed with the views expressed by Deputy Dr Browne. I know he is convinced of the justice of the point of view which he holds, but I think that some corporal punishment is necessary. I can never understand why this expression 'corporal punishment' is used so often today. In less extravagant days, people called it slapping, 'biffing'. The rule, as deputies know, is that children may be slapped on the open hand. When some questions were put down on this subject during the course of the last year, I looked up what material there was in the Department. I was amused to come across a reference to the subject in the *Irish School Monthly* for March 1955 entitled 'Punishment in the Schools'. It referred to a country which, beyond saying any more about it, is a friendly democracy, and where, it says, physical punishment in the schools is forbidden and as a result juvenile delinquency has practically disappeared, only to be replaced by adult delinquency by juveniles. It goes on to give some general examples of that adult delinquency, which I need not go into, and refers to it as having reached terrifying proportions. I might say, too, that in his Encyclical letter, *Divini Illius Magistri*: the Christian Education of Youth, Pope Pius XII said that disorderly inclinations amongst children must be corrected. That was a direct reference to methods of correction.

Browne: Does the Minister realise that there are thousands of schools in which corporal punishment is not used in other countries and in which they get good results?

Lynch: I will not deny it.

Lynch added: 'Irish teachers are not sadists and only in very rare instances do we get a case where a teacher might have gone beyond the limits.' At the time of these exchanges, we now know the Department of Education was turning a blind eye to the systematic physical and sexual abuse of children in institutional care. How likely was it that officials had any reliable information concerning the number of cases in which teachers in schools controlled by religious orders had 'gone beyond the limits'? Certainly, many of the pupils who attended such schools have memories of incidents that suggest that the limits were either too broad or were frequently exceeded. Even where slappings were only directed at pupils' hands, they were often ferocious and charged with venomous emotions. Too often, punishment also included contact with the pupil's head and the use of irregular implements.

On 16 July 1958, Browne rose yet again to challenge the Minister for Education about one particular case in which the department's own rules had clearly been broken. From his question, it is clear that the consequences of such a transgression did not necessarily include dismissal or even demotion. Browne asked Lynch whether he had completed his investigation into a corporal punishment incident, which was the subject of a court action, at Ballyhooley National School, and 'if so, what are his conclusions concerning the culpability of the teacher involved; and what action he proposes to take in the matter?'

> Lynch: The investigation of this case has been completed and appropriate official action has been taken in the matter. It is not the practice to disclose the nature of the official action taken in such cases.
>
> Browne: Could the Minister tell me whether that person is still employed as principal of the school?
>
> Lynch: That is so.
>
> Browne: Does the Minister really believe, in view of the decision of the court, that this is a fit person to be principal of a school?
>
> Lynch: I do.

Even today, not everyone agrees that corporal punishment harmed themselves or others who experienced it, and some lament its complete abolition from schools in the context of contemporary reports of serious disciplinary problems in Irish classrooms. Nevertheless, the vast majority of parents do not want its reintroduction in schools for their children. In Ballyhooley and elsewhere, on 1 February 1982, families heaved a sigh of relief. Young people no longer live their daily lives in fear of teachers inflicting physical pain at school.

In 2004, in a bizarre twist to the story of Irish corporal punishment, pop-singer Brian McFadden (previously 'Bryan' when a member of Westlife) released a song that suggested he had been beaten at school and that this experience was an intrinsic part of his upbringing as an 'Irish son'. While he received much publicity, the singer also incurred the wrath of one school which he had never attended but which featured in the video of his song. As McFadden was a mere infant when corporal punishment was abolished, many greeted his claim with great scepticism.

ANN LOVETT, RIP

Granard, Co. Longford, 31 January 1984

It was the most poignant of scenes. Ann Lovett lay dying when the schoolboys found her. She herself was only 15 years old. Beside her, at the little grotto built in honour of Mary, mother of Jesus, lay a stillborn baby boy. Ann had concealed her pregnancy and had tried to deliver the child on her own, taking with her a pair of scissors to cut her umbilical cord.

Daylight was already fading when the three lads made their way down the green lane that passed the grotto. They spotted a schoolbag at its entrance and heard moaning. When they discovered her, Ann Lovett was covered in blood. She died later in Mullingar Hospital.

The death might have gone unnoticed beyond the small community of Granard. Ann was just another in a long line of Irish girls and women who concealed their pregnancies. Some gave birth and kept their babies; some had babies and killed them or abandoned them. We shall never know what Ann Lovett intended to do. The father of her child, the man who got this girl pregnant, has never been identified. She was below the legal age of consent.

What we do know is that frequently such pregnant girls have been an embarrassment to their families and to their communities, and they have not always received the sort of support they needed to cope with their predicament. One of the reasons we know this is because of the outpouring of stories that followed the publication of details of Ann Lovett's death. An anonymous caller to the *Sunday Tribune* alerted news editor Brian Trench to what had happened and, just one week after Ann's death, her story was published. There was a deep sense of national shame and shock which, later that same year, was to be exacerbated by the Kerry babies affair.

Ann's baby suffocated during birth, while she herself died of shock from exposure and loss of blood. What kind of society drives women to such extremes? Television pictures of Granard showed that it might as well have been any quiet little town or village in rural Ireland. Nobody suggested that what had happened in Co. Longford was unique. Her parents, family and school all denied knowing that Ann had been pregnant. Many of the people of Granard deeply resented the media's close attention to their local problem.

On RTÉ radio and in the newspapers a flood of stories told of similar experiences and episodes. Irish people were aghast. The death of Ann Lovett at Granard, on 31 January 1984, was a human tragedy. No amount of soul-searching or changes in sex education and contraceptive services could put things right for the Lovetts. Ann's family never entirely recovered from what happened. Within months, one of her sisters died from an overdose. It was not long before her father also died.

It is impossible to say whether or not Ann Lovett became pregnant as a result of consensual sex. Today, most single women who by accident or design or rape find themselves expecting a baby no longer face the level of condemnation that women of earlier generations generally did. Moreover, the option of having an abortion seems more acceptable and practical. Could a death like that of Ann Lovett happen again? Yes, it could. However, hopefully, the chances of it doing so are less now than they were in 1984.

KERRY BABIES

Tralee, Co. Kerry, 12–14 April 1984

In 1984, circumstances surrounding the birth and death of two babies in Co. Kerry appalled the public and led to an official investigation into Garda methods in the case. The baby found at Cahirciveen had been stabbed repeatedly, and the baby at Tralee battered. Coming within a couple of months of Ann Lovett's fate at Granard, these deaths cried out for an explanation.

An investigation was launched across the whole of the beautiful Iveragh Peninsula. After ten days, the Gardaí discovered 'from a private source' that Tralee General Hospital was holding what it called 'an inconclusive file' on Joanne Hayes of Dromcunnig Lower, Abbeydorney. They learnt that Hayes had given birth to a full-term or near full-term baby prior to her admission to hospital, but had denied to hospital staff that she had had a baby and refused to say what became of it. The Gardaí also found that there was no new baby at Joanne's home and that no funeral had been held by the family. Hayes already had, and was supporting, another child by the man believed to be the father of her missing baby. Detectives travelled to Kerry from Dublin to assist in the investigation.

On 1 May 1984, the Gardaí called for the first time at the Hayes farmhouse to question Joanne Hayes. The farm of just under sixty acres included a herd of some sixteen milch cows and two houses. Joanne's family was by no means poor by the standard of the community in which they lived. As it happened, on the day the Gardái called, Joanne had gone back to work as a receptionist at a sports centre in Tralee. The atmosphere in the house was very tense. Members of the immediate family, and a relative named Bridie Fuller who lived with them, went subsequently to the Garda station in Tralee to be interviewed. Each of the Hayes family and Bridie Fuller started their interviews with the Gardaí by making statements that were false. Joanne first said that she had not given birth, but later claimed that she had had a miscarriage at four to six months. Other members of the family denied knowing that she was pregnant. Under questioning, they eventually changed their stories and the Gardaí then charged Joanne Hayes with murder. She replied, 'I am guilty.' Joanne's brother Mike was charged with endeavouring to conceal the birth by secretly disposing of the dead body. He replied, 'I helped conceal the child.' However, the Gardaí charged them both in respect of the baby found at Caherciveen, which was not actually Joanne's baby.

So what had happened to the baby to whom Joanne Hayes did give birth and which would become known later as the 'Tralee baby'? His father was a married man called Jeremiah Locke, by whom Joanne had already had both a miscarriage and a baby girl. Locke was three to four years older than Hayes and worked with her at the Tralee Sports Centre as a groundsman. Despite his being older, the tribunal later established to investigate the Kerry babies affair stated: 'Obviously, it takes two people to have an affaire [*sic*], but Joanne Hayes was the main or dominant force in the liaison between herself and Jeremiah Locke.' Joanne had been pleased to have her first baby with Locke and ignored the advice of her family and of a local Garda that she should break off her relationship. However, she was unhappy to find that she had become pregnant by him for a third time and tried to conceal the pregnancy, seeking no medical advice or treatment of any kind. During her pregnancy she learnt that Locke's wife was also pregnant by him. Locke and Hayes had a row about this and their affair cooled.

About midnight on 12 April 1984, Joanne went into labour at her home. When born, her baby was not at all well and never succeeded in establishing its breathing properly. No effort was made to obtain medical assistance. Immediately after the birth, Joanne's mother expressed annoyance at the prospect of their having to rear another child for the baby's father, especially when the child did not appear to be strong. Other relatives also rebuked Joanne. She panicked and, as the baby cried, put her hands around its neck and stopped it crying by choking it. The baby did not breathe again. She also used a bath brush to hit the baby subsequently. None of her family tried to stop her. The family now sent for the eldest son, Ned. He arrived up into the bedroom and exclaimed, 'Why in fuck's name did you do a thing like that? We could have reared it.' The family decided that it was for Joanne herself to get rid of the corpse. She was told to get Locke to help her.

Instead of summoning Locke, Joanne put her dead baby's body in some old hay near the house. She then tossed the afterbirth on the grass quite near by. She had lost a lot of blood and was becoming more ill. Later that day, she was brought to a local doctor who urged her to go to hospital immediately. The doctor seems to have believed that she may have had a miscarriage, or even that she was still pregnant. However, Hayes was worried that her baby's body might not be safe from discovery or from vermin, and returned home. That night or the following morning, she put the body into two bags and dropped it down in a pool of water some 200 yards from the house, on the Abbeydorney side. Only then did she go into hospital, where she denied that she had been pregnant. A scan showed that she was not telling the truth. Nevertheless, she was discharged home after a few days. Her visit to a doctor and her stay in the hospital allowed Joanne to pretend to those who had known she was pregnant that she had lost the baby naturally. However, any hopes that the family harboured of simply getting on with their lives and keeping their secret were destroyed following the coincidental discovery of a baby's body at Caherciveen on 14 April, the day after Joanne gave birth.

The fact that the Hayes family confessed to killing a baby and concealing its body is not altogether surprising in the circumstances. The fact that they ostensibly confessed to killing and concealing the particular baby found at Cahirciveen gave rise to severe criticisms of the Gardaí's methods. On 2 May 1984, just one day after they made their confessions, the body of Joanne's baby was found in the pool where she had dumped it at her family's farm near Tralee.

An official tribunal of inquiry subsequently determined that the Gardaí had not assaulted or physically abused any members of the Hayes family whilst questioning them on 1 May. However, it also found that the family all believed that they were in custody and not free to leave the Garda station until they satisfied the Gardaí that they had a role in the birth and death of the Cahirciveen baby. The Gardaí had allowed their own strong suspicions about a connection between Joanne and the Caherciveen baby to progress unreasonably into certainty. For her part, Joanne's belief that she was in custody increased when the Gardaí refused to take her to the family farm so that she might point out to them the place where she had hidden her dead baby. The tribunal found that this refusal was 'completely unjustified', that searches carried out that day by the Gardaí themselves were 'deplorably inadequate', and that their failure to find the Tralee baby at the Hayes farm was 'inexcusable'.

The Gardaí carried out no proper reappraisal of the case, even after the results of blood tests and other contradictory evidence became known. The Gardaí resorted to unlikely and far-fetched theories, including one involving 'superfecundation' (two separate fathers for each twin), and another based on the assumption that Joanne's confession meant that there 'must be' a *third* dead baby undiscovered between the Dingle and Iveragh peninsulas and that *this* was a twin of the Tralee baby. Charges against Joanne Hayes were subsequently dropped. An internal Garda inquiry into the conduct of the investigation was inconclusive. Accordingly, on 13 December 1984, the government appointed Judge Kevin Lynch to constitute a tribunal of inquiry into the Kerry babies cases. On 3 October 1985, Lynch presented his report, on which the account given above relies for its facts.

At the time, there was growing criticism of the methods the Gardaí were using in the course of their investigations, especially in respect of those involved in political and paramilitary activities. A 'heavy gang' of Gardaí was allegedly forcing suspects to confess to murders by exerting unreasonable physical and psychological pressure. The Kerry babies case brought this issue out of the political arena and into a more general domain, and the public did not like what emerged.

Some people were critical of Judge Lynch's tribunal report, feeling that he actually went too easy on the Gardaí, while casting Joanne Hayes in the role of temptress or witch. At the time of the Kerry babies crisis, Joanne Hayes was a competent 25-year-old working woman who wilfully had a relationship with a married man and who had been happy to have his baby. She knew about and had access to contraception which she previously used but decided to have unprotected sex and got pregnant as she was aware that she might.

She concealed her pregnancy for a time, but it is by no means clear that she did so because of some overwhelming sense of shame. Having learnt that her lover had also made his wife pregnant, Joanne deliberately battered their second child after it was born. A feminist could plausibly argue that she freely chose her destiny and that she was lucky to escape jail. Today, finding herself pregnant in similar circumstances, a woman might readily take a flight from Kerry to have her baby aborted in London.

Nell McCafferty is among those who have written books about the Kerry babies case. She is highly critical of the way in which the tribunal was dominated by men and condemns the manner in which it made the sexual behaviour of Joanne Hayes a matter of public knowledge and curiosity. She also places events in the context of the anti-abortion campaign that had convulsed Irish society from 1981 and that led to a constitutional amendment being adopted in a referendum in September 1983. She pays particular attention to the role of the bishop of Kerry and to the position of Kerry doctors in respect of that campaign and its implications. Her book, *A Woman to Blame* (Attic Press, 1985), highlights some of the weaknesses and the unsavoury aspects of the tribunal's work, and reminds us that many women around Ireland expressed their support and sympathy for Joanne Hayes during her ordeal.

People's shock and disgust at the Kerry revelations helped to change attitudes towards single mothers, and stiffened our resolve to provide State supports for women in crisis.

The identities of the Cahirciveen baby and his parents have never been established. The dead baby was baptised and named John by a local undertaker, who has also tended to the baby's grave and who, early in 2004, placed an engraved marble slab there. That slab, alone in the cemetery, was later deliberately smashed by someone wielding a heavy object such as a sledge-hammer.

THE 'X' CASE

Supreme Court, 5 March 1992

The girl, aged 14, was pregnant. Her baby's father, who was both the father of one of her friends and a friend himself of her own parents, had raped her. She and her parents decided that she would go to England for an abortion. She was about to follow a well-trodden path. More than 100,000 Irish women have travelled to Britain for abortions since the Abortion Act 1967 was passed there. More than one-third of all first pregnancies in Ireland are aborted abroad.

On 6 February 1992, the pregnant girl and her parents went to England and made arrangements for an abortion. The family had already contacted the Gardaí to see if an embryonic tissue sample might be used in evidence against the rapist in any future trial. By doing so, they alerted the Gardaí to the fact that the girl intended to procure an abortion. The Gardaí notified the Irish Attorney-General and the latter sought an injunction in the High Court to stop her from having an abortion. Rather than simply proceeding then to terminate her pregnancy, the girl and her parents dutifully returned to Ireland to await the outcome of the case. She was named 'X' in the proceedings in order to protect her identity

The High Court granted the Attorney-General his injunction, and there was much public comment on the effective internment of an innocent young girl within the borders of the Republic of Ireland. However, the Supreme Court overturned that ruling. It decided that, under the written Constitution of Ireland, abortion is permissible for a citizen in or outside the State where the continuation of the pregnancy poses a real and substantial threat to the life (as distinct from the health) of the mother. Delivering his judgment in the Supreme Court, Mr Justice Egan stated:

> X confided in her mother that when she learned that she was pregnant she had wanted to kill herself by throwing herself down the stairs and, on 31 January, she again said much the same to a member of the Garda authorities. In between, on the journey back from England she told her mother that she had wanted to throw herself under a train when she was in London and that she would rather be dead than be the way she was. Again in the presence of another member of the Garda Síochána when her father commented that the situation was worse than a death in the family, she commented: 'Not if it was me.'

On her return from England, X was brought by her parents to a very experienced clinical psychologist. He was of the opinion that she was capable of suicide.

The decision of the Supreme Court shocked and disappointed those who had campaigned vigorously to close off completely the possibility of abortion being introduced into Ireland. Abortion had been a crime in Ireland ever since 1861, when sections 58 and 59 of the Offences Against the Person Act were passed by the parliament of the United Kingdom. The 1861 Act had been explicitly confirmed in Ireland by section 10 of the Health (Family Planning) Act 1979.

Article 40.3 of the Constitution of 1937 provided that the State 'guarantees in its laws to respect and, as far as practicable, by its laws to defend and vindicate the personal rights of the citizen'. A number of earlier Irish cases had implied that the right to life of the unborn was protected by this provision. However, there was always a possibility that the courts might be forced to choose between the life of a mother and the life of a foetus. Anti-abortion groups argued that this choice was seldom if ever a real medical necessity, and they had set about persuading people that the Constitution ought to be tightened up on the issue. In 1983, lobbyists had succeeded in convincing the government to hold a referendum, which was passed. This resulted in a specific prohibition on abortion being included in the Constitution for the first time. However, the new wording recognised that mothers also had a right to life. In deciding to support the amendment, most anti-abortion groups allowed their eagerness to have the right to life of the unborn explicitly enshrined in the Constitution overwhelm the reservations of those who warned them that the particular amendment was ambiguous and that it could have implications that might not be welcomed by them.

The amendment which in 1983 became Article 40.3.3 of the Irish Constitution declares that:

> The State acknowledges the right to life of the unborn and, with due regard to the equal right to life of the mother, guarantees in its laws to respect and, as far as practicable, by its laws to defend and to vindicate that right.

At first it appeared that the amendment might seriously impede the provision of abortion services to Irish women. For, in and after 1986, the Society for the Protection of the Unborn Child (SPUC) obtained injunctions preventing a number of organisations from furnishing women with information that encouraged or facilitated abortion. Even the addresses and telephone numbers of foreign abortion agencies could not be disseminated.

However, in 1992, things began to go wrong for the anti-abortion lobby. Firstly, the Supreme Court's judgment in the X case made it clear that not only may a woman travel abroad for an abortion if her life is at risk but that, in those circumstances, she may even stay at home in Ireland and have an abortion. Then, in October 1992, the European Court of Human Rights ruled that the Irish ban on information about foreign abortion agencies was a breach of Article 10 of the European Convention on Human Rights, which guarantees freedom of expression. The ban was held to be 'overbroad and disproportionate' because it prohibited organisations from providing information to everyone, including women whose lives were at risk.

The government responded to the X case by holding another referendum on abortion. This involved three separate proposed amendments, of which the electorate accepted two. The two that were accepted in 1992 ensured that there would be no repetition of the internationally embarrassing X case and that Ireland could continue to adopt a pure anti-abortion policy domestically, while leaving its back door open for pregnant women to slip away to evil England for an abortion. These two amendments provided that the freedom of people to travel abroad would not be limited and that information on abortion services abroad could be obtainable in legally definable circumstances. Those circumstances were later defined in the Regulation of Information (Services outside the State for Termination of Pregnancies) Act 1995. However, some of the outstanding injunctions against organisations that had earlier disseminated information about foreign abortion agencies were not actually lifted by the courts until 1997.

While people voted in 1992 in favour of the two amendments to the Constitution that allowed travel and information, they rejected a third and important proposal dealing with the substantive issue in the X case. Unlike the first two amendments which were permissive, the third proposal was restrictive, and would have narrowed the grounds on which abortion is permitted in Ireland following the judgment in the X case. It would have ruled out invoking the possibility of suicide as a ground for abortion within Ireland, although still allowing that abortion could be permitted where a physical illness or disorder posed 'a real and substantial risk to her life'. The rejection of this proposal meant that the situation remained as defined in the X case. In other words, abortion was still permissible in certain narrow circumstances where the mother's life was at risk, including from possible suicide. Successive governments have never legislated to regulate the safe termination of such pregnancies. Doctors are exposed to criticism and to possible civil or criminal liability in the event of their attempting an abortion in Ireland.

The fact that the ruling in the X case still prevailed was underlined in the C case which, in 1997, involved a similar judgment regarding a 13-year old who had been raped and who was pregnant and suicidal. In that case, the child was in the care of the Eastern Health Board, which sought permission to take her to England. Her father was persuaded by anti-abortion lobbyists to appeal to her not to have an abortion. She proceeded to do so.

Following the X and C cases, anti-abortion lobbyists feared that the floodgates might open. They suspected that some doctors would certify many Irish women as suicidal in order to facilitate the termination of their pregnancies within the Republic of Ireland. So the campaign to tighten Irish anti-abortion law continued throughout the 1990s. Lobbyists persuaded politicians to commit themselves to holding a new referendum on abortion. Bertie Ahern indicated that a Green Paper on Abortion would be prepared as a prelude to a referendum. This was published on 10 September 1999. A useful, mature and somewhat inconclusive document, its appearance meant that the ball was back in the government's court. Opposition groups argued that the situation to which the X case decision gave rise might best be dealt with by simply passing appropriate legislation to regulate abortion in Ireland in cases where the mother's life was at risk from a continued pregnancy or birth. However, the government finally decided that it would keep its promise and go once more to the people with yet another proposal for an amendment to the Constitution. Again, this was intended to rule out possible suicide as a ground for abortion.

The particular proposal which was now brought forward won strong support from the Catholic bishops, who saw it as a step in the right direction. But it divided anti-abortionists, who objected to the fact that it would protect the embryo only from the time of implantation and not from the moment of conception or fertilisation. The poll took place on 7 March 2002. Partly because some anti-abortion lobbyists urged people to vote against it, the proposal was narrowly defeated and the law remained unchanged.

One bizarre coincidence possibly influenced voters. Shortly before the referendum, the man convicted of raping the girl whose pregnancy led to the X case in 1992 appeared in court once more. This time he was found guilty of a serious sexual assault on a 15-year-old girl. It emerged that, since being released from jail following his conviction in relation to his sexual relations with X, he had managed to acquire a taxi licence. The new assault was on a customer in his taxi. His victim was congratulated by the judge for having the presence of mind to memorise the number on the man's taxi badge. Nevertheless, the perpetrator was sentenced to just three and a half years in jail, having previously been sentenced, on appeal, to four years for the rape of the girl in the X case. Critics contrasted the length of his sentences with a proposed maximum sentence of twelve years for pregnant women procuring abortions illegally, were the proposed referendum to be passed.

The referendum of 2002 did not go the government's way, but Bertie Ahern could console himself that he had delivered on his promise to the constituency which wanted an abortion referendum. This possibly helped him to win the general election that took place two months later.

Irish law on abortion remains unsatisfactory. Politicians are unwilling to provoke further controversy by legislating for abortion even within the narrow circumstances permitted by the Supreme Court's interpretation of the Constitution. Moreover, that interpretation in no way facilitates the creation of embryos for medical research. The development of embryonic cell research seems likely to occur slowly in Ireland.

The last two decades of the twentieth century were remarkable for the level of gynaecological detail involved in public discussions about abortion in Ireland. The debate was somewhat unreal, given the easy availability of abortion services in Britain for all but the poorest or most helpless Irish women. In the light of the X case, voters have consciously rejected attempts to preclude the risk of suicide as a ground for abortion, and opinion polls show that many also support its provision within Ireland in cases where pregnancy results from rape or incest. The X case marked a turning point in the abortion saga in Ireland, and helped to change the public's perception of the issues involved in banning abortion outright.

'FREE' EDUCATION

Dún Laoghaire, 1966–1995

On 10 March 1967, Donogh O'Malley, the Fianna Fáil Minister for Education who is widely credited with having introduced 'free' secondary education in the Republic of Ireland, died suddenly, aged just 47. That reform had benefited great numbers of Irish families who were delighted to find that they had access, free of charge, to post-primary schooling. Henceforth, such educational costs would be met by the State out of public revenues.

Surprisingly, neither Moody and Martin in their *Course of Irish History* nor R. F. Foster in his *Modern Ireland: 1600–1972* include this highly significant social development in their chronological lists of events in twentieth-century Ireland. However, the former work does include an acknowledgment in its text of the impact of what is remembered as O'Malley's personal initiative. J. H. Whyte notes (p. 355): 'The free education scheme proved popular beyond all expectation, and the number of pupils in post-primary schools shot up from 143,000 in 1965/6 to 301,000 in 1980/81.' While other factors also contributed to that increase in numbers, there can be no doubt that making it easier for families to keep their children in school was something for which Donogh O'Malley is still fondly remembered.

What this change meant for particular families was well expressed by another Fianna Fáil Minister for Education who paid an eloquent personal tribute to O'Malley. Speaking in Limerick at the annual convention of the Association of Secondary Teachers on 22 April 2003, Minister Noel Dempsey declared:

> If people like Donogh O'Malley decided forty years ago that there was no need for change, think of the Ireland we would live in today. He and others made brave decisions that brought about the greatest social revolution in the history of the State. I am one of the beneficiaries of the brave decision to make second-level education available to all.
>
> Many of you in this room, and many hundreds of thousands of people across this country are, like me, among the first of a family ever to benefit from third-level education. Doors were opened for me and for others in my family that would have been unimaginable for my parents.
>
> And we owe that opportunity to the vision and the selflessness of the whole of Irish society — a society that posed questions that had been ignored for too long, that was ready to accept that the modern world required new skills, and that old ways could not survive.

Nearly one month later, on 15 May, addressing the annual congress of the Irish Vocational Education Association, Dempsey further observed:

> The OECD review of the Irish education system in the mid-1960s — 'Investment in Education' — is also widely acknowledged as a defining moment in Ireland's recognition of the vital link between education and the social and economic development of our nation. It created a sea change in people's expectations and ambitions and laid the foundation for major investment in education, which ultimately played such a crucial role in driving the transformation that came to fruition in recent years. Donogh O'Malley responded and his contribution to education has been of huge national significance and should never be forgotten.

It was on 10 September 1966 that Donogh O'Malley announced that there would be free secondary education. He did so at a meeting of the National Union of Journalists in Dún Laoghaire, much to the consternation of the Department of Finance and his Cabinet colleagues. The extent to which Taoiseach Seán Lemass knew in advance of details of the speech is a matter of debate, as is the extent to which O'Malley personally deserves credit for the system of free secondary education that was subsequently developed.

An extensive system of free transportation to school was also put in place, and this greatly helped students to take advantage of the new opportunities. Those new opportunities are sometimes said to have made possible the subsequent strong growth in Ireland's economy, with a 'well-educated workforce' being represented as a necessary precondition for the location of many industries here.

The perceived success of what has come to be regarded as Donogh O'Malley's secondary school scheme, and the public's association of it with Fianna Fáil, was one of the inspirations behind the later decision of the Labour Party to press for free third-level education for undergraduates. Sharing power in a coalition government, Labour had an opportunity to have its policies adopted. During 1994, Labour's Niamh Bhreathnach, then Minister for Education, committed herself to abolishing university fees. Like Donogh O'Malley, she is said to have done so without having first fully cleared her initiative with her Cabinet colleagues. Bhreathnach had been elected to the Dáil to represent Dún Laoghaire, the harbour town where Donogh O'Malley made his announcement of free secondary education, and the departure point for generations of Irish emigrants who had for too long flocked ill-educated to Britain for employment.

On 8 February 1995, the Dún Laoghaire deputy and minister gave the Dáil details of how exactly the government was going to abolish undergraduate fees in publicly funded third-level institutions from January 1996. The subsequent provision of open access to colleges and universities was popular among those sections of society who had any prospect of sending their children there, notwithstanding objections that it benefited the rich as much as it did the middle classes, and more than it did the poor. In fact, said its opponents, there was no reason to believe that the waiving of fees increased the number of students from lower income families attending third-level institutions. Cynics suggested that the Labour Party was seeking the votes of middle-class people and pointed out that there were and are, apart from fees, many other expenses associated with going to college that deter the truly poor. Critics also pointed out that the State already heavily subsidised the universities, even before fees were abolished.

Certainly, Bhreathnach's measure, when it was introduced, made life easier for any families struggling to pay third-level fees. Perhaps these would, in any event, have incurred debts or found other ways of paying for the education of their children. Nevertheless, it is remarkable that Minister Bhreathnach did not benefit politically from her initiative, losing her seat at the next general election in a notable expression of ingratitude by the middle classes and of the electorate's dissatisfaction with her party's performance in government.

There is of course a strong political argument in favour of concentrating increased public expenditure on primary-level education, where the greatest number of people in need can be helped. During 2004, for example, a study for the Department of Education revealed severe literacy problems among primary schoolchildren in disadvantaged areas. There is a strong argument against waiving fees at third-level if it means that such areas of educational and social need are thus deprived of public expenditure. Nevertheless, the wealthy had already been able to claw back much of what they paid in third-level fees by means of tax avoidance through educational covenants. This had involved a considerable loss of revenue to the State prior to Bhreathnach's simultaneous abolition of such covenants when she introduced free education for undergraduates at third-level. It is also believed to be the case that some went to college who would not have done so, had the fees not been abolished.

After 1995, the State struggled and failed to fund the university sector at the level of revenue that might reasonably have been expected to accrue to colleges, had fees been maintained and gradually increased. Poorer students who went to college still struggled to stay there, especially in Dublin, as rental and other costs increased and as the government failed to provide adequate maintenance grants. At the same time, with more young people staying longer in full-time education, a third-level qualification came to be seen by many employers as an essential prerequisite for someone seeking long-term employment in many jobs.

Many regard the introduction of free second-level education as a significant moment that changed us, boosting the personal prospects of individuals and the future of the Irish economy. There is still disagreement about the significance of the subsequent decision to abolish university fees. If the first event helped to change our idea of what is appropriate in terms of State support for education and to express our appreciation of the socio-economic importance of secondary education, the latter initiative focused our minds on the possible limits of State support.

Violence

This country of ours is violent,
I think to myself this morning with surprise —
I only lately realised that dancehall fights
were not as usual everywhere, nor everywhere excused
as young men going wild. I mean in Connemara, not
Belfast.
Half-murdering your neighbour at a dance
at Christmas and St Patrick's Day
was not, it seems, considered de rigueur
for young men everywhere but there it is:

MARY O'MALLEY, 'Violation'
FROM *The Boning Hall*, 2002

THE LATEST ATROCITY

Mostly Northern Ireland, 1968–2005

People remember particular moments. For some it was Bloody Sunday; for others, Bloody Friday; or Dublin or Enniskillen or Omagh or London — or any other place in the terrible topography of the latest atrocity. It may have been a single, horrible incident — a father shot dead while at dinner with his children, or young musicians ambushed on the road. Or it may have been a massacre, like the IRA firebombing of the La Mon House Hotel, outside Belfast, that killed twelve people in February 1978.

Such moments of madness, or badness, were milestones on the road leading to a greater understanding of the fact that violence cannot resolve conflict in Northern Ireland. It has been a long and blood-spattered road.

Slowly but surely the gap widened and the balance shifted between those who were prepared to condone violence in order to achieve their ends, and those who rejected physical force. The politics of manipulating the latest atrocity for narrow political advantage became the politics of reconciliation, up to a point.

On 5 October 1968, a civil rights march in Derry was attacked and broken up by the Royal Ulster Constabulary (RUC). Gerry Fitt and other nationalist leaders were among those wounded by blows from RUC batons. On 4 January 1969, a march from Belfast to Derry by a small group of civil rights activists was savagely attacked by loyalists at Burntollet Bridge in Co. Derry. The marches had tested the patience of those who resented the demands of the nationalist minority in Northern Ireland. Television reports of these two events, and the evident complicity of the security forces in such oppression, had a powerful impact on public opinion in Ireland and beyond.

On 9 August 1971, the United Kingdom government further inflamed passions by introducing internment without trial. Internment was administered in a partisan and inefficient manner, catching in its net nationalists who were politically active, while failing to suppress the IRA.

On 30 January 1972, one of the worst atrocities of the recent troubles in Northern Ireland was perpetrated in Derry. Members of the Parachute Regiment of the British army attacked a big civil rights march, which had been banned by the authorities, killing thirteen people and wounding many more. Their murderous behaviour galvanised nationalist sentiment. Official attempts to gloss over what they had done included the publication of the Widgery Report, which was quickly discredited as a whitewash. The massacre became known as 'Bloody Sunday'.

In the days following Bloody Sunday, some British property in the Republic of Ireland was the object of attacks. A crowd of people cheered while the British Embassy in Dublin burned on 2 February 1972. The crowd was described by Taoiseach Jack Lynch next day in the Dáil as 'representing the different organisations, the trade unions, state bodies, students and, indeed, people from every walk of life'. I was one of those students. However, I slipped away as the fire took hold, feeling that a bad situation had been made worse by the actions of a few men who were clearly organised and determined to destroy the building. The government let the embassy burn as a means of venting public anger and so avoiding even more explosive consequences. Nevertheless, conscious of a threat to the security of the State itself, Lynch rose in the Dáil the next day to condemn 'a small minority — men who, under a cloak of patriotism, seek to overthrow the institutions of this State — [who] infiltrated what was necessarily a peaceful demonstration, infiltrated essentially peaceful groups, and fomented violence.'

When one of the most ardently nationalist members of the Dáil, Neil Blaney, made an inflammatory speech, there followed what Garret FitzGerald, a former Taoiseach, has called 'an instinctive and spontaneous reaction by all subsequent party speakers that was clearly designed to calm emotions'. FitzGerald adds, significantly, that 'from that moment onwards Irish government policy became directed primarily towards seeking peace and stability in Northern Ireland, both for its own sake and also in order to protect our State against the possible overflow effects of Northern Ireland violence' (*Reflections on the Irish State* (Dublin, 2003) p. 177). His observation reflects the fact that any change of attitude in the Republic towards Northern Ireland was not entirely devoid of self-interest. People in the Republic were sorry for the plight of the northern Catholics, but were also beginning to do quite nicely on the economic front. Prominent members of Fianna Fáil, among others, had facilitated a split in Sinn Féin on the basis that elements which they supported, and which became the 'Provos', would concentrate their activities on the northern side of the border and, hopefully, forget about fomenting revolution in the Republic.

As atrocity followed atrocity, we were forced to examine our assumptions. Three weeks after the burning of the embassy, John Taylor, a leading Unionist politician, was shot and seriously injured in Northern Ireland. Jack Lynch immediately praised Taylor and described his attempted assassination as 'the action of evil men with an evil purpose which cannot be condoned in any circumstances by any of us'. The government took steps to ensure, by means of the controversial provision known as 'section 31', that those who advocated paramilitary violence remained off the radio and television airwaves.

An important moment in the evolution of new political thinking was the publication, later in 1972, of Conor Cruise O'Brien's *States of Ireland* (Hutchinson). The author provided an intellectual framework for debate, within which both traditions might be allowed to enjoy what later became known as 'parity of esteem'. On 24 March 1972, the UK government suspended local government at Stormont and introduced a more even-handed form of direct rule from Westminster.

Yet, there were continuing horrors on both sides of the border, and on both sides of the Irish Sea. In Belfast, on 21 July 1972 (Bloody Friday), the Provisional IRA detonated more than twenty explosions, killing 19 people and injuring 130. Any warnings the Provos gave were wholly inadequate and were possibly calculated to create confusion. This was a vicious premeditated attack, intended to put pressure on the United Kingdom government following the breakdown of secret talks that had been taking place between ministers and nationalist paramilitaries, including Gerry Adams.

The atrocity of 21 July 1972 is forgotten by many who remember other bloody moments. It was remarkably savage. That afternoon, between 2.10 p.m. and 3.15 p.m., no fewer than nineteen bombs were exploded by the Provos in various parts of Belfast. Seven civilians and two soldiers died, and more than 120 people were injured. The murderers' youngest victim was Glynn Stephen Parker, aged 14. The first bomb went off at Smithfield Bus Station, having been left in a car in an enclosed yard. Other bombs were also left in locations where civilians gathered. The *Belfast Telegraph* wrote: 'This city has not experienced such a day of death and destruction since the German blitz of 1941.' *The Irish Times* commented: 'Throughout the 32 counties Irish men and women should ponder how a virulent Nazi-style disregard for life can lodge in the hearts of our fellow countrymen.'

Almost two years after Bloody Friday, car bombs exploded in Dublin and Monaghan, killing 33 people on 17 May 1974. British security forces are believed to have facilitated or even organised, with loyalist paramilitaries, the explosions. The full truth of what happened that day is still unknown.

On 21 July 1976, Christopher Ewart-Biggs, the British Ambassador to Ireland, was blown up by an IRA landmine in Co. Dublin. On 10 August that same year, a car being pursued by soldiers in Belfast went out of control and hit and killed three children. This led to the foundation of the 'Peace People' movement, led by Mairead Corrigan and Betty Williams. They subsequently won the Nobel Prize for Peace, but their movement ran out of steam. While it briefly flourished, it had created a way in which people could publicly distance themselves from those who carried out violent acts.

Parts of Birmingham, Manchester and other English cities have also been devastated by explosions related to the troubles. Massive IRA 'spectaculars', such as the bombing of Canary Wharf in London on 9 February 1996, left innocent people spectacularly dead and provided a model for other undemocratic forces to emulate.

But if a single moment of political violence in Ireland was more significant than any other since 1972, it was the bombing of a 'Poppy Day' ceremony in Enniskillen on 8 November 1987. That IRA attack on the commemoration of war dead touched people in a special way, not least because of the subsequent courage of Gordon Wilson, who was caught in the blast and whose daughter died holding his hand. The bomb was planted by the Provos, who at first, in the face of public outrage, lied about the mode of its detonation. Gordon Wilson forgave his daughter's killers and went on, until his death, to play an important role in the search for reconciliation.

On 15 August 1998, four months after the signing of the Good Friday Agreement, a bomb planted by the so-called 'Real IRA' exploded in the centre of Omagh and killed 29 people and two unborn babies. It was the worst single incident of the troubles in Northern Ireland, although the car bombs in Dublin and Monaghan together killed more people on one day. The Omagh bomb confirmed people in their commitment to the peace process, and allowed even Sinn Féin for once to condemn an atrocity for which republicans were responsible.

Yet, notwithstanding the Good Friday Agreement, the IRA and other paramilitary organisations have not entirely gone away. In the case of the IRA, this became blindingly clear in December 2004 and early 2005 when the involvement of some members of that organisation in robbery, intimidation, money-laundering and murder was exposed to the public gaze in an unprecedented way. Some who had watched Sinn Féin's progress in elections both north and south of the border recalled with unease the questions asked by Danny Morrison, Sinn Féin's director of elections, at his party's 1981 Ard Fhéis: 'Who here really believes we can win the war through the ballot box? But will anyone here object if with a ballot box in this hand and an Armalite [rifle] in this hand we take power in Ireland?' Shortly afterwards, his party began to contest elections.

Some acts of violence were mercifully less murderous than intended. Just how bad would have been the consequences for Ireland had Prime Minister Margaret Thatcher and her senior ministers been killed by the IRA bomb that exploded at their Brighton hotel on 12 October 1984? And what cycle of unspeakable reprisals might have been sparked had an attack on a Dublin pub gone as planned? On 21 May 1994, persons thought to belong to the loyalist UVF went to place a bomb at the Widow Scallan's in Pearse Street. Their target was a Sinn Féin/IRA meeting taking place upstairs, but their victims would have included customers who had packed the bar downstairs to watch a boxing bout on television. The UVF bombers were confronted by an IRA guard, whom they shot dead. They fled, leaving their bomb. Although the detonator exploded, fortunately for all present and for the future of the peace process, the main explosives were not ignited.

Those who died in the troubles before 1999 were, that year, individually recalled in a thick book, *Lost Lives*, by David McKittrick, Séamus Kelters, Brian Feeney and Chris Thornton (Mainstream: Edinburgh, 1999). Many more people have been physically or psychologically maimed for life.

Perhaps almost as significant in its own way as Bloody Sunday in Derry, or the slaughter at Enniskillen, was the vicious murder of Robert McCartney in Belfast on 30 January 2005. He was beaten and stabbed to death by members of the IRA, who were drinking in the same pub as he was and whom he had annoyed by making certain statements. McCartney's death spurred his sisters into launching a campaign for justice that damaged Sinn Féin's reputation and that increased pressure both on members of the IRA to desist from common criminality and on the IRA itself to disband.

We have learned slowly, while others paid for our education. One was Ronnie Hill, caught in the Enniskillen blast in 1987. A father of four, he soon lapsed into a coma. Noreen Hill was suffering from cancer, but she dedicated her life to nursing her damaged husband. After Ronnie had been in hospital for four years, Noreen established a nursing home at Holywood, Co. Down, to take care of him and other patients. In December 2000, more than thirteen full years after Enniskillen and never having come out of the coma, Ronnie passed away. Noreen was holding his hand when he died.

SEX ABUSE REVEALED

Ulster Television, 22 October 1995

Towards the end of the twentieth century, the public became aware that some Catholic priests and members of religious orders had been sexually abusing Irish children. Of course, the priests were not unique in this respect. Most child abuse is committed by lay people, including some parents, close relatives, teachers and sports coaches, and abuse has also been committed by some non-Roman Catholic ministers of religion.

Evidence of systematic child abuse on the island of Ireland first came to light in Northern Ireland. In the 1980s, the activities of paedophiles at the Kincora Boys' Home, a Protestant institution in Belfast, were revealed and the ringleader, William McGrath, convicted. McGrath was not only a worker at Kincora but also an influential political activist and agent of the British Intelligence Service MI5. It is claimed that some civil servants, Protestant ministers, politicians and security personnel were involved in a cover-up of what went on. If they were, then they escaped the consequences of any involvement.

People north and south of the border were slow to appreciate the scale of the sex abuse problem. However, a special programme on Ulster Television about a Catholic priest, Fr Brendan Smyth, made it impossible to ignore the reality of what such abuse means for its victims. It would take another television programme, shown on RTÉ, to propel the Irish government into apologising for the State's failure to protect children. Thereafter, television continued to drive the debate, while bishops and government ministers dragged their heels.

During the twentieth century in the Republic of Ireland, the Catholic Church had played a central role in running institutions for children. This suited an impoverished State that long struggled to survive after winning independence from the United Kingdom in 1921. It also suited the Catholic Church, because such institutions were a source of some revenue from the State and an outlet for the energies of many nuns and clergy. Ireland is said to have had a high proportion of its boys and girls institutionalised, relative to Britain. Some of those children had committed crimes, but most simply came from broken or deprived homes.

As Ireland grew prosperous and self-confident during the last four decades of the twentieth century, children began to enjoy greater social protection. Mounting concerns about the response of the Irish State to emerging evidence of child sexual abuse led to the collapse of a coalition government led by Albert Reynolds, on 17 November 1994: Labour had refused to support the appointment of Harry Whelehan, Attorney-General, as president of the High Court. It was felt that the authorities had not acted promptly enough to extradite Fr Brendan Smyth to Northern Ireland, where that priest was wanted in respect of serious sexual abuse charges. Smyth eventually went north of his own volition and was jailed.

Yet even after this, the issue of child abuse still did not receive the official attention that it merited. However, on 22 October 1995, a special programme on the Fr Brendan Smyth case was screened by Ulster Television (UTV). UTV can be received by most viewers within the Republic. The extended edition of *Counterpoint* was entitled 'Suffer Little Children'. It included a particular shot of Smyth that has been repeated subsequently in many other TV programmes on both sides of the border. This shot showed him lumbering across a street, his stocky body and thickset features appearing to register little sign of shame at his having been found out.

The *Counterpoint* programme had an enormous impact on the public both north and south. It made viewers wonder how Smyth had for so long got away with his crimes on both sides of the border and on both sides of the Atlantic Ocean. Smyth himself came to be regarded by many Irish people as the personification of corruption within the Catholic Church. Having served a period of imprisonment in Northern Ireland, he was brought south to the Republic, where he pleaded guilty to a total of 74 charges of indecent and sexual assault committed during 35 years, and was again jailed. He was soon joined by other clerics in an unholy pantheon of sexual abusers.

Public anger mounted, but the reaction of the Irish government was still curiously muted. The print media now ran story after story about some priest or other who had raped an altar boy or abused a sick child. Priests and former priests began to appear in court, frequently, in connection with sexual offences. People were appalled by what they were reading and hearing, and adults who had been abused as children came forward on popular national radio programmes to recount their experiences.

It was soon widely recognised that sexual abuse had taken place within both local parishes and institutions run by religious orders. At some such institutions, there was also a level of physical abuse that far surpassed even the harsh beatings that were common in many Irish schools until the last decades of the twentieth century. Some of the abused believed that the physical abuse itself was sexually charged, and nuns as well as priests were implicated in the affair. In 1996, RTÉ screened *Dear Daughter*, a film by Louis Lentin, that revealed through its interviews what life had been like during the late 1950s and early 60s for children at the Goldenbridge orphanage, Dublin, run by the Sisters of Mercy.

During the late 1990s, decent priests and nuns became depressed. They were already struggling to cope with a heavy workload, as few young people were joining them in their particular way of life, and weekly attendance at church was falling dramatically in some areas. Some priests were cursed or even spat upon as they walked down the street. Not long before, no person would have dared to show disrespect to a priest. When Fr Brendan Smyth died in jail in August 1997, he was buried at night to avoid adverse publicity or disruptive protest.

While members of the general public were sympathetic towards the majority of priests and nuns, many of whom were ageing, there was diminishing public sympathy for the institutional Catholic Church itself. The hierarchy seemed to be gripped by inertia, if not actually in denial about the reality of abuse. The bishops appeared to resent or even despise the media's revelation of the truth.

The Irish State also responded poorly to the emergence of stories about child sexual abuse. Ministers dragged their feet and appeared to hope that the whole problem might blow over. It did not. However, a production screened by RTÉ in April and May 1999 finally pushed the Irish government into announcing a series of measures ostensibly intended to investigate institutional child abuse fully and to provide compensation and justice for the victims or 'survivors' of such abuse. That RTÉ production was a series of three one-hour documentaries by Mary Raftery, entitled *States of Fear*. Although newspapers and RTÉ Radio programmes had for some time been reporting the subject of child abuse, and even a number of RTÉ Television programmes had dealt with it to some extent, *States of Fear* had a special impact. It was widely discussed in the media. On 11 May 1999, just as the last programme in the *States of Fear* trilogy was about to be transmitted that night, the Irish government made a major announcement. It apologised publicly to those who had been abused as children in institutions. This meant, in effect, that the government also accepted partial responsibility for what had happened down the years and effectively accepted at least some legal liability for damages done. An official inquiry into aspects of child abuse was launched.

Then, during 1999 and 2000, TV3, the Republic of Ireland's only privately owned television service, screened a three-part series of documentaries, collectively entitled *Stolen Lives*. The series kept public attention focused vividly on the effects of child abuse. However, one of the three programmes, entitled 'Philomena's Story', was strongly criticised by the Sisters of Mercy and the Catholic archdiocese of Dublin as unfair and untruthful, most particularly in respect of an allegation of group rape. Criticism of the programme raised questions about the broadcasting of emotional and uncorroborated allegations relating to alleged events long past. The nuns initiated legal proceedings in respect of the programme, which continue at the time of writing.

Yet, even after such programmes, the State's response to the abuse scandal has continued to come in for much criticism. In September 2003, Judge Mary Laffoy resigned as chairperson of the official Commission to Inquire into Child Abuse, blaming the government for failing to support her work with adequate powers and resources. During the following month, the Comptroller and Auditor General published his annual report, which revealed many inadequacies in an agreement between the government and religious orders in respect of liability for compensation for survivors of abuse. To this day the government's manner of handling the problem continues to be controversial.

Meanwhile, the remarkable role of television in unravelling the cover-up of child abuse did not end with the transmission of *States of Fear* or *Stolen Lives*. Ulster Television, RTÉ and TV3 having played their part in the unfolding story, now the BBC stepped forward. On 19 March 2002, BBC2, which is widely received throughout Ireland, transmitted a programme entitled *Suing the Pope*. It included moving interviews with victims of abuse in the Irish diocese of Ferns, where Brendan Comiskey had long been the presiding Bishop. Some of the worst abuse of children that is known to have taken place in Ireland had occurred in Ferns when one Fr Seán Fortune worked there.

Bishop Comiskey refused to engage in depth with the BBC programme-makers, but he was caught on camera stepping from his big car and facetiously singing the title of a popular feminist anthem, 'I will survive' (he sang 'we'). He then proceeded literally to shut a door of the church in the face of the TV reporter. Later, with RTÉ preparing to repeat the BBC's programme, Comiskey stepped down.

The central role of broadcasting in the unravelling of the Irish child abuse scandal has been remarkable. The print media helped to tell and to explain the story, with articles by Bruce Arnold for the *Irish Independent* and Patsy McGarry of *The Irish Times* being among the most notable. Popular daytime national radio talk shows, especially those of RTÉ's Marian Finucane, Pat Kenny and Joe Duffy, have also played an important role. But it has been the sight and sound of survivors of child abuse on television that has driven the Church and State into admissions and action. In fairness, it should be said that the Catholic religious orders in Ireland today are generally appalled by what has emerged in respect of the past behaviour of some of their members. It must also be admitted that some in the media have occasionally been over-zealous and unfair to members of the Catholic Church and have had to apologise for certain errors.

During the past decade, revelations in the media appear to have changed the public's understanding of sexual abuse. These revelations may have alienated some individuals from the Catholic Church, or from religion altogether.

VANISHED

Moone, Co. Kildare, 9 November 1995

The telephone receiver swings at the end of its cable, off the hook. A cold breeze chills the phone box in the tiny village of Moone, Co. Kildare. Here, Jo Jo Dullard was last seen late at night on 9 November 1995. The 21-year old from Callan, Co. Kilkenny, missed the last bus home. So she hitched a lift from Naas to Kilcullen, and another lift from Kilcullen to Moone, going south. At Moone, Jo Jo telephoned a friend to tell her what had happened. Jo Jo broke off the conversation for a moment, only to return to tell her friend that she had just been offered yet another lift. That was the last that anyone ever heard from her. She is still missing.

It is believed something terrible happened to Jo Jo Dullard. She was returning to Callan from Dublin to start a new job. Hers is just one of a number of mysterious disappearances that, in recent years, have baffled the Gardaí and left women frightened. At the end of the twentieth century, Irish women were reminded of their vulnerability. But it was not only women who disappeared without trace, to the consternation of their families and loved ones.

Suspicions abound about who may have been responsible for some of the women disappearing, but nothing is proven. In February 2000, hunters out late at night happened upon one man in the act of forcing a woman into a car boot on a lonely country lane in Co. Carlow, and he was captured. The perpetrator was a carpenter in his mid-twenties. Nobody knows if Jo Jo Dullard or any other woman still missing was treated similarly before they vanished. Their disappearance was a brutal reminder that women are not safe in modern Ireland.

Another brutal reminder was the vicious rape of a woman at Cratloe Woods, Co. Clare, by a gang of violent Limerick teenagers in January 2004. Her boyfried was beaten and locked in the boot of their car. Had he not escaped and raised the alarm, perhaps they too would be counted today among the vanished.

The women who have vanished include Annie McCarrick. She went missing on 26 March 1993. Annie was a young American who loved Ireland. Living in Sandymount at the time of her disappearance, she was reported to have been seen taking a bus to Co. Wicklow. She liked walking in the country. There are reports that she may have been in Johnnie Fox's pub, in the hills, later that same evening.

Jo Jo Dullard disappeared two and a half years after Annie McCarrick. Within the three years of the moment Jo Jo vanished, a number of women went missing in what some members of the public came to imagine were circumstances linked to the activities of a serial killer. However, that assumption may be incorrect.

In August 1996, at Tullamore, Co. Offaly, Fiona Pender's partner said goodbye to her as he left for work early. Fiona was 25 years old and seven months pregnant. She was happily looking forward to the arrival of her baby. Fiona was never seen again. Her parents had recently lost one of their other two sons in a motorbike accident and the strain of Fiona's disappearance proved too much for her father. He committed suicide.

In February 1997, Ciara Breen vanished from her family home in Dundalk. The 17-year old slipped out through her bedroom window to meet up with some friends of whom her mother, Bernadette, disapproved. Ciara was never seen again. A man was later questioned about her disappearance. On the day Ciara disappeared, her mother also received news that she herself had cancer.

In February 1998, Fiona Sinnott was last seen alive. The 19-year old from Bridgetown in Co. Wexford was a single mother who had a turbulent relationship with her child's father. She was said to have been on her way to see a doctor about pains in her chest and arm when she vanished. However, as she had previously gone off and stayed with friends on occasions, the alarm was not raised about her disappearance for more than a week.

Two and a half years after Jo Jo Dullard disappeared, on 28 July

1998, an 18-year-old woman vanished into thin air near her home in Newbridge, Co. Kildare. It was a lovely summer's day, the sort of day when it is hard to believe that anything horrible might suddenly happen to someone walking on a residential road in a small Irish town. Deirdre Jacob was back from a teacher training college in England to spend some time with her family. She was in good spirits, expecting her boyfriend to travel over from London to join her in Ireland. As with Annie and Jo Jo, and many others who have gone missing, there is no reason to believe that she did away with herself, or somehow devised a bizarre and complex scheme to cut all ties with her family and friends. One moment she was shopping in Newbridge, talking to people, heading for home. She was seen just hundreds of yards from her parents' house. Then she was gone, without a trace. The Gardaí found nothing. Nobody heard anything. She has never been seen since.

The fact that these young women were never found and that their disappearance was so mysterious led to pressure being put on the Gardaí to improve their performance in relation to the location of missing persons and to the correlation of evidence in such cases. Unease at shortcomings in Garda procedures in the case of missing persons has fed into a wider unease at the performance of Ireland's police force. In October 1998, the Gardaí established 'Operation Trace'. The operation utilised new computer technology, but it has not resulted in the finding of any connection between the circumstances in which these women disappeared. It would be wrong to assume that there is any such connection. The absence of specific crime scenes in the case of the missing persons mentioned above, and the resultant lack of evidence relating to their disappearance, makes any investigation of their cases particularly difficult.

Over the years, a number of commentators have remarked on the fact that a disproportionate number of women have disappeared in Co. Kildare. One such disappearance and associated murder was finally solved thanks to advances in DNA technology ('genetic fingerprinting'). Almost 23 years earlier, on 22 December 1979, Phyllis Murphy (23) was last seen alive near a bus stop in the town of Newbridge, Co. Kildare. Weeks later, her body was discovered in a wooded area of the Wicklow Gap. The Gardaí never closed the case, and two decades after her killing, an experienced detective, Brendan McArdle, sent some semen samples taken from suspects in 1980 to an

English laboratory for testing. His action resulted in the conviction for murder and sentencing to life imprisonment of a former army sergeant from Kildare town, on 31 October 2002. No such suspect has been proven to be connected to more than one disappearance and murder of an Irish woman.

It has been known for people to go missing quite unexpectedly, and to turn up alive later. It is also the case that men as well as women vanish without trace in peculiar circumstances. Perhaps the most poignant such incident in recent years involved Trevor Deely, a young man from Naas, Co. Kildare, who was working in a Dublin bank. He was last seen near the Grand Canal at Baggot Street, at about four o'clock on the morning of 8 December 2000. Trevor had been out celebrating Christmas with friends, and his last known movements have been quite well documented. His image was captured by a number of closed-circuit television cameras attached to various Dublin buildings. It was a wet and windy night and he appears to have been walking home when he simply vanished.

Yet, throughout the years of all these disappearances, there have been two families whose misfortune seemed particularly harsh. Their children disappeared and have never been found. In March 1977, little Mary Boyle, not yet aged 7, vanished in Co. Donegal. A few years before her disappearance, a young girl was abducted and murdered about thirty miles from Mary Boyle's home. Did Mary fall into a bog, or was she too kidnapped and killed? Nobody knows. And nobody knows what happened to Philip Cairns nine years later. His parents have never given up hope that their son may be alive. He went missing on 23 October 1986, aged just 13. He had come home from school for lunch and was on his way back to classes when he vanished. His schoolbag was found, but the Gardaí could detect no clues from it to help them in their search for Philip. The bag was found days after his disappearance on a laneway that had earlier been searched thoroughly. A number of his books were missing from it. Given the emergence of so many accounts of paedophilia in Ireland in recent years, it is not surprising that some have speculated that Mary Boyle and Philip Cairns were the victims of sexual predators. Some men now known to have committed sexual crimes are said to have lived not far from Philip's home. There is no evidence to support such speculation. More recently, when Robert Holohan (11) disappeared from Midleton, Co. Cork, on 4 January 2005, people feared also that he may have been abducted by paedophiles, even foreign paedophiles, and there was some feverish reporting in sections of the media. However, Robert's body was found eight days later and a young neighbour, aged 20, was charged with his manslaughter.

There is no definite pattern that connects the events surrounding disappearances in recent decades. It is not even established that any of those who vanished were attacked, although it is quite possible. Certain people who vanished received more publicity than others, and some Irish people disappeared abroad in circumstances that received little media attention. At least one Irishman is missing in India, and another in Florida, USA, in what seem to be suspicious circumstances. Women other than those already mentioned have also vanished. From time to time, people on the missing lists have turned up much later, either alive or dead. Two books have given detailed accounts of missing Irish persons. They are Barry Cummins's *Missing: Missing Without Trace in Ireland* (Gill & Macmillan, 2003) and Valerie Cox's *Searching: The Stories of Ireland's Missing People* (Blackwater Press, 2003).

The official Garda website now has a section for missing persons, following the example set by an unofficial website, www.missing.ws. The latter was created by a priest in Little Bray, Fr Aquinas Duffy, after the disappearance of his cousin, Aengus Shanahan. On 11 February 2000, 20-year-old Aengus vanished without trace off the streets of Limerick City. A 'National Missing Persons Helpline' has also been established at 1850-442-552. According to Fr Duffy's website:

> It is important to note that any person over 18 years of age is entitled in law to go missing of their own free will. Indeed, hard as it may be to imagine, some missing persons may not want to be found. But families who have a son or daughter missing just want to know that their loved ones are OK. Knowing this alone would be a source of great help. Every year, there are 1,800–2,000 people reported missing to the Gardaí. 99% of these cases are resolved. For the 1% that are not resolved (20 + a year), their families must live with the uncertainty.

This website also refers its visitors to a Missing Persons Association.

It is not known if more Irish people disappear today than in previous years and centuries. Certainly, such disappearances now receive considerable publicity and have a great impact on the public mind. Increasing mobility, especially the proliferation of vehicles on our roads, makes it easier for any potential abductor to move without being noticed from one part of the country to another, and to transport a victim for disposal elsewhere.

AN ATTACK ON DEMOCRACY

Newlands Cross, 26 June 1996

The brutal slaying of Veronica Guerin shocked Ireland. It changed our understanding of the dangers of investigative journalism, and awoke us to a serious threat to society from organised criminal gangs. On 26 June 1996, she was shot dead as she waited in her car for the lights to turn green. The then Taoiseach, John Bruton, called her killing 'an attack on democracy'.

On an earlier occasion, Veronica had been shot in the thigh by an assailant who wanted to stop her writing about particular aspects of the criminal underworld. On that occasion, she had been preparing to go out to a party being given by the *Sunday Independent* for its staff and columnists. I was at that party and I remember how surprised we were to learn of the unprecedented attack. It came as a great shock when the line was later crossed between assaulting or intimidating a journalist and assassinating one.

Guerin was the first journalist in Ireland to be murdered because of her work. She was not the last. On 28 September 2001, Martin O'Hagan of the *Sunday World* was gunned down near Lurgan. His killing has received far less attention both at home and abroad than that of Veronica Guerin, partly because his particular 'beat' meant that people outside Northern Ireland have tended to regard him as just another unfortunate victim of the troubles. However, he too died because he reported on crime, albeit crime committed by a gang of loyalists with an occasional political agenda.

Guerin was not yet 40 years old when she was killed at Newlands Cross, on the road from Naas to Dublin. Her assassin came and went by motorbike. She was married, with a young child, and one criminal had even threatened to rape her son. She insisted on continuing her work, and her employers capitalised on her high profile by mounting an advertising campaign that promoted her stories and helped to make Veronica Guerin a household name. Independent Newspapers were criticised after her death for not having done more to support and protect her, and even for not forcing her to stop. She did not wish to stop, believing passionately that the public has a right to know about the criminal underworld.

It cannot be said that the deaths of Guerin and O'Hagan have led to the investment by any media organisation of very significant new resources in an investigative unit dedicated to honouring their memories by exposing criminals. Nor can it be asserted with confidence that the shock of their deaths resulted in such an improvement in Irish policing that the operations of gangs like those which murdered Guerin and O'Hagan were permanently inhibited.

It is possible to exaggerate the power of organised criminals in Ireland. Some academic observers have discerned what they describe as a 'moral panic' in the reaction of politicians and the media to Guerin's murder. They say that statistics do not support any perception that violent crime is spinning out of control, and they fear that editors and political strategists have used Veronica Guerin mainly to boost the circulation of their newspapers or to increase the power of the State.

However, many others worry that statistics on crime do not capture the full picture, and that the behaviour of gangs importing illegal drugs has had a particularly destructive effect on the social fabric of poorer communities. Irish people who oppose ordinary criminals, and who oppose paramilitaries involved in criminal violence, have felt more vulnerable since the deaths of Guerin and O'Hagan. Successive governments have been grappling with the problem of violent, organised crime rather than solving it, and the public is disturbed by reports of incompetence or corruption within the Gardaí and the Police Service of Northern Ireland.

Guerin's murder spurred the State into adopting a number of new measures aimed at making life difficult for criminals, including the establishment of a Criminal Assets Bureau to confiscate the proceeds of crime. This was certainly an improvement on the situation where criminals had brazenly enjoyed the fruits of their illegal activity. Furthermore, following Guerin's murder, those whom the State believed to have been involved either directly or indirectly in her killing were targeted, and some were jailed for other offences. In 1998, Paul Ward was convicted of her murder. However, later on appeal he succeeded in having that conviction overturned when the credibility of a state-protected witness was successfully impugned. This was disappointing for those who had hoped that the use of 'supergrass' informers as witnesses in important cases might prove useful in defeating organised crime. Subsequently, John Gilligan was found not guilty of ordering Guerin's murder, but was jailed for twenty-eight years on drugs charges.

A film released in 2003 and starring Cate Blanchett paid due respect to Guerin's memory. So, too, have a number of editions of *Evil Empire* by Paul Williams. Williams is a popular crime journalist, whose own stories have appeared regularly in the *Sunday World* and who himself has been threatened with serious violence by criminals because of what he has written. *Evil Empire* is a fascinating account of John Gilligan and his gang, and of the murder of Veronica Guerin. Williams clearly respected Guerin's skills as a journalist, and admits that he had even envied her on occasions. He recalls how she had first arrived on a front page at the *Sunday Tribune*, having flown to South America and tracked down Eamonn Casey, the former bishop of Galway, whom she then interviewed exclusively.

However, a number of Irish journalists have been less kind to her. The first book on Veronica Guerin and her killing, by Emily O'Reilly, did her memory few favours. Published quickly, O'Reilly's book has become a source on which people rely for their information about Guerin's life and work. In 2003, it was distributed afresh and unchanged, in large quantities, to coincide with the release of *Veronica Guerin*, the film.

It includes various harsh criticisms of Guerin, and nine pages are devoted to an account of affidavits sworn by John Traynor. Traynor, she writes, was an associate of the 'self-confessed chief murder suspect'. He himself had assaulted Veronica Guerin. According to Paul Williams, experienced Garda officers have described Traynor as an 'extremely clever, manipulative and duplicitous' gangster. One BBC reporter referred to O'Reilly's book as 'the second fall of Veronica Guerin'.

O'Reilly admits: 'I had rarely read what she wrote, because I did not take a great interest in crime' and 'as an area of journalistic or intellectual interest, crime did not excite me'. Yet, she has no problem concluding: 'Veronica was not revealing truths that would otherwise have been hidden' and 'even if she saw herself as involved in a crusade against dangerous people, her journalism contributed nothing to their downfall'. Others disagree with this judgment. Veronica's journalism helped to bring dangerous people into the public light: if many of their ilk are still operating today, it is not because Veronica Guerin surrendered to their intimidation.

Veronica Guerin's brother, Jimmy Guerin, has paid her an eloquent tribute in his recent book, *Justice Denied: Crimes in Ireland* (Blackwater Press, 2004). Chronicling a number of the most high-profile killings in Ireland in recent history, he devotes almost seventy pages to his sister and deals directly with some of those whom he believes treated her inadequately or improperly when she was alive, or treated her memory and reputation unfairly since she died.

Veronica Guerin was killed for attempting to tell the truth about men who were bent on evil and who would stop at nothing to protect their criminal empire. She and Martin O'Hagan deserve to be honoured as people who died for their profession and who helped to highlight the threat to freedom and democracy that is posed by violent criminals.

A FATE WORSE THAN DEATH

Fairview, Dublin, 29 July 1999

A social outing in Ireland can end in brain damage or paralysis, 'a fate worse than death', in the words of one judge. Assaults on strangers in recent years have frequently been gratuitous, involving no connected theft of personal items. People have been punched, kicked, bitten and stabbed. Knocked to the ground, they may have further blows and boots rained down upon them and some have even been jumped on by their assailants. Bottles and knives are used. Women as well as men commit savage assaults. When young people are out late at night in Irish cities, especially in Dublin, their parents worry about their safety.

Politicians and others have linked street violence to the assailants' abuse of alcohol and drugs. It has also been claimed that a macho culture is breeding contempt for human dignity and is encouraging young men to attack others — just for the hell of it. That macho culture is not confined to Ireland. Films such as *The Fight Club* are suspected of exacerbating such a culture. Some groups of middle-class school-leavers have taken to attacking one another when abroad on celebratory cheap trips, after completing their Leaving Certificate examinations, and a number of boys have been seriously injured in such attacks at foreign resorts. There have been similar incidents at home in Ireland.

Some of the random violence has been connected with other crimes. Offering resistance to a mugging, even where perhaps only a mobile phone is at stake, can increase the likelihood of a sudden and fierce assault on the victim.

One of the worst violent attacks in Dublin took place at Annesley Bridge Road, Fairview, on 29 July 1999. The incident was to receive more publicity than most such incidents because the injuries sustained by the victim were so especially dreadful, and also because the victim was a visitor from abroad whose plight received international attention.

Guido Nasi was an Italian student who came to Ireland to learn English. He was 17 years old and it was his first time living away from home. He and some friends were playing football in Fairview Park. They were joined for a short while by some Dublin youths but, as these departed, Nasi realised that his wallet was missing. He chased and grabbed the youth whom he believed had stolen it. Two of the boy's acquaintances struck Nasi. As the confrontation continued, a man intervened and advised the boys to flee before the Gardaí arrived. As Nasi turned away, that same man hit him on the head with a bottle partly filled with lager. Nasi fell to the ground, banging his head on the pavement.

Nasi was taken to hospital in a dazed state, but was still able to walk. However, he rapidly deteriorated and he went into a coma that lasted for weeks. He ended up almost totally paralysed from the neck down. His attacker was caught and he confessed. The court heard that the assailant, aged 29 at the time of the assault, was an alcoholic who had been drinking for most of the day of the attack. The court was told that the assault was 'fuelled by drink and rage'.

A letter from Guido Nasi was read to the court. It had been prepared with great difficulty and with the assistance of others. Its tone captured the sense of loss and shock experienced by victims of random violence. He asked:

> Why can't I read or write? Why can't I go to school, which I enjoyed so much and which gave me so much satisfaction? Why am I living such a monotonous life without all the activities of young people of my age which are my rights? Why, when my friends have finished university, will I be still waiting to finish school? Why will I always be separated from my friends when they go ahead and I stand still? Why me? Why?

The perpetrator came from a family with a history of criminal violence. He was sentenced to eight and a half years in jail. During an unsuccessful appeal by the assailant against the length of that sentence, Mr Justice Hugh Geoghegan said that the phrase 'a fate worse than death' came to mind when one contemplated Guido Nasi's condition. The assailant had informed the court that he deeply regretted 'the terrible, catastrophic injuries inflicted on Mr Nasi'.

Nasi is the only child of a single mother. She was reported to have made financial sacrifices to give him a chance to come to Dublin and to improve his prospects in life. A vegetarian, he was tall and lively, and wore his hair in dreadlocks. His plight after the attack outraged most Irish people, but it also shamed them. Moral and financial support was proffered to him and to his mother, and the Lord Mayor of Dublin made a special appeal to people for help. Two years after the attack, Guido Nasi was back in Dublin, in a wheelchair, to thank the Irish people for the support he had received. His condition had improved slightly following treatment at an Austrian clinic, but he faced a bleak future. He was reported to have limited power in one hand and to have managed to complete a collection of poetry, entitled *Just Look into My Eyes: Verses from a Silent Bed.*

For many Irish people, the attack on Nasi was not surprising. While he had decided to confront a suspected pickpocket, there was no excuse for what had ensued. Other youths had been assaulted who had given their attackers no pretext whatsoever for violent assaults. It seemed that walking in the park or down a street was becoming a lottery.

There has been no consistent pattern to street attacks. If some street violence has appeared to have a racist and xenophobic edge to it, much does not. Most victims have been both Irish and white. If there is an element of public panic fed by tabloid headlines, there has been a real basis for people's fears and anxieties. While the Gardaí publish crime statistics which suggest that the incidence of assault may not be as spectacularly high as some suppose, many families know directly or indirectly of someone who has been attacked. And the violence can erupt in suburbs as well as in city centres.

In 1999, Raonaid Murray was stabbed to death walking home on a quiet path in Glenageary, Co. Dublin, from a nearby disco. She was 17. During 2002, a brawl outside a filling station in Goatstown left one youth fighting for his life. A Cork student received severe head injuries after an unprovoked attack. Another was killed in a separate incident. A Kilkenny hurler lay in a coma for days after being attacked outside a nightclub. Young men and women told stories of being suddenly hit in the face, stabbed or knocked down from behind for no apparent reason. The phrase used by a lawyer in Guido Nasi's case to describe his assailant's behaviour, 'fuelled by drink and rage', again springs to mind to explain such incidents.

One particular assault, on 31 August 2000, attracted much attention. Brian Murphy, aged 18, was killed outside Club Anabel at the Burlington Hotel in Dublin 4. The Gardaí did not receive the full co-operation of all relevant witnesses. The four young men charged with his manslaughter had attended the prestigious Blackrock College. On 8 March 2004, as their trial concluded, Murphy's mother addressed the court. Her moving account of how the family was devastated by their loss was published in full the following morning by *The Irish Times*. Another mother's sad story appeared in the *Irish Independent* on 18 December 2004. Miriam Higgins told the court about her son, Alan (17), who was murdered for his mobile phone in Dublin on 12 October 2002. His killer, at whose home the Gardaí found €1,500 worth of cocaine, had told the court: 'I just stabbed the bloke [more than once, with a steak knife carried in the killer's pocket]. I am very sorry. It wasn't meant to happen that way.' On 11 November 2003, at Mountmellick, Co. Laois, Darragh Conroy (14) was beaten to death with a hammer that was wielded repeatedly by another teenager who wanted his mobile phone.

Brian Murphy's death and that of another teenager shortly afterwards were linked in the public mind with excessive drinking by young people, and with the aggressive promotion of alcohol in nightclubs. With the price of drinks pegged at certain hours by some pubs and clubs, youths throughout Ireland were encouraged to increase the pace and amount of their consumption. Reckless mixtures of shorts and Red Bull, and other potent combinations, appeared to have been regarded by some young people as a daring statement of their individuality or flair. A further factor in the growing problem of violence was said to be the taking of performance-enhancers by some sports players, leading to what is known in certain circles as 'roid rage' (a play on the words 'steroid' and 'road rage'). However, the suggestion that the use of steroids might be significant in explaining more than a handful of assaults is hotly contested by schools. The government took the view that a relaxation of licensing laws had exacerbated the problem and tightened the regulations again. On 15 June 2004, the Oireachtas Committee on Health and Children made a number of additional recommendations aimed at curbing excessive drinking. They also highlighted the role of sports sponsorship and of advertising generally in glamorising alcohol.

A lack of effective regulation in relation to the type and quality of supervision at nightclubs has created problems, and some bouncers have used excessive or dangerous force when they encountered even reasonable objections to the exercise of their unofficial authority. This has heightened the hazards that have come to surround a night out for young people in our cities.

Racism has also been a factor in some attacks. Groups involved with immigrants report frequent verbal abuse of African, Chinese, Romanian and other people visiting or working in Ireland. This abuse sometimes spills over into physical violence. One particularly savage racist attack took place on Dublin's Pearse Street in June 2000. The principal victim was actually white. David Richardson of Bristol, England, was in Dublin with his black wife to visit their son, Christian. Christian had got a job in telemarketing in Ireland. David Richardson was set upon, beaten and stabbed, and almost died. He had dared to remonstrate with youths who taunted his family with shouts of 'Niggers out'. David Richardson's injuries were expected to have lasting effects. His assailant was subsequently jailed for seven and a half years.

On 15 March 2005, three men convicted for their part in violent disorder at a pub in New Ross, Co. Wexford, on a night in 2003 when Lars Forsmark was beaten to death there, walked free from court. Their sentences were suspended. There was no evidence that any of them had struck Forsmark, and the judge observed that, 'Everyone deserves a second chance'. Unfortunately, no second chance is available to the victims of assault who die violently or who are permanently disabled.

———

Random attacks have changed our perception of the quality of our lives, and have made us feel less secure in our own towns and cities.

HIT AND RUN

Raphoe, Co. Donegal, 14 October 1996

Richard Barron, a cattle dealer, died at Raphoe, Co. Donegal, on 14 October 1996. Although Barron appears to have been killed in a hit-and-run motor accident, Mr Frank McBrearty Jr allegedly confessed to Barron's killing. The Director of Public Prosecutions decided that McBrearty ought not to be prosecuted.

The circumstances of Barron's death and McBrearty's 'confession' gave rise to controversy about the role of certain Gardaí who were stationed locally. Inquiries by Mr Justice Frederick Morris into Garda activities in Donegal revealed a saga of ineptitude, corruption and malpractice. The arm of the State that is meant to protect citizens from violence has been weakened in recent years by the violence and ineptitude of some of its own members, in Donegal and beyond.

There has always been a great deal of public sympathy and support for the Gardaí, notwithstanding their faults and occasional lapses, and the dangers and difficulties they face are still very much appreciated. Rumours or reports of bribery are extremely rare and minor incidents involving the solicitation of payment in relation to motoring offences, for example, have been dealt with promptly. Nevertheless, in recent decades people have seemed more ready than at other times to criticise the Gardaí publicly, and to fret privately that the force may not be up to the job of policing a modern society. The erosion of confidence caused by events such as those surrounding the deaths of Richard Barron and John Carthy (below), or by leaks from the force, has been exacerbated by the willingness of Gardaí to contract the 'blue flu', a fictional illness which saw large numbers withdraw their labour in pursuit of higher pay. This action cast them in a new light for any members of the public who had hitherto harboured the notion that individual Gardaí were selflessly dedicated to their duty.

In earlier years, concerns about the integrity of the Gardaí tended to centre on the compromising of the force through occasional political interference in the investigation or prosecution of influential individuals, and the moving of insistent investigators to stations distant from their homes. In so far as the Gardaí themselves were regarded with scepticism, it tended to be in relation to peripheral matters such as their ability to earn enough overtime to become landlords, or their involvement as bouncers at various and sometimes dubious nightspots. Thirty years ago and earlier, there were certainly accusations that Gardaí sometimes assaulted those whom they arrested, but it was generally felt that such assaults were probably deserved in some way. They also occurred out of sight and were generally directed at people in the lower social classes, who had limited opportunities to articulate an effective protest through the media or the courts.

During the early years of the twenty-first century, the Gardaí have stood loudly accused of occasional gross ineptitude, deviousness, breaches of confidence, boorishness, assault, and even worse. Such accusations no doubt reflect unfairly on the great majority of the force, but the force has not helped itself by failing to treat many complaints seriously and by engaging in a form of industrial action that appeared devious, if not dishonourable. They have also failed to be seen to embrace enthusiastically the sort of computer technology that is a symbol of any organisation eager to meet the challenges of the modern world. The Gardaí's failure to reform internal systems and to adopt the best possible procedures is, rightly or wrongly, connected in the public mind with their failure to solve a number of cases in which young women in Ireland have mysteriously disappeared without trace. Concerns about the force's methodology were heightened by their handling of the case of Dean Lyons, a heroin addict charged with the grisly murder of two people at Grangegorman, Dublin, on 8 March 1997, and later detained notwithstanding the fact that another man confessed to the crime.

The Gardaí have also been seen openly to hit people, some of whom belonged to the more privileged classes. The most spectacular example of this occurred on May Day 2003, during a 'Save the Streets' protest by a mixed bag of protesters, quite a few of whom were students. Some of the protesters may have provoked the Gardaí by word or deed, and their methods of protesting were not entirely above reproach. However, some Gardaí were caught on camera, that day, flailing young people with their batons. The widespread use of video cameras in one form or another, and the greater awareness of civil rights together with the availability of free legal aid, make it more likely than ever that such Garda conduct will not go publicly unnoticed. Since the late 1990s, millions of euro in compensation have been paid from the public purse in out-of-court settlements of assault claims against the Gardaí. The fact that the consequences for the Gardaí involved in such cases appear to have been negligible, in terms of disciplinary action, has exacerbated the public's growing frustration with the way the force is managed. It should be added, however, that a number of Gardaí who were prosecuted in respect of their behaviour on May Day 2003 were subsequently acquitted.

It is also the case that the force depends on the government to fund it adequately and to pass the laws necessary to police properly a modern and complex state. Such funding and legislation have not always been forthcoming. Moreover, concerns and expectations in relation to civil liberties have also become more demanding, and this has put additional strains on the Gardaí who were used to conducting interrogations of suspects or arrested persons out of the presence of lawyers and in the absence of audio or video recorders. The Gardaí are expected to aspire to higher standards than ever at a stage in our history when criminals are vicious and violent and when it is increasingly difficult to differentiate between paramilitaries and so-called 'ordinary decent criminals'. Particularly shocking was the killing of Det. Garda Jerry McCabe and the serious wounding of Det. Garda Ben O'Sullivan by IRA robbers at Adare, Co. Limerick, on 7 June 1996.

The 'blue flu' of 1998 was a watershed in the relationship between the Gardaí and the public. During that unorthodox withdrawal of labour, with most Gardaí calling in sick, Garda Commissioner Pat Byrne told the Garda Representative Association (GRA) that his force could 'never be the same as it was on April 30th last'. The first outbreak of 'flu' occurred on 1 May 1998, and its subsequent recurrence prompted the government to find a way to settle the dispute. The public was contemptuously amused.

However, it was not the fact that the Gardaí got away with blue flu that worried people most, but the possibility that some members of the force were getting away with 'blue murder' when it came to their treatment of members of the public. The Gardaí's own response to complaints became increasingly unsatisfactory. Internal Garda investigations into certain incidents proved so unwieldy and unsatisfactory that two official tribunals of inquiry were established by the State. Thus, firstly the Morris Tribunal was set up in April 2002, mandating Mr Justice Frederick Morris to inquire into certain matters relating to the behaviour of the Gardaí in Donegal. Some of these matters had earlier been investigated inconclusively by a Garda team under the supervision of Assistant Commissioner Kevin Carty.

For its part, the Barr Tribunal was established in July 2002, mandating Mr Justice Robert Barr to inquire into the facts and circumstances surrounding the fatal shooting of John Carthy at Abbeylara, Co. Longford, on 20 April 2000. An armed and disturbed Carthy had held the Gardaí at bay for some time before emerging from his home and being shot dead by the Gardaí. The Oireachtas itself had earlier attempted to investigate what had happened, but a parliamentary committee overreached itself when it strayed into areas requiring judicial decisions and procedures. Judge Barr himself had earlier been strongly critical of Garda methods and evidence in the cases of Paul Ward, accused of the murder of Veronica Guerin, and Colin Murphy, prosecuted in relation to the awful bombing of Omagh on 15 August 1998.

While the Morris and Barr tribunals got on with their work, at times painfully slowly, further allegations were made about the failure of the Gardaí to act properly and promptly on information relating to cross-border security, and particularly relating to the bombing of Omagh in 1998. On the one hand, some were concerned that the force may have put the safety of its informants ahead of that of members of the public, particularly in relation to the movements of a certain car. On the other, Garda eagerness to convict Colin Murphy of involvement in that mass murder led to Barr accusing some of them of 'outrageous behaviour' and 'persistent lying on oath'.

Indeed, over the years, accusations about Garda ineptitude or collusion in relation to the Northern Ireland troubles have ranged across the spectrum. There were suspicions that the force had been lax in its pursuit of those loyalists and any members of the United

Kingdom security forces responsible for planting the Dublin and Monaghan car bombs and for attempting to bomb the Widow Scallan's pub. However, some Gardaí were also alleged to have colluded with the IRA. A retired Canadian judge, Peter Cory, was appointed to inquire into two such allegations. One related to the 1989 murder of two senior RUC officers attending a meeting with senior Gardaí in Dundalk. Following the presentation of Cory's report on this murder, the Irish government decided to order further enquiries. However, in respect of the IRA murder of Lord Justice Maurice Gibson and Lady Cecily Gibson on 25 April 1987, Cory found that he could 'come to no other conclusion but that there is simply no evidence of collusion on which to base a direction to hold a public inquiry'. The Gibsons had been driving across the border after a holiday. Cory conducted his investigations as part of a cross-border review of six outstanding complaints of alleged collusion between security forces and paramilitaries on both sides of the border.

The response of the Irish State to public concerns about the Gardaí has been slow and, seemingly, resentful. While eager to demand and support the implementation of elaborate measures in Northern Ireland for the supervision of the police and the protection of human rights there, following the acceptance of the Good Friday Agreement, the Government of the Republic of Ireland was remarkably slow and unwilling to match new institutions north of the border with bodies of similar weight and substance in the south. In that context, during 2003, when the Minister for Justice proposed to introduce new penalties for Gardaí who leaked or sold information, his action was as much seen as a measure to protect Gardaí from investigative journalism and public scrutiny, as it was regarded as a necessary step to prevent some mercenary members of the force from selling private information to newspapers, or to discourage careless gossip that breaches the confidentiality of dealings with the Gardaí at all levels. Such was the degree of public dissatisfaction that, on 8 January 2004, when RTÉ's *Primetime* programme screened a special and controversial report on Garda abuse, its reporter, Brendan O'Brien, concluded: 'Confidence in the force has been badly dented in recent years.'

Scandals

They hold such broken attitudes
that once were strong enough to hold
their own in gleaming city-states —
now the marble flows in them
like burst mercury, making them fragments
of a dance to ring the room:
damaged patriarchs and footloose caryatids.

CAITRÍONA O'REILLY, 'Statuary: 1. The Crouching Boy'
FROM *The Nowhere Birds*, 2001

WHERE'S THE BEEF?

Manchester, England, 13 May 1991

The programme had a major impact on the public's perception of the Irish beef industry, dominated by Larry Goodman and his company, Anglo-Irish Beef Processors. It blew the whistle on malpractice and confirmed the worst fears of consumers about official neglect of their interests and about the misuse of European taxpayers' money in the agricultural sector.

The ITV programme was broadcast throughout the United Kingdom on 13 May 1991. Produced by the *World in Action* team of Granada Television, Manchester, it opened dramatically with images of money and meat and, placed among them, a photograph of Larry Goodman. The narrator intoned: 'For over twenty-five years, this man has been the boss of a powerful international organisation that is dedicated to killing.'

As shots of cattle being gutted and of blood flowing filled the screen, the narrator continued: 'He is Irishman Larry Goodman, Europe's biggest beef baron. For almost twenty years, Goodman's companies have made a killing out of European taxpayers.' Anyone dozing in an armchair when the programme started was now probably sitting bolt upright. The viewer's attention was held as Patrick McGuinness, a former Goodman accountant, talked about how easy it was to abuse the system of subsidies for beef processors

The programme's allegations became even more serious as Barry Desmond, a Labour Party TD and sometime government minister, began to speak of his receiving threatening phone calls from Northern Ireland, telling him to 'lay off Larry Goodman'. Goodman was next described by the programme presenter as 'Europe's Mr Meat, the man who makes his money putting the beef into Britain's supermarkets while picking up millions from taxpayers who have been handing out money for nothing'. Goodman was described as 'the main supplier of Britain's top supermarkets'.

Viewers heard that Goodman had left school early. They saw the modest terraced house in the small town of Ardee, Co. Louth, which served as Goodman's corporate headquarters. This was contrasted with the rural mansion where he now lived, and where he had a swimming pool, a Mercedes car and a helicopter among other luxuries. Goodman companies were said to have facilitated the evasion of tax by making irregular payments to their employees.

The programme showed an old clip of film in which Goodman claimed: 'We stand for integrity.' However, it was claimed that veterinary stamps were forged in Goodman's factories. Viewers were told that the Irish Department of Agriculture had declined to participate in the programme.

The Irish taxpayer was being exposed to particular liability and risk, according to *World in Action*. This was in respect of export subsidies and guarantees that Goodman was being given by the Irish State when dealing with Iraq and other lucrative markets. As export subsidies were considered, a photograph of Taoiseach Charles Haughey was shown hanging on a meat hook next to one of Larry Goodman.

World in Action noted that Goodman's publicly stated policy was 'to buy only the best beef', but claimed: 'In practice, he bought everything.' It was revealed that old, frozen meat from European intervention stores (some thirteen years old) was repackaged as having being killed ostensibly within the previous year or two. Some of it was said to have been green and dirty, and some of it refrozen. 'No matter what shape it was in, it was reboxed', according to a former worker. One investigation by Customs officials in Waterford, in 1986, found irregularities but was said to have been kept secret at the time. It was alleged that Goodman's companies cheated buyers abroad by, for example, providing meat to Muslims that purportedly was killed in the appropriate ritual fashion but that actually was not. *World in Action* reported that Goodman claimed that any irregularities were the responsibility of subcontractors.

Larry Goodman declined to be interviewed. The programme's researcher, Susan O'Keeffe, approached him outside his local church and asked him about the allegations of bogus veterinary stamps, false documents, rotten meat and irregular payments. Viewers saw him smiling tightly as he sat into the driver's seat of his Mercedes and made off without any comment. In a statement issued later, his group of companies said that it did not knowingly breach any EC regulations.

World in Action told of financial donations to Fianna Fáil from the Goodman group and of Charles Haughey having publicly promoted Goodman's activities. Haughey's photograph was again displayed on a meat hook. He was said to have endorsed Goodman with grants and to have launched Goodman's most important investment programme. Viewers heard that when Barry Desmond criticised Haughey's role in Goodman's affairs, he had been accused by Haughey of 'national sabotage' and had received anonymous phone calls of a threatening nature.

The programme also revealed that a major European Commission investigation of Goodman had been avoided, and it asked what role, if any, Ireland's EC Commissioner, Ray MacSharry, had played in persuading a Dutch bank to hold off taking firm action to recover a large sum of money owed to it by Goodman. MacSharry denied asking his Dutch counterpart to intervene with the Dutch bank

Viewers also learned that the Irish parliament had been recalled specially in order to rush through emergency legislation in favour of Goodman's business when a particular financial crisis threatened it, in the aftermath of the Iraqi invasion of Kuwait and of Iraq's defaulting on its debts. This emergency legislation had allowed the courts to appoint an examiner rather than a liquidator. The programme ended by noting that in the forthcoming year, 'Larry Goodman's companies will again be claiming millions in taxpayers' handouts.'

One government minister responded immediately to the programme. This was Desmond O'Malley, a strong critic of the relationship between Goodman and the Irish State. Leader of the Progressive Democrats, the minority party in government, O'Malley insisted on an investigation. On 24 May 1991, just eleven days after the *World in Action* broadcast, Dáil Éireann passed a resolution establishing a tribunal to inquire into the programme's allegations regarding illegal activities, fraud and malpractice, and into related matters. Fianna Fáil, the much larger partner in government, was not entirely pleased. Taoiseach Charles J. Haughey reminded the House of the importance of the beef industry to the Irish economy and noted that it faced 'major market challenges'. He added:

> For a number of years now one of the most persistent and venomous political campaigns ever has been waged in an attempt to discredit the Government over the affairs of the Goodman companies. The whole basis of this attack is, by innuendo and association, to create the impression that Mr Goodman and his companies enjoyed some unique ill-defined protective relationship with the Fianna Fáil Government of 1987–89, a kind of relationship that they did not have with the previous Fine Gael-Labour Coalition Government. Nothing could be further from the truth as the records clearly show.
>
> One of the very first decisions of the Fine Gael-Labour Coalition Government on coming into office in late December 1982 was to grant export credit insurance for the first time in respect of beef exports to Iraq to Mr Goodman's company, Anglo-Irish Meats Limited. Concerns were expressed at the time about the unacceptable financial risks in the midst of the Iran-Iraq war, but these were overruled. Incidentally, this was done on the basis of a proposal put to the Government by the Minister for Trade, Commerce and Tourism, the late Deputy Frank Cluskey, former leader of the Labour Party.

Another Fianna Fáil deputy, Dermot Ahern, who represented the Louth constituency in which Goodman's HQ was located, attacked *World in Action*. Later, in 2002, Ahern would become Minister for Communications, the Marine and Natural Resources, with responsibility for Irish broadcasting policy. He was appointed Minister for Foreign Affairs in September 2004. The future minister with responsibility for broadcasting told the Dáil in 1992:

> I should like to place on record my abhorrence at the *World in Action* programme. I watched the programme and was absolutely horrified at several aspects of the programme. Indeed, the very first statement made was: 'This man makes his living out of killing.' That is no way to start a programme that sets out to be

> objective, as the programme describes itself. I give the programme some credit for subjects they have covered in the past, particularly in relation to the Birmingham Six and other such cases. The programme in question was anything but objective. It was disgraceful and it did a disservice and a dishonour in its portrayal of our Taoiseach on a meat hook. To cap it all off, a decent man was hounded at his place of worship on a Sunday morning. It was despicable for the lady who made that programme to try to justify such treatment later on. The woman said she was not lying in wait for that man, but most people who saw the programme believe — quite rightly — that it was a set-up job and that innuendo was involved in the way in which the church was photographed before Mr Goodman was approached by the camera.

The president of the High Court, Mr Justice Liam Hamilton, was appointed to head the inquiry and to write a report. When he died in 2000, by which stage he had been promoted to the position of chief justice, RTÉ noted that Hamilton's inquiry had been attacked in some quarters for its length and cost, and that he had also been criticised for 'his reluctance to draw conclusions in the final report'. In fairness to him, the terms of reference of the tribunal were so wide ranging as to present its sole member with huge logistical and organisational problems. He was thought by some colleagues to have aged noticeably during the long and difficult years of the inquiry.

During the inquiry, I was approached as a communications academic and asked by a representative of Anglo-Irish Beef Processors (by then in examinership) to undertake a review of certain RTÉ radio and television coverage of the tribunal. I did so, subject to a legal agreement confirming that my report would be entirely independent. I found that general RTÉ news coverage of the tribunal that I examined was unbiased and balanced, and that coverage by *The Pat Kenny Show* and *Today at Five* was, on the whole, fair and objective. I expressed some criticisms of the coverage of the tribunal on certain agricultural programmes and on *Today Tonight*. I defended the behaviour of RTÉ reporter Jerry O'Callaghan who had donned a disguise and strayed on to private property without the permission of its owners in his attempts to get at the truth about what appeared to be fraudulent behaviour in the beef industry.

Cynicism about the tribunal, which enriched many lawyers, was subsequently reinforced when the only prosecution to result immediately from its work was that of the journalist and researcher Susan O'Keeffe. She was prosecuted for refusing to reveal her sources, but the case against her collapsed and she was not convicted. The British Campaign for Freedom of Information, which presented her with an award in 1995, pointed out: 'Despite the possibility of a two-year prison sentence she continued to refuse to name her informants throughout, upholding a vital journalistic principle that protects the flow of information to the public.'

—

Those deterred by the prospects of reading Hamilton's full report might prefer Fintan O'Toole's *Meanwhile Back at the Ranch* (London, 1995), which is largely a reconstruction of the events at the heart of the tribunal's investigations. O'Toole, a journalist, has written extensively about the beef industry and, in an article in *The Irish Times* on 18 September 2003, pointed out that there are still unanswered questions about Goodman's dealings. Those unanswered questions have not deterred Larry Goodman from continuing to operate a successful business and from prospering personally.

BIG FELLA ON A BALCONY

Orlando, Florida, 20 February 1992

It was just another call for the Florida cops. They did not know that the man causing a disturbance at the hotel was possibly the richest person in Ireland, or that his arrest would lead to the exposure of political malpractice and widespread tax evasion in his home country.

What was Ben Dunne doing on the seventeenth floor of that American hotel in February 1992? He denied having threatened to commit suicide by jumping from a balcony, although he was clearly overwrought. A woman in his hotel bedroom had to be treated medically for a drugs overdose. It emerged later that she worked for an escort agency.

It transpired that Dunne was on a golfing holiday, not his first in Florida. As before, he had brought along as his guests Irish friends and business acquaintances. He left these in the evenings to return to his hotel suite, where he summoned up call girls to keep him company. One was Denise Wojcik, who made her way to his door at 1.30 a.m. on 20 February 1992.

Wojcik had lost her job as a librarian and lived in a trailer with a female friend and that friend's baby. She joined Dunne in his room for a cocaine binge, sharing a bath and listening to his rambling fantasies. He had acquired a big cellophane bag of cocaine and had thousands of dollars in cash stashed in his room. The cocaine made

Dunne paranoid and he began to act wildly. In 1981, he had been kidnapped for a ransom and seemed to fear that he was now again under threat. Shouting 'Get the police, get the police', he left his room to stand on a corner of a balcony that hung seventeen floors over the lobby far below.

Also staying on the seventeenth floor of the Florida hotel that night were members of U2, the famous Irish band who were about to start a US tour. Bono and other members of the band witnessed from the lobby below what was happening, but it was said later that they were unaware that the Irishman at the centre of the commotion was Ben Dunne. Dunne was removed from the balcony by police officers, before being cuffed at his wrists and ankles and 'hog-tied'. He was carried on a pole through the lobby and taken to jail.

Dunne was charged with cocaine trafficking. That charge was later dropped, apparently because of doubts about the legitimacy of the procedure used to search Dunne's apartment and because Dunne agreed not to contest a separate prosecution for possession of two grams of cocaine. The Florida court decided not to impose a jail sentence, but merely ordered him to undergo evaluation and treatment for drug abuse in a specified London clinic.

Other members of the Dunne family had had quite enough of Ben and his behaviour. They decided that he could not be allowed to continue to run the family business in the manner to which he had grown accustomed.

The rise of Dunnes Stores has been one of Ireland's great business success stories. The growth of the company paralleled the emergence of the new Irish State from decades of economic torpor. Dunnes has long supplied the Irish public with food and clothing of good basic quality and value, earning the loyalty and affection of many customers in the process. Ben Dunne Jr and his siblings inherited a highly successful business from Ben Dunne Sr, and made it even more successful.

Until he was arrested in Florida, Ben had run Dunnes Stores as he saw fit. He was widely regarded as a man without airs or graces, but he had signed large cheques whenever he wished. That now changed. His brother and sisters moved to restrict his freedom, and a family row ensued. His sister, Margaret Heffernan, ousted him as chairman in 1993. During the row, details of unorthodox payments to politicians and political parties emerged.

Some of the unorthodox payments had been to Charles Haughey, Taoiseach and leader of Fianna Fáil. Others were to Michael Lowry, a leading member of Fine Gael and sometime government minister, whose company provided refrigeration services to Dunnes Stores. It transpired that Dunnes Stores had paid £395,000 to contractors for refurbishment work at Lowry's home in Co. Tipperary. However, these payments were treated in Dunnes' accounts as though made for work on a shop in Dublin. They allowed Lowry to evade tax and to avoid questions about the propriety of a politician receiving payments in this fashion. Dunne also gave other money to Lowry, as well as making three large contributions to the Fine Gael Party amounting to £180,000. The latter payments were ostensibly made with the motive of assisting Fine Gael to be 'a stable opposition to the government'.

The family row at Dunnes lifted the lid on a scandal that no government could ignore. In February 1997, Taoiseach John Bruton appointed a senior judge, Brian McCracken, to inquire into payments made by Ben Dunne to politicians. McCracken was quick and efficient. He issued his report within months, finding that Lowry had an 'unhealthy business relationship' with Dunne. McCracken believed that this was 'particularly disturbing in view of Michael Lowry's position as a public representative, and subsequently as chairman of the Fine Gael Parliamentary Party and ultimately as a Cabinet Minister'.

McCracken also discovered a complex financial web that had been used to hide a series of payments to Charles Haughey. Dunne made four donations amounting to £1.1m at the request of Des Traynor, a friend and business associate of Haughey. In late 1987, Traynor had approached Noel Fox, a chartered accountant and one of Dunne's close advisers, and explained that he was seeking to put together about half a dozen people to contribute £150,000 each towards settling Haughey's financial problems at that time. When Dunne heard of this and was told of the need for confidentiality he said, 'I think Haughey is making a huge mistake trying to get six or seven people together. . . . Christ picked twelve apostles and one of them crucified him.' Dunne then agreed to pay the entire amount required and eventually paid even more than that amount to Haughey.

One of the most memorable stories told to the McCracken Tribunal concerned a particular meeting that Ben Dunne claimed to have had with Haughey. It related to a payment other than those already mentioned. Dunne told the McCracken Tribunal that he was playing golf one day and that, at the time, he happened to have three bank drafts in his pocket. He had had the bank drafts for £70,000 sterling each made out in fictitious names by a company in the Isle of Man in November 1991. The tribunal found that 'Mr Ben Dunne has said that they were drawn for personal reasons, and the Tribunal did not consider it necessary to explore what these were'! After the golf game, he telephoned Charles Haughey and it was arranged that he would call to Haughey's home on his way home. He did so, and got the impression that Haughey 'was not himself but looked down and depressed'. As he was leaving, he took the three bank drafts out of his pocket and handed them to Haughey and said, 'Look, this is something for yourself.' Dunne added that Haughey responded, 'Thank you, big fellow.' Haughey claimed to have no recollection of this meeting, but later admitted that the money had been lodged to his account. This £210,000 was in addition to the £1.1m already paid by Dunne to Haughey.

While Haughey and Lowry benefited most from Dunne's largesse, Dunne was also a major donor to the Fine Gael Party, and even made a personal donation of £15,000 to the Labour Party towards the cost of the political campaign to elect Mary Robinson as president in 1990. The latter contribution was considered by the McCracken Tribunal to have been 'a spontaneous gesture' and was made following a chance meeting between Dunne and Labour's Ruairi Quinn in the Barge pub in Portobello, Dublin.

The tribunal undertook extensive inquiries throughout the public service as to any possible instances in which Haughey might have used his influence for the benefit of Ben Dunne or Dunnes Stores, but found no wrongful use of his position in this regard. It found that, at the time of the initial request to Dunne for money to help Haughey, Dunne had only a casual acquaintanceship with Haughey.

After the first payment was made, his contacts with Haughey became much more frequent. Dunne's evidence was that he thought it quite wrong that the Taoiseach of the country should be facing financial problems, and that he had a very high regard for Haughey's ability. While the tribunal found no reason to doubt the truth of this evidence, it found it 'hardly sufficient in itself to explain the generosity shown by Mr Ben Dunne', and added:

> It is no part of the function of the Tribunal to conduct a psychological study of Mr Ben Dunne. However, it does appear to the Tribunal that a possible motive for the actions of Mr Ben Dunne, in the absence of any ulterior political motive, was simply to buy the friendship, or at least the acquaintance, of a person in a very powerful political position. Mr Ben Dunne appears to have had many friends in the business community, but few, if any, in the political community.

Haughey did arrange a meeting for Ben Dunne with the chairman of the Revenue Commissioners but was found to have made no representations in respect of that meeting. McCracken also found that neither Dunnes Stores nor Ben Dunne ever requested Michael Lowry to make any personal or political intervention on their behalf. However, in July 2003, Dunne told the Moriarty Tribunal of an approach to Lowry 'to do something' to speed up a rent review of a building rented by the State-owned Telecom Éireann from a company in which Ben Dunne had an interest. Mark FitzGerald, a trustee of Fine Gael and a business colleague of the independent arbitrator conducting the review, gave evidence that Lowry, his party colleague, had contacted him and asked that he 'organise it' that the rent be doubled. It was not.

McCracken found it 'quite unacceptable' that a member of Dáil Éireann, and in particular a Cabinet Minister and Taoiseach such as Haughey, should be supported in his personal lifestyle by gifts made to him personally. McCracken stated: 'The possibility that political or financial favours could be sought in return for such gifts, or even be given without being sought, is very high, and if such gifts are permissible, they would inevitably lead in some cases to bribery and corruption.' McCracken also described Dunne's relationship with Lowry as 'an appalling situation', where a government minister and chairman of a parliamentary party was 'consistently benefiting from the black economy from shortly after the time he was first elected'.

The McCracken Tribunal had opened a can of worms. Haughey's resistance to it led to further enquiries and to investigations which uncovered a particular tax scam involving Irish investors and Ansbacher Bank in the Cayman Islands. In his book, *The Ansbacher Conspiracy*, Colm Keena writes: 'If he [Haughey] had come out with his hands up it might have prevented the tribunal from discovering the Ansbacher deposits. . . . Some people urged him to confess but the habits of a lifetime were too hard to overcome.'

The repercussions of Ben Dunne's disgrace in Florida have continued to ripple through Irish society to this day. Dunne himself appears to have overcome his personal difficulties and is active today as a businessman in the fitness sector.

TAX CHEATS' CHARTER

Leinster House, Dublin, 14 July 1993

It was a gift for tax evaders, but it dismayed those who had hoped that Labour's good performance in the general election of 1992 might herald a new era in Irish politics. Following the election, the party had found itself with 33 seats. It formed a coalition government with Fianna Fáil under Taoiseach Albert Reynolds.

Within a year, the tax amnesty, which senior Labour politicians supported, fostered a cynicism about Irish public life that has continued to have a corrosive influence to this day. The election had been an expression of outrage at what was emerging from scandals in Irish society. Yet, the tax amnesty was a slap in the face for those who wanted radical reforms.

Officially entitled the 'Waiver of Certain Tax, Interest and Penalties Act 1993', the amnesty became known by its detractors as the 'tax cheats' charter'. Its supporters have pointed out that it brought the Exchequer a windfall of hundreds of millions of pounds and freed money for investment in Ireland that might have remained hidden overseas. Its critics claimed that wealthy business people were able to benefit from the amnesty at a time when ordinary workers were paying top rates of taxation.

Passed by Dáil Éireann at Leinster House on 14 July 1993, the Waiver Act disgusted Pay As You Earn (PAYE) taxpayers who had their income tax deducted at source by employers. They had long complained about the high level of income tax evasion in Ireland, and some had taken to the streets to march in protest on the issue. They were disappointed when Tánaiste Dick Spring and other Labour politicians lent their support to the new measure. The Fianna Fáil Minister for Finance and future Taoiseach, Bertie Ahern, had let it be known that he was strongly against the amnesty, but he failed to oppose it when the Cabinet met to make a decision on the matter. It has been suggested by one Labour apologist, Fergus Finlay, that his party's ministers were so convinced that Ahern would successfully oppose the amnesty that they were caught off guard when he mysteriously stayed quiet. This version scarcely explains Labour's failure to vote against the provision, from which 'every sleazebag in the country' (as Finlay himself put it in 1998 in his memoir, *Snakes and Ladders*) was able to benefit.

The 1993 Act permitted a person with unpaid arrears of tax to pay an amount without having to pay also any related interest to which he or she ought to have been liable. Only a proportion of certain arrears need be paid and, moreover,

> . . . proceedings shall not be initiated or continued for the recovery of any fine or penalty to which the person may be liable under any of the specified provisions in relation to arrears of tax . . .

It was also agreed that there would be no 'naming and shaming' of those taking advantage of the amnesty. Confidentiality was assured. Moreover, the amnesty of 1993 allowed evaders not only to cough up what they owed without facing penalties but actually to substitute a single payment of 15 per cent for *all* income tax and capital gains liabilities arising before April 1991 and in respect of which tax had not been paid. This made those who had declared their income on time and who had paid their full taxes feel like fools. It was a reward for evasion. The Revenue Commissioners later estimated that their tax take from the incentive amnesty represented hitherto undeclared income of 'over £1 billion, perhaps £1.25 billion'.

There was a precedent for the 1993 measure. However, at the time of its implementation, Fianna Fáil's earlier tax amnesty of 1988 had seemed somewhat more reasonable to people who were then 'tax compliant'. This was partly because it had been granted when the financial activities of golden circles in Irish society were less loudly publicised than later, and partly because Charles Haughey's 1988 amnesty was meant to be a 'last chance' for evaders. It was intended to put the State's tax affairs in order so that there could be no excuse for further evasion. The public then knew little about Mr Haughey's own finances or about his financial backers. According to the Revenue Commissioners, the amnesty of 1988 had resulted in over 300,000 payments with a total value of £497 million. The year 1988 also saw one of the most fundamental changes in Irish taxation and revenue structures when 'Self-Assessment' was introduced for some income tax, followed by corporation tax and capital gains tax.

During the 1980s and 90s, certain people sought to rationalise and even to justify tax evasion in Ireland on the grounds that tax rates were so high that they constituted a disincentive to enterprise and investment. Implicit in this argument was the idea that people are entitled to take the law into their own hands when it comes to revenue liability and are entitled to pay whatever they themselves believe to be appropriate or fair.

In practice, successive governments did not treat tax evasion as a crucial priority. It was widely believed that tax evasion was common among the self-employed, but the powers and resources of the Revenue Commissioners were inadequate to collect what was due, and most politicians seemed to be in no hurry to remedy that deficit. The new Financial Services Centre in Dublin was itself a monument to tax avoidance, if not evasion.

It was precisely because of the public's impatience with official attitudes towards tax cheats, and with the slow pace of social and economic reform generally, that the Labour Party fared well in the general election of 1992. Its subsequent decision on the tax amnesty has dogged the party ever since. However, it was not the last tax amnesty.

The later tax 'incentive' of 2001 did not dare to speak its name. This was unsurprising when the Progressive Democrats, Labour's successor as partner in government with Fianna Fáil, were led by Mary Harney. For she had roundly condemned tax amnesties when the coalition of Albert Reynolds and Dick Spring collapsed. On 22 November 1994, Harney said in Dáil Éireann:

> Larry Goodman, for his efforts, got an amnesty. What do the

> victims of child sexual abuse get from the State? They get no compensation for their pain and suffering. The victims of crime get absolutely nothing. . . . I mention these two things because the hallmark of the next Government must be fairness and the creation of a fair society. Tax amnesties are the very opposite to fairness and justice because what tax amnesties do is tell those who do not pay their fair share that they will get a reprieve and will pay less while those who are compliant, who work hard, who make an effort and have a sense of public duty are told that they will be penalised all the way.

The Revenue Commissioners had vehemently opposed the 1993 tax amnesty, believing that they were already on the trail of major cheats who would be forced to pay up. They feared that the implementation of the measure could result in defaulters creating new bogus non-resident and offshore accounts instead of coming clean. Indeed, it was to address the fact that much 'hot' money had either remained in, or found its way into, such accounts that the coalition government of 2001 now introduced its own amnesty, albeit an amnesty not as generous as earlier ones. Ironically, this government was led by not one but two former opponents of tax amnesties, its Taoiseach being Bertie Ahern and its Tánaiste Mary Harney. Was it any wonder that this pair did not describe their scheme of 2001 as another amnesty? Is it any wonder that Irish people are cynical about tax evasion and about politics?

Under the 'incentive' scheme of 2001, Revenue promised tax defaulters:

- Exposure to interest and penalties will be capped at 100% of the tax — in other words account-holders will have to pay the tax and up to the same amount again in interest and penalties. Under the normal regime operated by Revenue much higher interest and penalties could arise.
- Revenue will not take steps to initiate the prosecution of related tax evasion offences through the courts.
- Details of the payment to Revenue will not be published.

Politicians across the Dáil furiously denied that this 'Voluntary Disclosure Scheme' was another let-off. Labour's future leader, Pat

Rabbitte, thought that the scheme was pragmatic: 'To be honest, I couldn't call it an amnesty,' he remarked. 'This is going to be extremely punitive. Anyone who doesn't come out with their hands up by 15 November faces very serious consequences.' According to Fine Gael's Jim Mitchell, it was 'a last chance to avoid jail'.

Describing this latest 'last chance' of 2001 as 'the "it's not an amnesty" amnesty', Pat O'Brien wrote in the KPMG consultancy's online Tax Monitor in May 2001: 'If it is not an amnesty, then what is it? Surely an offer not to prosecute criminals amounts to an amnesty?' O'Brien, a partner in the accountancy firm KPMG, was highly concerned about the measure. He was not alone. Dundalk's *Argus* newspaper commented, on 11 May 2001:

> If it looks like a tax amnesty and smells like a tax amnesty, then the chances are it is a tax amnesty, even if the Revenue Commissioners say it is not.

Not all the members of the Labour Party appeared to be singing from the same hymn sheet. According to a report in the *Munster Express* of 11 May 2001, a Labour member of Waterford County Council, Fiachra Ó Ceilleachair, told a meeting of the Labour Party National Executive in Leinster House:

> The tax evaders are effectively avoiding their responsibility to contribute towards the public services we all value and would like to see increased investment in.

Yet another sort of tax amnesty was embedded in the Residential Tenancies Bill published in 2003. This was introduced to require landlords to register details of all tenancies with a new board. However, the register was not to include the identity of the landlord or tenant or the rent, and there was no intention that the landlord's details would be passed to the Revenue Commissioners. A spokesperson for the Minister for the Environment and Local Government said: 'The job of the Board is to manage the rental market on a day-to-day basis. It is not to act as tax master.'

In such circumstances, few people were surprised to learn, in January 2004, that the Revenue Commissioners were still allowing people who had made false declarations in the tax amnesty of 1993 to settle their tax affairs privately and without being prosecuted. On RTÉ's *Morning Ireland*, on 20 February 2003, a senior spokesman for the Revenue Commissioners protested that this was 'definitely not' yet another tax amnesty: 'We would say it's not an amnesty at all. It's an opportunity for taxpayers to clean up their affairs and it's one that's available to all taxpayers.' He pointed out that the thousands of people involved would have to pay their full tax with interest and penalties. However, they could do so without being named, shamed or prosecuted for their crimes.

On 15 June 2004, the Commissioners announced they had collected €1.5 billion from all the special investigations mounted following the revelation of various scandals, which was additional to the yields from the amnesties of 1988 and 1993. The special investigations had been into Ansbacher (yielded €42.7m), NIB (€50.4m), Moriarty Tribunal (€6.3m), Flood/Mahon Tribunal (€18.7m), bogus non-resident accounts (€749m) and offshore (€651m).

If the tax scandals of the 1990s and 2000s changed the level of compliance with tax laws in Ireland, many citizens still suspect there will always be some other 'last chance' amnesty for tax evaders and that few, if any, will ever be jailed.

A BLOODY DISGRACE

Mespil Road, Dublin, 22 February 1994

On a chilly February morning in 1994, RTÉ announced on the radio that the Blood Transfusion Service Board (BTSB) wanted certain people to contact it 'just in case'. It was a moment that many families will never forget. Women had contracted Hepatitis C as a result of receiving contaminated blood transfusions. Most had been given transfusions of a blood product known as 'Anti-D' in connection with their pregnancies.

Haemophiliacs, as a group, had also suffered as a result of gross negligence on the part of the BTSB. Haemophilia is a condition that results in people not being able easily to stop bleeding, but it may be ameliorated by certain blood treatments. Already, in 1994, Irish haemophiliacs were struggling to come to terms with the consequences of an earlier disaster. During the 1980s, more than a quarter of the 400 members of the Irish haemophilia community had been infected with HIV, when a contaminated blood product was imported from the United States and used by the BTSB. At first, the HIV infection of Irish haemophiliacs seemed to be entirely an unforeseen consequence of the sudden emergence of AIDS. However, it later transpired that some of the infections might have been avoided by the BTSB, which failed to treat some of its blood products in a way that had been developed elsewhere to neutralise any possible HIV content.

Whatever excuses might be offered for the way in which the HIV problem had been handled in the 1980s, it should have been crystal clear from no later than 1994 that something was seriously amiss at the BTSB on Mespil Road, Dublin. However, rather than rush to help the infected in every way possible, successive governments for too long allowed lawyers to determine the State's response to those directly affected by the blood scandals. People who requested State investment in a trust fund for haemophiliacs were even lectured by Taoiseach Charles Haughey on the need not to undermine the government's authority in financial matters. Michael Noonan, who was Minister for Health during part of the time that victims experienced great difficulty in getting information or justice, subsequently became leader of Fine Gael. Some political analysts believe that Fine Gael's relatively poor performance in the general election of 2002 was due to Noonan's earlier association with the hard-nosed legalistic strategy on the part of the State towards Hepatitis C victims. Just months before that election, the public was reminded of his ministerial role when RTÉ screened *No Tears*, a four-part dramatisation of the Hepatitis C affair, in January 2002.

The manner is which the BTSB, not once but three times, allowed people to contract HIV or Hepatitis C beggars belief. Here was an organisation that was the pride of Ireland, widely supported and acknowledged as providing a great service to the nation. Yet, when things began to go wrong, it seemed to be entirely unable to respond in an adequate manner.

Judge Thomas Finlay later recalled the achievements of the BTSB, including from 1970 the manufacturing of Anti-D Immunoglobulin which is said to have resulted in an annual reduction of over 100 in the number of Irish babies born dead, and the avoidance of many more being born severely handicapped. In 1997, in his official report into aspects of the affair (*Report of the Tribunal into the Blood Transfusion Service Board*, p. 32), he wrote:

> The setting up of a national self-sufficient blood transfusion service in the 1960s and 1970s in a country the size of Ireland, was a very great and beneficial scientific achievement.
>
> The development of a self-sufficient unit for the production of Anti-D made exclusively from the plasma of Irish voluntary donors in sufficient quantities to meet the entire needs of the country was a particularly noteworthy and splendid aspect of that

> development, of which Dr O'Riordan and his colleagues were justly and understandably proud.

However, the judge further noted:

> For the supply of home produced Anti-D to fall short of requirements at any time so as to involve its replacement or supplementation by imported products, would have been a major admission of failure.

In striving to maintain the domestic supply of Anti-D, the BTSB departed from normal practice in respect of blood care. Originally, the source of plasma for manufacturing Anti-D was post-menopausal women who could safely donate blood every three months. Certain voluntary male donors were also used. However, it was later decided to utilise blood from patients undergoing therapeutic plasma exchanges, which involved them in both receiving and donating three times each week for approximately twenty-five weeks, thus greatly boosting the supply for the manufacture of Anti-D. This decision 'was in the teeth of the BTSB's own guidelines against using blood from a donor within six months of that donor's receipt of a blood transfusion', as Judge Finlay later found.

The big problems began in the years 1976 and 1977 when plasma taken from a certain woman during a series of blood transfusions was, without her knowledge, given over to the BTSB. That plasma was used to make Anti-D, which was then administered to many other people. The unwitting donor later became known as 'Patient X' during investigations into what occurred. Patient X had become jaundiced during the course of her therapeutic plasma exchanges, and also showed other symptoms that would normally alert medical authorities to the fact that her plasma might not be suitable for use in making blood products of any kind. Indeed, on ten occasions between 19 November 1976 and 8 December 1976, information about samples of the plasma of Patient X was apparently recorded on forms signed by the deputy national director of the BTSB. On each of the ten forms, a column providing for a statement of the clinical diagnosis of the donor (Patient X) had the words 'infective hepatitis' contained in it. Investigating the affair twenty years later, Judge Thomas Finlay, in 1997, found:

> It cannot therefore be doubted that by the middle of December 1976, the entire senior medical staff concerned for the BTSB with this question of the plasma obtained from Patient X . . . were all aware of a diagnosis of infective Hepatitis and the display of jaundice by the patient.
>
> Notwithstanding this knowledge, further supplies of plasma were obtained from Patient X on 10, 17 and 19 January 1977. These supplies of plasma or part of them were included in pools of plasma used to manufacture batches of Anti-D on dates between 14 February 1977 and 4 July 1977 (Report of Tribunal, p. 19).

It would have been bad enough had that been the full extent of recklessness on the part of the BTSB in respect of Patient X. Unfortunately, it was not. During 1977, the BTSB was informed by the Rotunda Maternity Hospital that three of its patients who had received doses of Anti-D made with the plasma of Patient X had themselves been subsequently diagnosed as having Hepatitis. The doctors of these three patients even explicitly suggested to the BTSB that their Hepatitis might be associated with their having been the recipients of doses of Anti-D. Nevertheless, although the BTSB thereupon ceased to make new batches of Anti-D from the plasma of Patient X, it continued to issue batches which had already been manufactured from the plasma of Patient X. Finlay was to find that 'no decision was taken at any time to either prohibit the further issue of batches of Anti-D derived in part from the plasma obtained from Patient X or to recall batches which had already been issued, although a decision was taken as indicated in July, not to manufacture any more batches'. One of the batches issued in 1977 was the origin of the Hepatitis C with which Mrs Brigid McCole was infected. She later came to play a leading role in the uncovering of the truth, prior to her untimely death.

In acting in respect of Patient X and her blood, the BTSB contravened fundamental principles in respect of blood transfusions. For example, in the first instance, the donor should have been asked for her consent. Patient X was not asked for hers, and later said that she would never have given it because she had earlier in her life been infected with tuberculosis. Moreover, blood should not be taken from a donor sooner than six months from the date of the last infusion or injection of blood into that donor. This rule was ignored because the

BTSB needed blood for its Anti-D manufacturing programme. By failing to allow a period of six months to elapse, the BTSB reduced the chances of spotting that a donor herself had been infected by donated blood. Even more obvious, if not fundamental, was the fact that the blood of any donor with a history of jaundice should have been excluded permanently from blood products being administered to others. Patient X was known to have had jaundice, but still her blood was used.

And then, once again in 1989, there was a major breakdown in normal procedures associated with blood transfusions. That year, a person later known as Donor Y underwent a therapeutic course of plasma exchange, during which blood supplied by the BTSB was given to Donor Y, and plasma from Donor Y was given to the BTSB. Some of the blood given to Y was infected from an unknown source (not Patient X). After Donor Y then became infected, Donor Y's infected blood was used to make Anti-D. Standard procedures were not applied in the case. In 1992, even after four tests were carried out on plasma which had been taken from Donor Y in 1989 and these had all proved positive for Hepatitis C, eighteen further batches of Anti-D containing that infected plasma were manufactured and twenty-one issued. Thus, due to gross negligence on the part of the BTSB, batches of the Anti-D blood product made from the plasma of two separate donors were distributed. This negligence resulted in great suffering and deaths.

Five years after Finlay presented his pithy 1997 report into the BTSB, Judge Alison Lindsay delivered her much bigger official tome on 'Infection with HIV and Hepatitis C of persons with haemophilia and related matters'. It was criticised for lacking a convenient summary and for not laying blame sufficiently clearly. For example, information that the Fianna Fáil Minister for Health, Dr Rory O'Hanlon, had given the Dáil was found to be 'incomplete and unsatisfactory', but 'he was doing no more than placing on the record of the House, information which was given to him by officials in the Department'. Yet, a careful reading of Lindsay's report leaves one in no doubt that the BTSB was inadequately run and supervised. Apart from anything else, its medical records were 'unsatisfactory and incomplete'.

On 23 July 2003, two former senior officials of the BTSB were arrested and became the first people to face criminal charges in connection with the scandal. They appeared in the District Court accused of 'unlawfully and maliciously' causing a noxious substance, namely infected anti-D, to be taken by seven particular women, thereby inflicting grievous bodily harm contrary to the Offences Against the Person Act. Counsel for one of the accused wondered why it had taken longer than two decades to bring the charges.

—

Glenys Spray and Rosemary Daly have both written vivid accounts of how the whole blood scandal mangled the lives of those infected with Hepatitis C or HIV and the lives of their families. Their books, Spray's *Blood, Sweat and Tears* and Daly's *A Case of Bad Blood*, are a convincing indictment of the State, which failed to protect women from the consequences of gross negligence by public officials.

FLOODGATES

Newry, Co. Down, 3 July 1995

Local government in Dublin was straining under the weight of its own corruption for too long. The Gardaí had failed to root out that corruption, despite undertaking a number of investigations. An advertisement placed in national newspapers, on 3 July 1995, ultimately led to at least some of the truth coming out at the Flood Tribunal and elsewhere. Hard evidence confirmed what many had suspected for years about the conduct of local government in Ireland.

The advertisement was placed on behalf of Dublin-based clients by Messrs Donnelly, Neary and Donnelly, a firm of solicitors in Newy, Co. Down. It offered a £10,000 reward for information leading to conviction on indictment of persons for corruption in respect of the rezoning of land. The clients who had retained the firm of Northern Ireland solicitors were Michael Smith and Colm Mac Eochaigh. Both were qualified lawyers and both had an interest in environmental matters. Later, in 1999, Smith was to be appointed chairman of An Taisce, the National Trust. Originally, says Smith, they had intended to employ a solicitor within the Republic of Ireland to administer the scheme but were surprised to find that even solicitors who were generally perceived to be somewhat radical seemed reluctant to become involved in what they were proposing. Smith then looked north of the border, to his friend Kevin Neary.

Within months of the advertisement's appearance, it is said, dozens of persons had approached the solicitors in response. Among the most notable was James Gogarty, who was to play a major part in the events that followed. Smith ensured that a steady drip of information was fed to journalists, although Ireland's libel laws inhibited the media from publishing some of it. Eventually, however, enough got into print and circulated among politicians to ensure that corruption in local government in Dublin could no longer be ignored.

On 4 November 1997, on foot of a resolution of both houses of the Oireachtas, the Minister for the Environment and Local Government appointed a special tribunal of investigation. Mr Justice Feargus Flood had agreed to be its 'sole member', or chairman. The tribunal was instructed 'to inquire urgently into and report' on certain 'definite matters of urgent public importance'. These included the identification of certain lands and the planning history of those lands. The tribunal was 'to ascertain the identity of any members of the Oireachtas, past or present, and/or members of the relevant local authorities who were involved directly or indirectly in any of the foregoing matters' and 'to ascertain the identity of all public officials who considered, made recommendations or decisions on any such matters and to report on such considerations, recommendations and/or decisions'. It was instructed to discover

> the identity of all recipients of payments made to political parties or members of either House of the Oireachtas, past or present, or members or officials of a Dublin local authority or other public official by Mr Gogarty or Mr Bailey or a connected person or company within the meaning of the Ethics in Public Office Act, 1995, from 20th June 1985 to date, and the circumstances, considerations and motives relative to any such payment; [and] whether any of the persons referred to . . . above were influenced directly or indirectly by the offer or receipt of any such payments or benefits.

Having regard to acts 'which may in its opinion amount to corruption', the tribunal was asked to make recommendations. It was specifically advised to seek discovery of all relevant documents, files and papers in the possession of Donnelly, Neary and Donnelly Solicitors. The tribunal was also asked, specifically, to look at certain activities and donations involving Ray Burke TD.

On 14 February 2000, counsel for the Flood Tribunal publicly recalled the circumstances that had led to its establishment. He noted:

> For many years there had been serious public disquiet concerning allegations of corruption relating to the planning process and, in particular, the planning process in so far as it relates to the Dublin area. This concern led to a number of intensive Garda investigations.

He said that, in 1974, following the appearance of an article by Joe McAnthony in the *Sunday Independent*, a Garda investigation had been carried out into land rezoning in the Swords area. This resulted in no criminal prosecution.

> In February 1989, the Gardaí commenced another investigation into allegations of bribery and corruption in the planning process. This investigation lasted approximately fifteen months and an official of An Bord Pleanála — who has since retired — was charged with offences contrary to the Prevention of Corruption Acts 1889–1916 and the Forgery Act 1913. This prosecution resulted in an acquittal. A former senior executive building surveyor employed by Dublin Corporation was also prosecuted. He was convicted in the Central Criminal Court and was sentenced.
>
> In 1993, while Dublin County Council was in the process of making a new development plan for the County of Dublin, a series of articles appeared in *The Irish Times* alleging that a number of unnamed Dublin County councillors had received bribes in return for their votes on rezoning issues. Following these allegations, a further Garda investigation commenced in July 1993. In the course of the investigation it is understood that Gardaí contacted, *inter alia*, each of the 78 members of Dublin County Council either personally or by telephone. At the conclusion of the investigation a file was forwarded to the Director of Public Prosecutions who decided there should be no prosecution.
>
> In each of these Garda investigations, the investigating officer stressed that there was great difficulty in investigating allegations of bribery and corruption in the planning process.

Having referred to the newspaper advertisement placed from Newry, counsel continued:

> In the *Sunday Tribune* of 27 July 1997, Mr Raphael P. Burke, the then Minister for Foreign Affairs, was named as the recipient of an alleged political contribution by Mr Michael Bailey of Bovale Ltd in 1989. On 8 August 1997, the *Sunday Business Post* published an article alleging that JMSE Ltd had paid Mr Burke £30,000. On 7 August 1997, Mr Burke issued a statement in which, *inter alia*, he admitted receiving £30,000 as 'an unsolicited political contribution' from Mr James Gogarty on behalf of JMSE Ltd. He denied receiving any money from Mr Bailey or Bovale Developments Ltd.

On 10 September 1997, Burke made a personal statement in Dáil Éireann which purported to set out the facts as he saw them. On 7 October 1997, he resigned as Minister for Foreign Affairs. Attempting to explain why he had appointed Ray Burke to the Cabinet when rumours of his corruption were rife, Taoiseach Bertie Ahern claimed to reporters that he had been 'up every tree in north County Dublin' (the Minister's constituency) to check out the truth of allegations and had found nothing. In respect of Ray Burke, the Flood Tribunal had its terms of reference amended to allow it to inquire not only into his role in respect of corruption in local government, but also into aspects of his former role as the minister responsible for issuing communications licences, including that for Century Radio, from whose promoters he received a donation. The fact that, in June 1989, Burke also received a donation of £30,000 from Rennicks, a corporate subsidiary of Tony O'Reilly's Fitzwilton group, has been a cause of concern. O'Reilly's Independent News and Media is Ireland's single most powerful media organisation. It invested heavily in a national MMDS television relay system for which Burke issued licences.

The Flood Tribunal has been unwieldy and slow. Its proceedings have enriched lawyers out of public monies to an extent that many citizens find obscene and objectionable. Mr Justice Flood retired and was replaced by Mr Justice Alan Mahon. It became clear that the format of the Flood/Mahon Tribunal meant that investigations might ramble on almost indefinitely. Nevertheless, despite its flaws much has been revealed about the planning process in Dublin that was only whispered about in private beforehand. There is no reason to believe that Dublin is or was exceptional in respect of such matters, but no similar inquiry has been launched into corruption in other local authority areas. A parade of colourful characters including, among others, George Redmond, Joseph Murphy, Liam Lawlor, Ray Burke, Frank Dunlop, builders Brennan and McGowan, and the Bailey brothers, has ensured that the proceedings of the tribunal received much publicity. However, there has been no rush of prosecutions on foot of the revelations, and it is far from certain that the Gardaí have been provided with sufficient resources and powers to ensure that the kind of corruption revealed at the tribunal is even today being effectively prevented. The placing of a small advertisement by a Newry solicitor certainly led to a change in the level of public knowledge about corruption. Whether or not it has resulted in the passage of new laws and the adoption of new systems that will make such corruption far less possible is unclear.

DIRTY BUSINESS

Cashel, Co. Tipperary, 17 December 1998

A decision to investigate the major banks, taken by Dáil Éireann on 17 December 1998, marked the moment when people began to think that even the most powerful institutions in the land might not be above the law. The subsequent inquiry into DIRT accounts reverberated throughout Ireland, and nowhere more so than in the small south Tipperary town of Cashel. There, one man felt he had good reason to be annoyed at his local bank manager. He was not alone in his resentment.

The involvement of Irish banks in tax evasion, including the infamous Ansbacher offshore accounts in the Cayman Islands, has done much to damage the reputations of those establishments. By 1999, it came as no surprise to learn that a farmer in Cashel, Co. Tipperary, was suing his local bank for negligence. He alleged that he had been encouraged by Allied Irish Banks into evading tax and also into failing to avail of the tax amnesty of 1988. He claimed that, had he not followed its advice, his tax bill would have amounted to only about half of the £175,000 he was eventually obliged to pay when he failed to take advantage of the amnesty.

The banks themselves had long been benefiting quite happily from their own wrongdoing in relation to the evasion of DIRT and other liabilities. Tax evasion is a crime. Its victims are those members of the public who would otherwise have benefited from the expenditure by the State of revenues that remain unpaid in tax. They may include, for example, patients in need of vital operations or children in need of special education.

The first substantial indication that the political climate was changing with respect to the traditional tolerance of tax evasion came in 1998. On 17 December that year, Dáil Éireann passed a resolution requesting the Comptroller and Auditor General to investigate the activities of certain banks and other financial institutions to see if their accounts were properly completed and if they presented 'a full and true picture of the extent of those institutions' compliance' with particular legislation relating to deposits. He found that they did not.

Of particular concern to the Dáil was DIRT (Deposit Interest Retention Tax). The acronym may have been more suited to peat moss or fertiliser, but it was applied to the tax due on interest paid on deposit accounts. The relevant deposit-taking institution, whether bank or building society, was expected to assess accurately the amount of DIRT on each account and to return this amount to the Collector-General. However, from the moment that DIRT was introduced in 1986, bankers began to explore means of avoiding deductions. The number of non-resident accounts created from Ireland began to rise to an unprecedented and remarkable level.

On 17 December 1998, the Dáil, 'having been apprised of prima-facie evidence of a substantial risk to the revenues of the State' from the non-payment of due DIRT, asked its own Committee of Public Accounts to review the findings of the Comptroller and Auditor General in the matter and to 'determine how to proceed'. Public hearings of that committee were televised by TG4. They made interesting viewing for many citizens, as senior bank personnel were pursued by politicians. Cynics have claimed that the banks were relatively soft targets when it came to examining tax evasion. They were institutions that could easily afford to pay penalties for tax evasion without making a significant dent in their profits or market values.

The hearings were the high point in the career of the late Jim Mitchell, a Fine Gael TD and a former government minister, who was chairman of the Public Accounts Committee. Because it was very focused, and because the banks did not fight it every inch of the way, the committee's work was completed quickly and has been contrasted favourably to that of the Flood/Mahon and Moriarty tribunals in Dublin Castle. This is somewhat unfair, as the tribunals were given very different and far broader tasks. The immediate focus of the inquiry had been the evasion of DIRT from its very introduction in 1986 up to 1998.

The committee reported on 15 December 1999. It found that the practice of evading DIRT had been large-scale, systematic, and carried out by the banks over many years:

> The use of bogus non-resident accounts — already long established as a means of concealing capital and income from the eyes of Revenue — now took on an added dimension. Bogus non-resident accounts became a route to evading yet another tax, DIRT. Banks facilitated this, as they had long facilitated deposit splitting and bogus non-resident accounts prior to 1986.

Bank officials not only organised the opening and operation of bogus non-resident accounts for customers, but also established them for their own use. The committee concluded:

> It is now also apparent that the evasion of DIRT was practised in a wider culture of more generalised tax evasion. Specifically in addition to the simple evasion of DIRT, bogus non-resident accounts were employed as a means of concealing otherwise taxable income from Revenue so as to ensure the evasion of other taxes due on those monies. This phenomenon of bogus non-resident accounts and the accompanying technique of deposit splitting to evade tax dated in fact from the early 1960s.

From 1987, the Revenue Commissioners had decided that the poor economic climate in Ireland was such that it was inappropriate to push for inspection and access to bank account information, ostensibly lest money lodged in Irish financial institutions be moved elsewhere. However, the Public Accounts Committee described this capital flight argument as 'implausible'.

The work of the committee, and its report, were greeted enthusiastically by the media and by politicians. Financial institutions were subsequently obliged to settle with the Revenue Commissioners, although no bank official was then prosecuted for her or his role in the scam. There was a lot of looking to the future, and ensuring that a similar problem would not arise again.

The public has tended to grow cynical of the fact that the many and growing number of revelations about actual or apparent tax evasion have not been matched by people going to jail for that crime. Deposit account holders may have paid DIRT tax that was overdue, and also penalties, but even some of the biggest tax fraudsters appear to be immune from incarceration.

One must be careful not to equate an overseas account with tax evasion. When information about accounts in the Ansbacher Bank in the Cayman Islands was published by the State, it was stressed that no such assumption of criminal activity was being made. Moreover, the very fact that Irish people long had a relaxed attitude towards paying tax helped to ensure that enforcement laws were weak, especially when it came to technologically sophisticated means of transferring money across national boundaries. The fact that some of the most powerful and 'well-got' people in Irish society were themselves breaking the law was no great incentive to their political friends to get tough on tax cheats. There was one law for PAYE workers when it came to collecting taxes, and another for those whose income was not transparent and could not be taxed at source.

As the banks have continued to make big profits, critics fear that they have simply passed on to customers the cost and consequences of their involvement in the DIRT and other scandals. Thus, on 8 January 2001, the Council of Tipperary South Riding passed the following resolution, which it then circulated for endorsement to other councils and which it also sent to the major banks:

> That this Council calls on the Government to intervene regarding the latest policy on cheques encashment being operated by the major banks and regards this policy to be a greedy and blatant attempt to extract profits from their customers as a means of recouping the DIRT tax which the banks had fraudulently hidden and withheld from the Revenue Commissioners in criminal fashion, and which they later had to pay upon discovery and for which crime nobody has been seen to be prosecuted, convicted or punished.

Citizens' annoyance at tax evasion by the rich or at social welfare fraud by the poor tends to sit rather easily alongside a capacity to 'forget' to declare our own additional income or to benefit from the lower labour costs of the 'Black Economy', where workers expect cash and give no VAT receipts.

It also reflects a certain residual public ambivalence towards tax evasion that Beverley Flynn was not expelled from the Fianna Fáil Parliamentary Party for years after it became known that, in her former capacity as an employee of National Irish Bank, she had encouraged and assisted people to evade tax. It was only in April 2004, when the Supreme Court finally rejected her libel action against RTÉ, which had reported what she had done, that the Mayo TD finally found herself outside the fold. Even then, hints were dropped that she might not be excluded for long. Flynn let it be known that whatever she had done had been effectively encouraged by her employers, and was common practice at the time.

The extent to which senior managers in Irish banking had been indifferent to the consequences of tax evasion became glaringly apparent on 28 May 2004, when it was reported that former and current senior executives in Allied Irish Banks had themselves benefited directly from personal investments in an offshore company that was set up by the bank. The scheme involved a breach of tax law. A suggestion that some of the executives had not fully understood the nature of the activity was widely derided by the public and dismissed as 'hard to believe' by Taoiseach Bertie Ahern, speaking in the Dáil on 1 June 2004. It also emerged at this time that the banks had been overcharging customers for certain transactions and engaging in sharp practice in respect of their sale of various financial 'products'. Where the malpractice by John Rusnak that came to light in 2002 had constituted a massive fraud on the bank by an employee of its US subsidiary, Allfirst, the practices that were uncovered during 2004 looked to many like the bank itself cheating its customers. Nevertheless, and despite having had to repay millions to customers who were overcharged for certain transactions, on 22 February 2005 AIB managed to declare an annual profit of €1.4 billion before tax. This profit was unprecedented for an Irish company.

AIB was clearly not alone in offending. On 30 July 2004, High Court inspectors published their report into National Irish Bank. Described by the business editor of the *Irish Independent* as 'the most damning report ever written on an Irish financial institution', it was a catalogue of corruption, theft and tax evasion by that bank.

The extent to which Ireland's tolerance of tax evasion has really changed remains to be seen. The report of the DIRT Inquiry is a monument to its chairman, the late Jim Mitchell. It helped to change our sense that nothing could be done to check those who engaged in tax evasion, and it altered our perception of the nature of the problem. If our ambivalence towards revenue collection has been partly founded on habits formed over centuries by a colonised people in the process of attempting to outwit a colonial administration, then our painful realisation of the harm that an inequitable system of tax collection and an inadequate system of banking regulation can do to our own society may be an indication of the maturing of the independent Irish State.

Politics

Though creed-crazed zealots and the ignorant crowd,
long nurtured, never checked, in ways of hate,
have made our streets a by-word of offence,
this is my country, never disavowed.
When it is fouled, shall I not remonstrate?
My heritage is not their violence.

JOHN HEWITT, 'An Ulsterman'
FROM *An Ulster Reckoning*, 1971

BETWEEN BOSTON AND BERLIN

Brussels, 1 January 1973

On 1 January 1973, both the Republic of Ireland and the United Kingdom became members of the European Economic Community, now known as the European Union. Our period of membership has coincided with the economic and social transformation of Ireland.

As a country, today we are richer, more vibrant, more cosmopolitan and more self-confident than we were thirty years ago. As a state, the Republic of Ireland has benefited enormously from a transfer of funds from richer European countries. Many major infrastructural projects have been made possible by this source of revenue. Our joining the EU has also facilitated and become the excuse for social reforms, and citizens have learnt to embrace membership as a maturing or even liberating reality. Some people who originally saw membership as an infringement of our economic and political sovereignty are happily reconciled with it today, and find that their fears were exaggerated. Citizens feel freed from a dependence on Britain and are proud to be seen as 'good Europeans', especially when compared to the British. We endorsed closer integration of the EU by voting in referenda for the Single European Act on 24 May 1987, for the Maastrict Treaty on 18 June 1992, and for the Amsterdam Treaty on 22 May 1998. On 1 January 2002, the Irish punt was readily swapped for the common coinage of the euro.

We have not surrendered our independence. Thus, in a referendum held on 7 June 2001, Ireland rejected the proposed Nice Treaty. Some saw this as evidence of ingratitude, and of a grudging attitude to the proposed enlargement of the community to include countries that might reasonably expect to be assisted in the generous way Ireland itself had earlier been helped to adjust to the competitive realities of membership. Taoiseach Bertie Ahern described the outcome as 'an unexpected shock to our partners and to the applicant countries'. Although the Irish government proceeded to hold and carry a further national referendum on the Nice Treaty on 19 October 2002, the first result stands as a warning to Brussels that the ordinary citizens of Ireland and other countries must not be taken for granted. Voters were at least as worried by the growing power of EU institutions as by the community's continuing enlargement.

Strains between the Irish government in Dublin and the commission in Brussels have become evident down the years. The social democratic traditions of many European countries can foster a degree of EU economic regulation that is anathema to the main political parties in Ireland, which are conservative. Since the 1950s, the Republic has looked to American capitalism for investment and inspiration. Resulting tensions were articulated in a celebrated speech by Tánaiste Mary Harney, leader of the neo-liberal Progressive Democrats. Addressing the American Bar Association in Dublin on 21 July 2000, Harney suggested that we may be 'spiritually' closer to Boston than Berlin. Boston has a particular resonance for Irish people, not only because so many Irish have emigrated to that city, but also because it was the home of John F. Kennedy, whose visit to Ireland in June 1963 helped to nurture the seeds of optimism in an Ireland beginning to emerge from years of depression. Harney told the visiting lawyers:

> History and geography have placed Ireland in a very special position between America and Europe. History has bound this country very closely to the United States. Down the centuries millions of Irish people crossed the Atlantic in search of a new life in a new world. And that tradition of emigration laid the foundation for the strong social, economic and political ties between our two countries today. Geography has placed this

country on the edge of the European continent. One of our most significant achievements as an independent nation was our entry, almost thirty years ago, into what is now the European Union. Today, we have strong social, economic and political ties with the EU.

As Irish people, our relationships with the United States and the European Union are complex. Geographically we are closer to Berlin than Boston. Spiritually we are probably a lot closer to Boston than Berlin.

Ireland is now in a very real sense the gateway to Europe. This is especially true for corporate America, whose companies are investing here in ever greater numbers and in ever greater volumes. They see Ireland as an ideal base from which to attack the European market, the largest and most lucrative single market in the history of the world. Geographic location is not the key factor which influences these corporate decisions: many other places have probably more to offer if that was the deciding issue.

What really makes Ireland attractive to corporate America is the kind of economy which we have created here. When Americans come here they find a country that believes in the incentive power of low taxation. They find a country that believes in economic liberalisation. They find a country that believes in essential regulation but not over-regulation. On looking further afield in Europe they find also that not every European country believes in all of these things.

The figures speak for themselves. It is a remarkable fact that a country with just 1% of Europe's population accounts for 27% of US greenfield investment in Europe.

Political and economic commentators sometimes pose a choice between what they see as the American way and the European way. They view the American way as being built on the rugged individualism of the original frontiersmen, an economic model that is heavily based on enterprise and incentive, on individual effort and with limited government intervention. They view the European way as being built on a strong concern for social harmony and social inclusion, with governments being prepared to intervene strongly through the tax and regulatory systems to achieve their desired outcomes. Both models are, of course, overly simplistic, but there is an element of truth in them too. We in

> Ireland have tended to steer a course between the two, but I think it is fair to say that we have sailed closer to the American shore than the European one.
>
> Look at what we have done over the last ten years. We have cut taxes on capital. We have cut taxes on corporate profits. We have cut taxes on personal incomes. The result has been an explosion in economic activity, and Ireland is now the fastest-growing country in the developed world.
>
> And did we have to pay some very high price for pursuing this policy option? Did we have to dismantle the welfare state? Did we have to abandon the concept of social inclusion? The answer is no: we didn't.

Not everyone agrees with Mary Harney's estimate of the price we have paid for our economic policies. Critics believe that underlying inequities have been concealed beneath the foliage of growth and that these inequities may emerge more clearly than ever if and when there is a major recession. Meanwhile, critics fear, Ireland has become a harder and more selfish society as the decline of religious practice and the espousal of economic individualism corrode the public's appreciation of the value of social cohesion and community, and of international solidarity beyond Europe and North America. The term 'spiritual', used by Harney, is not one that all Irish people would immediately associate with our attempts to woo US investors and to maintain a social climate to their liking. Her speech in part springs from the fear that countries in eastern Europe or elsewhere, with their lower wages and lower costs and populations ready to support US foreign policy, might become the main platforms for US investment within the expanding European Union. As the level of education in such countries improves, the fact that Ireland is English-speaking and that its workforce is skilled may no longer be as significant as before. The Irish government has been particularly irked by EU efforts to enforce stringent economic policies on smaller countries, whilst larger member states have been given some slack to depart from the agreed norm.

———

The professed Irish affinity for Boston, as a symbol of the American way of doing business, may be 'spiritual' or simply mercenary. In any event, the strain of balancing on a tightrope between Boston and Berlin became very evident when, in 2003, the United States invaded Iraq and large numbers of US troops began to pass through Shannon Airport on their way to the Middle East. Taoiseach Bertie Ahern tried to please the Irish public who opposed war and who supported neutrality, attempted to maintain good relations with the French and Germans as they argued with Washington and London, and strove not to mortally offend President George W. Bush. An angered White House might cause severe disruption to future US investment in Ireland and create difficulties in continuing negotiations between Ireland and Bush's UK war ally in respect of the implementation of the Good Friday Agreement. However, fortunately, Ireland's turn to be president of the European Union came around in 2004. This allowed Bertie to play host in Dublin to all EU leaders, on 1 May, at a ceremony celebrating the enlargement of the community by the accession of ten new members. In his capacity as EU president that year, he also found himself attending the G8 summit in Georgia, USA, and welcoming President Bush to Ireland when the latter attended the joint US-EU summit at Dromoland Castle, Co. Clare. Suspended somewhere between Boston and Berlin, and making frequent use of the government's executive jet, Bertie strove manfully on behalf of the Irish people to butter our bread on both sides.

COALITION AND COMPROMISE

Dáil Éireann, 29 June 1989

On 29 June 1989, Charles Haughey failed in his bid to be chosen as Taoiseach by the deputies of Dáil Éireann. Following the general election that month, Fianna Fáil was once again the largest party in the Oireachtas. Haughey now faced an important decision: was he to yield power to the opposition, or would he forge an alliance to take his party into a coalition government for the first time in its history?

Fianna Fáil had long excoriated the very idea of coalition, not least when Fine Gael and Labour entered office under such an arrangement. Faced with losing power, however, Haughey chose to break with precedent. He formed a government with the Progressive Democrats. His decision was not entirely surprising. For one thing, he was highly ambitious. For another, during 1982, Haughey had headed a Fianna Fáil minority government that depended on the votes of Tony Gregory and other independent members of the Dáil. He ensured their support through his government's generosity to their constituencies.

The moment Haughey was forced to make a choice between losing power and forming a coalition was the moment that Ireland's recent preference for moderate and centrist governments was consolidated. There had been some 'interparty' governments in the past, from 1948 to 1951 and from 1954 to 1957, but these were both unwieldy and exceptional.

Opposition parties grew increasingly frustrated by the monolithic dominance of Fianna Fáil. This frustration drove conservative Fine Gael and leftist Labour to find ways of doing business together. In March 1973, they seized the opportunity and exploited the optimism of Ireland's having joined the EEC by proposing to the electorate that they were the parties to steer Ireland on its new course in Europe. No sooner was the ink dry on the Treaty of Accession, signed in January 1973 by Taoiseach Jack Lynch, than Liam Cosgrave succeeded Lynch to become Taoiseach of a Fine Gael-Labour National Coalition. In 1977, Lynch managed to return his party to power for four years, but that was the last time that any single party won an overall majority in Ireland.

Under the reforming leadership of Garret FitzGerald, Fine Gael and Labour demonstrated the ability of parties of different hues to work together in government for the good of the State. Both explained to supporters that getting some of your policies adopted in such circumstances was a sufficient reward for not insisting on the implementation of others. Either party on its own in government might have indulged its particular supporters and created social instability. FitzGerald was Taoiseach from 1981 until early in 1982, when he yielded to Haughey for a few months, and again from 1982 to 1987.

The years 1987 to 1989 were exceptional, with Fianna Fáil surviving as a minority government under Charles Haughey. The economy was deteriorating, and Fine Gael had decided not to oppose Fianna Fáil on a number of difficult measures. On 2 September 1987, the leader of Fine Gael, Alan Dukes, outlined his strategy at a meeting of Tallaght Chamber of Commerce. He said, 'Any other policy of Opposition would amount simply to a cynical exploitation of short-term political opportunities for a political advantage which would inevitably prove to be equally short-lived. I will not play that game.' Whether Dukes was being genuinely principled, or merely making a virtue of necessity in the light of Fine Gael's weaker electoral results, is a matter of opinion. Critics claim that he damaged his own party in the long run. Nevertheless, although Haughey expected to win an overall majority when he called an election in 1989, Fianna Fáil actually lost seats. Fine Gael gained four.

There was a special reason why the public was glad to see Fianna Fáil under Charles Haughey forced into coalition in 1989, especially in partnership with the Progressive Democrats (PDs). People distrusted Haughey, partly because of his role in the Arms Crisis, but also because of his political reputation as a bit of a ruthless chancer. The PDs had been formed on the initiative principally of Desmond O'Malley and other former members of Fianna Fáil. They broke from their old party because of their unease at the direction in which it was heading, in their opinion, not just politically but morally. A coalition formed with the PDs meant that Haughey was less likely to get away with misgovernment than if Fianna Fáil was in power on its own.

Since Haughey set a precedent, other coalitions have been led by Fianna Fáil's Albert Reynolds and Bertie Ahern. Although the Labour Party had earlier been in government with Fine Gael, Reynolds enticed it to switch allegiance to Fianna Fáil from 1992 to 1994. Then, Labour switched back again and joined with Democratic Left to form 'The Rainbow Coalition' under Fine Gael's John Bruton between 1994 and 1997. The Progressive Democrats have only worked in government with Fianna Fáil.

Ireland's voting system lends itself to the formation of coalition governments. A detailed variety of proportional representation, in which people may cast a vote for every single candidate, in the order of their preference, results in the wishes of voters being reflected quite closely in the distribution of seats to the various parties. For this reason, it is not surprising to find minority parties holding the balance of power. What is surprising is that there were not more minority or interparty governments before the closing decades of the twentieth century. Since 1973, the Republic of Ireland has known little else but government by coalitions. The appointment of programme managers and special advisers has helped to oil the wheels of coalition.

It is notable that no single political party in the Republic of Ireland has won an overall majority since the general election of 1977, and there have been only coalitions since 1989. These usually emerged from post-electoral negotiations rather than pre-electoral pacts, with those involved agreeing on a programme for government before entering office. Indeed, no government of any particular hue was re-elected from 1969 until 2002, when the Fianna Fáil-PD coalition was returned to power on foot of extravagant promises that it almost immediately set about breaking.

A foreigner, reading this political history, might assume that there has been political instability and turmoil. On the contrary, coalition has ultimately worked well as a moderating influence in Ireland. It has helped to build compromise and create a consensus, in which a broad range of social and economic interest groups have worked together for the welfare of the State. By avoiding extremes, a political climate was created that nourished both the Celtic Tiger and the Peace Process. Coalition has facilitated, in particular, a social partnership that has seen the successful conclusion of successive national pay agreements. However, as a form of government, its value may be sorely tested in the near future if Sinn Féin makes further significant strides in the Republic and comes to hold the balance of power in Dáil Éireann.

MATURE RECOLLECTION

RTÉ, Donnybrook, 25 October 1990

It was a political catastrophe for Brian Lenihan. Just as he seemed set to crown a long political career by becoming president of Ireland, he was revealed as an apparent liar. And he compounded his problems by going on national television and repeatedly using the phrase 'mature recollection' to explain his attempts to deny what he had earlier let slip to a research student.

It was worse than a political catastrophe: it was a personal disaster, because people were now laughing at a man whom many had long regarded fondly as an honourable if roguish politician and whose catch-phrase had been, hitherto, 'no problem' when facing any difficulty. Now, there was a problem.

Brian Lenihan lost the presidential election of 1990. Mary Robinson and her backers might not have won it without him. His error let her into office, and she became the Republic of Ireland's first female Head of State. She was also the first successful presidential candidate to have run for office without the backing of Fianna Fáil. Her election subsequently allowed Irish people to come to the conclusion that they had, as a nation, consciously chosen that model of a new kind of tolerant Ireland which she personified. Her elevation to office set the official tone for Ireland in the 1990s.

Robinson and her backers ran a clever campaign, and her

dedication and hard work were essential prerequisites to her ultimate success. But the electorate might still have chosen Lenihan, had it not been for a second major gaffe by another leading member of his party, Pádraig Flynn. Flynn's naked abhorrence of what Mary Robinson represented, in terms of liberal values and mildly socialist rhetoric, spilt over into a vitriolic public attack on her that sealed Lenihan's fate.

Fianna Fáil had long determined who became president of Ireland. So, at the outset of the campaign of 1990, the party had no reason to believe that Brian Lenihan would not be succeeding Patrick Hillery in Áras an Uachtaráin, the presidental residence in Dublin's Phoenix Park. He was an obvious candidate. Rumours of his ill health evoked sympathy rather than concern about his ability to conduct himself as president. He had a long track record of public service, including that of Minister for Foreign Affairs, and he was popular with parliamentary colleagues in all parties.

Mary Robinson appeared to be an unlikely horse to back in any race for the Phoenix Park. Indeed, some suspected that she was nominated by the Labour Party principally to attract new voters to that party, in the hope that those same voters would turn out for Labour at subsequent elections. However, she proved to be a formidable candidate. Called to the bar in 1967, Robinson was Reid Professor of Laws at Trinity College Dublin from 1969 to 1975. She became a senior counsel in 1980, and later was a founder and director of the Irish Centre for European Law. She appeared in many constitutional and human rights cases in Irish and European courts and came to be regarded as a fearless, outspoken defender of civil liberties. She represented Trinity College in Seanad Éireann (the Irish Senate) from 1969 to 1989. She had been a member of the Labour Party from 1976 until 1985, when she resigned from the party in protest at the terms of the Anglo-Irish Agreement, which her party supported that year and which she had helped to negotiate. She felt that the final version imposed a framework that was unacceptable to many unionists.

Robinson's personal commitment to civil liberties was brought home to me when I became acquainted with the late Johanna (Josie) Airey, a woman from Cork who, at the time that I met her in the late 1970s, was in the midst of a massive personal struggle for justice in respect of the breakdown of her marriage. She could not afford a lawyer to act for her. Airey's efforts, aided voluntarily by others, eventually brought the Irish government to the European Court of Human Rights. Throughout her struggle Airey was abandoned and sometimes harassed by the Irish State, and few people were interested in her problems. I reported on her difficulties for RTÉ. One person who did assist her was Mary Robinson, and I saw at first hand how Robinson's help kept Airey from despairing. Robinson's strong commitment to Airey's needs led to the latter's vindication, in 1979, under the Convention of Human Rights and, eventually, to the introduction of civil legal aid in Ireland. In two other leading cases before the European Court of Human Rights, Robinson helped to end the legal and social stigma of illegitimacy in Ireland, and to change the Irish law on homosexual behaviour.

When the leader of the Labour Party, Dick Spring, got together with a small group of his colleagues to discuss a possible candidate for president in 1990, Mary Robinson fitted the profile which they had in mind. She agreed to be nominated, but declined an invitation to rejoin the Labour Party. This was an astute move that allowed her to be viewed as an independent by many who liked her candidacy, but who would not usually vote Labour.

Robinson's aloof manner disguised a grasp of practicalities that served her well as a lawyer. She now embarked on a long and gruelling journey that took her around Ireland, availing of the opportunity to be photographed with 'ordinary people' and to convince them that rumours of her revolutionary politics and extreme liberalism were greatly exaggerated. The fact that the main opposition party, Fine Gael, failed to convince any of its senior members to run for office and had to fall back on Austin Currie, a respected public representative from Northern Ireland, helped Robinson.

Lenihan's fall from grace resulted from his attempts to portray himself as statesmanlike. There were rumours that he had been one of a number of government ministers who unsuccessfully put pressure on President Paddy Hillery not to dissolve the Dáil during a budget crisis in January 1982. If not exactly irregular, any such decision by Hillery would have been unprecedented and would have greatly helped the new leader of Fianna Fáil, Charles Haughey. Lenihan now publicly denied that he even made any such phone call. A presidential candidate ought not to be seen to have harassed a sitting president.

Unfortunately for Lenihan, he had earlier met Jim Duffy, a research student at University College Dublin. Duffy had taped an interview, during which Lenihan admitted that he spoke on the phone to President Hillery in 1982. In fact, Lenihan had confirmed that there were at least two or three phone calls, 'certainly', from the government side. He reportedly told Duffy that he got through to Hillery and remembered talking to him.

Details of Lenihan's interview with the UCD student soon found their way into the public domain. Matters then went from bad to worse for Brian Lenihan when he went on television to distance himself from the UCD interview. On RTÉ News, he looked right into the camera and repeatedly used the phrase 'mature recollection' to justify a new account of events. Now, he claimed that he had not actually spoken to the president in 1982 and that he had misinformed Duffy. As a direct result of that TV appearance, the words 'mature recollection' are widely used to this day by Irish people joking about denials that are utterly implausible and about political U-turns.

Even still, Lenihan might have recovered from this disaster. The public liked him, and his medical condition might be blamed for any lapse of memory. However, Robinson's chances were greatly boosted by a savage assault on her propriety by the Minister for the Environment, Fianna Fáil's Pádraig Flynn. Flynn was later to be appointed an EU commissioner. On a radio programme, during the closing days of the campaign, Flynn accused her of being pro-socialist and pro-abortion and claimed: 'She has the new interest in family, being a mother and all that kind of thing.' He added, 'None of us who knew Mary Robinson very well in previous incarnations ever heard her claiming to be a great wife and mother.'

Flynn was voicing sentiments that were, along with even stronger ones, being articulated by some of his party's canvassers on the doorsteps of Ireland. However, by making such a personal assault across the airwaves, he had overstepped what Irish voters regard as the bounds of decency and helped to tip the scales decisively in Mary Robinson's favour.

Yet, notwithstanding any offence caused by Lenihan's behaviour or Flynn's comments, Lenihan began to recover lost ground and Mary Robinson actually trailed him by 82,219 votes in the presidential election of 1990. It took the second preferences of the eliminated Fine Gael candidate to bring her eventual victory.

On the day of her inauguration, Mary Robinson stood at Dublin

Castle surrounded by the dark-suited stalwarts of a humiliated Fianna Fáil Party. Some looked as though they were choking on her victory. The image of a rose among thorns sprang to mind as Taoiseach and former taoisigh, a former president and government ministers gazed down on the brightly dressed new president. She had been voted into office because of a mixture of hard work on the hustings, clever positioning in the media, and bad judgment on the part of her opponents. In the course of her election she had persuaded many to support her who had never voted for the parties that promoted her.

In her first address to the people of Ireland as president, Mary Robinson said:

> The Ireland I will be representing is a new Ireland, open, tolerant, inclusive. Many of you who voted for me did so without sharing all my views. This, I believe, is a significant signal of change, a sign, however modest, that we have already passed the threshold to a new, pluralist Ireland.

It was a brave judgment by someone who, in the end of the day, could not be sure that she would have won, had not her main opponent and his supporters done themselves so much damage. But her words were not entirely without foundation and, in any event, the general manner in which Robinson conducted her presidency encouraged people to believe that they had consciously voted for the vision of Ireland which she personified. The 1990s was a period when most Irish people accepted that the State should be pluralist.

During her term of office from 1990 to 1997, Mary Robinson became the first Irish Head of State to pay an official visit to the United Kingdom, visiting London and meeting Queen Elizabeth. One distinctive feature of her presidency was the fact that she placed a special light in the window of her official residence as a mark of her concern for what she called 'the diaspora', this being her term for emigrants from Ireland and descendants of Irish emigrants around the world.

———

Robinson decided not to run for a second term in office, stepping down to take a position instead as United Nations High

Dublin 1978: A march organised by the Contraception Action Programme as part of a campaign to legalise contraception.

Derek Speirs/Report

May 1992: The news breaks of Bishop Eamonn Casey's affair with Annie Murphy.

Eamonn Farrell/Photocall Ireland

O'Connell Street, Dublin, 1995: A campaigner for the No vote in the Divorce Referendum.
Leon Farrell/Photocall Ireland

14 May 2001: Taoiseach Bertie Ahern and Celia Larkin host a reception at Dublin Castle to honour the elevation of Archbishop Desmond Connell to the College of Cardinals.
Eamonn Farrell/Photocall Ireland

Women at work: Fruit of the Loom factory in Co. Donegal in the 1990s.

Peter Barrow

The Marian shrine grotto in Granard, Co. Longford, where Ann Lovett died.

Derek Speirs/Report

Dublin 1992: A sit-down protest outside Government Buildings objecting to the Attorney-General seeking an injunction to stop 'X' having an abortion in England.

Derek Speirs/Report

Donogh O'Malley: His announcement of the free secondary education scheme in 1966 was, arguably, the most successful single political initiative in the history of the State.

Lensmen Press

Enniskillen 1987: The Remembrance Day bombing.

Pacemaker

March 1997: Father Brendan Smyth is extradited from Northern Ireland to the Republic.

Reuters

Larry Goodman, one of the figures central to the deliberations of the Beef Tribunal.

Eamonn Farrell/Photocall Ireland

Dublin 1986: Ben Dunne greets Charles J. Haughey.

Eamonn Farrell/Photocall Ireland

Dublin 1983: PAYE workers march to demand tax equity.

Derek Speirs/Report

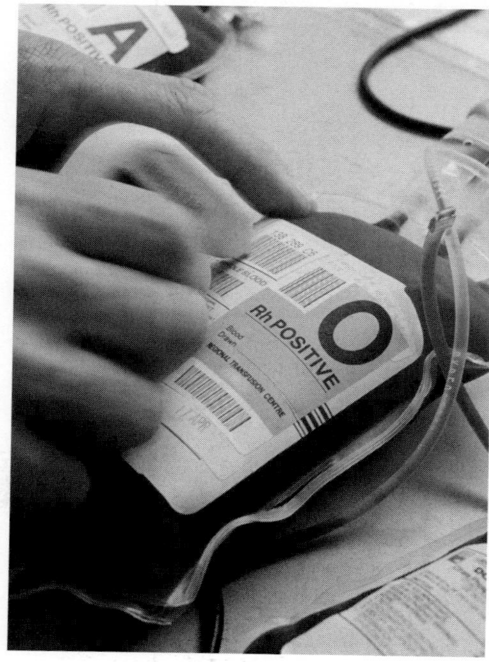

Blood for transfusion being barcode scanned. The scandal at the Irish Blood Transfusion Service from the 1970s onwards was, arguably, the greatest dereliction of duty in the history of the State.

Alamy

HAPPY NEW YEAR, NEW EUROPEANS!

CITY SPECIAL

Irish Independent

Vol. 82. No. 1 MONDAY, JANUARY 1, 1973 Price 4p

GOOD MORNING, EUROPE!

Historic moment as we go into E.E.C.

FROM DAVID HAWORTH, OUR MAN IN BRUSSELS

THIS MORNING we join a potential new superpower, which possibly will one day rival the U.S. and Russia. The formal enlargement of the European Common Market, to include Ireland, Denmark and Britain came at midnight last night.

The new nine-nation Common Market already represents the world's largest trading power, the second richest economy after the U.S., and the third most populous unit after China and India.

But the moment of enlargement will pass virtually unnoticed with no formal ceremonies here

The headquarters of the European Commission in Brussels — (Picture: courtesy E.E.C.).

1 January 1973: The headline in the *Irish Independent* on the morning on which the Republic joins what is now the European Union.

Irish Independent; courtesy of the National Library of Ireland

President-elect Mary Robinson and her husband Nick at home before moving to Áras an Uachtaráin.

Ian Cook/TLP/Getty

January 1992: Some people thought he would never go: the end of Charlie.

Derek Speirs/Report

Belfast 1998: A woman weeps as she watches Taoiseach Bertie Ahern and Prime Minister Tony Blair embrace at the signing of the Good Friday Agreement.

Reuters

December 2001: Forensic officials inspect the shipping container that contained the bodies of eight dead refugees.

Paul McErlane/Reuters

2004: Something you won't see anymore. In 2004, Ireland became the first member of the EU to ban smoking in public places.

Derek Speirs/Report

Ryanair has been the single greatest symbol of the Celtic Tiger, a phenomenally successful business that has revolutionised Irish and European travel habits.

Courtesy of The Irish Times

Dublin 1990: The West-Link bridge over the Liffey Valley is an integral part of the M50 orbital motorway. Here, people scramble for viewing positions prior to its official opening.
Derek Speirs/Report

1994 *Riverdance.* It started as an intermission item during the final of the Eurovision Song contest and went on to become an enormously successful global brand.
Used by kind permission of Abhann Productions Ltd; photograph © 2003 Joan Marcus

Dublin 1991: The opening of the Irish Museum of Modern Art at the Royal Hospital, Kilmainham.

Courtesy Irish Museum of Modern Art, Dublin

September 1979: The visit of Pope John Paul II to Ireland drew unprecedented crowds. It is estimated that over one-third of the population attended one or other of the Masses.

Anwar Hussein/Getty

1981: H-Block. The hunger strikes were the turning point in the evolution of contemporary Sinn Féin, north and south.

Eamonn Farrell/Photocall Ireland

1990: The Republic of Ireland qualifies for the finals of the World Cup, reaching the quarter-final before losing — by a single goal — to the hosts, Italy. No sporting event has ever galvanised the people in quite the same way; the squad received a hero's welcome on their return.

Inpho

Following attacks on the United States on 11 September 2001, Ireland declared a national day of mourning. Here, crowds stand in a three-minute silent tribute outside the Pro-Cathedral in Dublin.

Paul McErlane/Reuters

Commissioner for Human Rights. She was succeeded by another woman, Mary McAleese. While McAleese was more palatable to conservative Catholics, she shared some of Robinson's liberal views on feminism and certain other matters, and it was a sign of changed times that she was nominated by Fianna Fáil.

DOING THE STATE

Kinsealy, Co. Dublin, 11 February 1992

Rascal. Playboy. Accountant. Enigma. Reproached by Garret FitzGerald in 1979 for his 'flawed pedigree', Charles J. Haughey frequently represented himself as some sort of uncommon man with a common touch. He took money from rich patrons: he and they swore that he did them no favours in return. He mesmerised us with his personal wealth while sinking the economy in debt. He told untruths to a tribunal of inquiry, but no charge of perjury was ever proven against him. He spent his party's money on luxuries, but some voters envied his ostentation. He preached family values, while committing adultery. Having immersed the State in debt, he demanded fiscal rectitude and restraint from its citizens, but continued to live far beyond his own means. He compromised the integrity of the Irish body politic as no Taoiseach before or since has ever done. He resigned as Taoiseach on 11 February 1992. His resignation speech was an attempt to claim his place in history.

He was a man who appeared to imagine that his political style was a cross between that of the French emperor, Napoleon Bonaparte, and that of his own father-in-law and predecessor as Taoiseach, Seán Lemass. 'Arise and follow Charlie' was his party's electoral cry. His vanity was laid bare when the Moriarty Tribunal, set up to investigate payments to politicians, revealed on 6 October 1999 that Charles Haughey had, in 1991, spent nearly £16,000 on some fancy clothes at Charvet in Paris.

Charvet is a rich man's outfitters, to whom Haughey had been taking his custom at the expense of others. He was also living it up in Dublin at the exclusive Le Coq Hardi restaurant. There, he wined and dined his mistress and friends at great expense to others who included the Irish taxpayer. He indulged himself as Taoiseach at a time when unemployment and the national debt were soaring in Ireland, and when social services for the poor were very inadequate. He received special, favourable treatment from Irish banks that ostensibly respected his position as an important political leader while, simultaneously, appearing to be afraid of his power.

On one occasion, Haughey's private secretary and special adviser, Catherine Butler, accompanied him on a visit to the Charvet shop in Paris. He bought her an expensive scarf. She later described how the Irish diplomatic service was used to transport Haughey's shirts to Dublin. By convention, diplomatic bags are exempt from scrutiny at borders and are intended for use only for the transportation of materials relating to the official business of states.

There was a sharp contrast between his lifestyle and that of people struggling through an economic recession. However, so long as citizens could maintain the fiction that Haughey was somehow a self-made man whose heart was in the right place, he got away with playing the squire. Rumours of his long-running affair with Terry Keane, a social columnist in one of Dublin's newspapers, did not dent his popular image as some kind of statesman. Like many politicians, he was partly an actor. His gift of a teapot to Prime Minister Margaret Thatcher was a suitably ambivalent expression of his personality. Was it a friendly gesture or mockery?

Mockery and contempt were directed at Charles Haughey himself once it became known that he had been receiving hand-outs from rich patrons while Taoiseach. The fact that his mistress, when her relationship with Haughey ended, shared her recollections of their affair with the public did nothing to help him recover his dignity. He is even suspected of misdirecting to his own use certain funds collected for a liver transplant operation for Brian Lenihan, who was both a former Minister for Foreign Affairs and one of Fianna Fáil's elder representatives.

The titles of various books about Haughey indicate how he was perceived. They are *The Boss*, *The Statesman*, *The Legend of Charles Haughey*, *Sweetie*, *Short Fellow* (Michael Collins, hero of the Irish War of Independence, was known as 'The Big Fellow') and *The Modern Prince.* Haughey survived much political grief, perhaps because the public had a certain 'sneaking regard' for him. In 1970, his dismissal as Minister for Finance and his subsequent trial on charges of conspiring to import arms illegally did not terminate his political career. He was suspected of misusing State funds to arm paramilitaries north of the Irish border. The fact that the charge did not damage him permanently was partly because he was acquitted in court and partly because many people did not object to a little military support for the nationalists of Northern Ireland, especially when they were under imminent threat from loyalist forces. Haughey's reform of the succession law and his awarding of tax breaks to artists and writers pleased liberals and made the citizens of Ireland feel better about their society. For a long time, people chose to believe that his financial affairs were barely on the right side of regular. His acquisition of Innishvicillaun, a spectacular Kerry island where he built a second home, was seen as a flamboyant indulgence that could be tolerated in a prince of state. His personal retention of valuable gifts to him as Taoiseach, from the Saudi royal family, was not widely condemned. Many hoped that, because he had manifestly done himself so proud financially, he might somehow be able to see us all right economically at the end of the day.

I once interviewed him at length for RTÉ in the run-up to a general election. The interview was recorded at Kinsealy, his grand Georgian home in north Co. Dublin. On the room's crowded walls hung not only a large portrait of his father-in-law, Seán Lemass, but also a painting of himself by Robert Ballagh. It was the early 1980s, and, not long before our meeting, François Mitterand had made a declaration of his 'health and wealth' to the French people whom he was asking to elect him as president. As my final question, I asked Haughey if he would consider making a similar declaration. His eyes narrowed and he said in a cold, steady voice that he hoped that Irish politics would never descend to such a level.

Grudging respect for Haughey changed to grudge and disrespect as the extent of his financial chicanery was revealed, and his colourful lifestyle now looked just tawdry. The contrast between the state of the nation and the state of Mr Haughey's lifestyle in the 1980s and 1990s later became a recurrent theme of political exchanges, as in Dáil Éireann on 14 December 1999:

J. O'KEEFFE: It was 'Arise and follow Charlie' then but they [Fianna Fáil] do not want to know him now. These are very selective quotations.

AN LEAS-CHEANN COMHAIRLE [DEPUTY SPEAKER]: The Minister, without interruption.

R. BRUTON: What was going on when we were being told to tighten our belts?

MR DEMPSEY: Unemployment was running at 16 per cent.

O'KEEFFE: Charvet shirts were £250.

DEMPSEY: Emigration was soaring and personal tax rates were as high as 65 per cent. The London *Times* reported that the international moneylenders were about to 'pull down the shutters'.

BRUTON: *Le Monde* had excellent advertisements for Charvet.

D. AHERN: That is an infantile argument.

On 15 July 1997, in the yard of Dublin Castle, Haughey was booed by members of the public as he left a hearing of the McCracken Tribunal that was then investigating payments to him by Ben Dunne. The moment became all the more awful for him when one lone and die-hard supporter rushed forward and grabbed his hand only to seem unwilling to let it go again. He was also booed when he appeared in Cork at the funeral of Jack Lynch.

Haughey's bullying style of party leadership and his toleration of sharp practice encouraged emulation by sycophants. The rot had been spotted early by George Colley, one of Haughey's rivals within Fianna Fáil, who in May 1967, urged young members of his party not to be 'dispirited if some people in high places appear to have low standards'. Colley failed to stop Haughey's rise and died prematurely. Haughey's government went on to tap the telephones of journalists, and some of his supporters were suspected of other forms of intimidation.

Haughey escaped some of the possible consequences of his actions and has been given credit more than once for positive achievements during his long career as a government minister and Taoiseach. In his parting speech to the Dáil on 11 February 1992, he quoted from Shakespeare's *Othello* to sing his own praises and to tell the world that he had done the Irish State some service. Such vain presumption failed to recognise the destructive and corrosive influence of his deeds and personality. He urged deputies 'to foster a sense of pride in all our democratic institutions':

> Above all, I thank the people of Ireland for the support they have given me over such a long period of years and indeed for the great deal of affection they have shown me from time to time. As I leave office, I bid them a fond farewell and wish them every success and happiness. The work of Government and of the Dáil must always be directed to the progress of the nation, and I hope I have been able to provide some leadership to that end in my time. I have always sought to act solely and exclusively in the best interests of the Irish people. Let me quote Othello:
>
> I have done the State some service; they know't
> No more of that.

Haughey continued:

> The past 35 years have seen a total transformation of Irish society. Even if not all our high hopes have been realised, there is much to be proud of in the economic and social progress that has been made, and in recent years I believe we have laid good foundations for durable advance.

He concluded:

> Let the record speak for itself. If I were to seek any accolade as I leave office it would simply be: he served the people, all the people, to the best of his ability.

Since his resignation as Taoiseach, the Irish State has come to 'know't' quite a lot more about Haughey and his backers. Citizens have also learned about his hypocrisy in bolstering conservative Catholic campaigns against contraception and divorce while he himself had a mistress. A glimpse at those parts of the speech by Othello (Act v, Sc. 2) which Haughey did not quote in the Dáil reveals some lines that his detractors might think are more appropriate as a monument to his memory: 'Then, must you speak of one that loved not wisely but too well; . . . of one whose hand, like the base Indian, threw a pearl away richer than all his tribe.'

—

Haughey, in retirement, appeared from time to time at the Dingle regatta or at some other public event. He was not shunned, and some expressed a sort of sympathy or admiration for him. In November 2004, Taoiseach Bertie Ahern made soothing public sounds about Haughey's political legacy. Nevertheless, the abiding judgment of history on him is likely to have more to do with shame or disgrace than with glory or dignity. He threw away the pearl of his statesman's status. His political epitaph might be those words he used to describe a series of extraordinary events that culminated, on 13 August 1982, in the arrest of a vicious double murderer in the apartment of his attorney-general, Patrick Connolly: 'grotesque, unbelievable, bizarre and unprecedented'.

THE GOOD FRIDAY AGREEMENT

Belfast, 10 April 1998

The agreement reached in Belfast on 10 April 1988 was a major development in the saga of troubles that have plagued Northern Ireland ever since that political entity was created in December 1920. The prime ministers of the Republic of Ireland and the United Kingdom were delighted, and the media went into overdrive. This was good news, breaking on Good Friday, just in time to allow the negotiators and their advisers to go home for Easter. The over-used word 'historic' was justified as a description of their achievement. It is still justified today, notwithstanding subsequent complications and difficulties.

The 'Belfast Agreement' immediately became better known as the 'Good Friday Agreement'. It was an important compromise between nationalists and unionists, and between the governments of the Republic and the United Kingdom. It proclaimed 'parity of esteem' for all people, 'in the diversity of their identities and traditions', while accepting formally the right of the majority in Northern Ireland to continue to live separately from the Republic of Ireland. The Belfast Agreement affirmed that 'it would be wrong to make any change in the status of Northern Ireland save with the consent of a majority of its people'. It also acknowledged:

> It is for the people of the island of Ireland alone, by agreement between the two parts respectively and without external impediment, to exercise their right of self-determination on the basis of consent, freely and concurrently given, North and South, to bring about a united Ireland, if that is their wish, accepting that this right must be achieved and exercised with and subject to the agreement and consent of a majority of the people of Northern Ireland.

The Agreement was the fruit of a 'peace process' involving much work by many people. It expressed compromises that people had felt unable to make at an earlier date, especially at the time of the Sunningdale Agreement. Partly for that reason, Séamus Mallon of the Social Democratic and Labour Party (SDLP) is said to have referred to the talks leading up to the Good Friday Agreement as 'Sunningdale for slow learners'. On 9 December 1973, at a conference at Sunningdale in England, the British and Irish governments had agreed to a form of administration for Northern Ireland that required the involvement of both communities, but their scheme was fatally flawed because it had not won sufficient unionist backing to survive for long. The Sunningdale Agreement collapsed in the face of loyalist intimidation, and with it went a generation's hopes for peace. Later, on 15 November 1985, Taoiseach Garret FitzGerald and Prime Minister Margaret Thatcher signed an 'Anglo-Irish Agreement', which was intended to maintain some of the even-handedness in governing Northern Ireland that the Sunningdale Agreement had been designed to achieve. The 1985 agreement also failed to command majority support within the province itself, and was not the basis for a lasting peace.

A quarter of a century after Sunningdale, the Good Friday Agreement gave people new hope that Northern Ireland could be governed with the consent of both sides. The agreement included three 'strands', devoted respectively to democratic institutions for Northern Ireland, a North/South Ministerial Council and British-Irish arrangements.

The first strand of the Good Friday Agreement provided for a democratically elected assembly for Northern Ireland. This allowed Westminster to restore certain powers to a local legislature at Stormont, but these were subject to safeguards guaranteeing cross-community consent. Under this arrangement David Trimble of the

Ulster Unionist Party (UUP) became the assembly's first 'First Minister', while Séamus Mallon of the mainly nationalist SDLP became 'Deputy First Minister'. Each party in the assembly was entitled to be represented proportionally at ministerial and committee level.

The second strand of the Good Friday Agreement committed all parties to a new cross-border ministerial council, bringing together those with executive responsibilities in Northern Ireland and the Irish government. The council was given no powers of its own, but depended for its development and progress on the approval of the Oireachtas in Dublin and of the Northern Ireland Assembly in Stormont. Both unionists and nationalists were given an effective veto on its operations. However, if a holder of a particular ministry did not wish to participate in this council, for whatever reason, the Taoiseach in the case of the Irish government and the First and Deputy First Minister in the case of the Northern Ireland Administration were empowered to make alternative arrangements.

The third strand of the Good Friday Agreement created a consultative British-Irish Council 'to promote the harmonious and mutually beneficial development of the totality of relationships among the peoples of these islands'. The council was designed to involve representatives of the Irish and UK governments, as well as of the devolved institutions of Scotland, Wales and Northern Ireland (and representatives of the Isle of Man and the Channel Islands for good measure). These representatives were expected to 'exchange information, discuss, consult and use best endeavours to reach agreement on co-operation on matters of mutual interest'. This third strand also formally recognised the existence of a special relationship between the governments of Ireland and the United Kingdom, which had previously found expression in the Anglo-Irish Agreement of 1985.

In addition to establishing new structures under its three strands, the Good Friday Agreement also promised certain other safeguards and rights for Northern Ireland, including the establishment of a Human Rights Commission and the promotion of the Irish language. It promised a new beginning to policing in the province and a return as soon as possible to 'normal' security arrangements 'consistent with the level of threat'. Prisoners associated with paramilitary organisations were to be released earlier than expected. The Irish government also undertook to improve the protection of human rights within the Republic.

The Provisional IRA had declared a ceasefire in August 1994, but this broke down in February 1996. It was restored in July 1997, and Sinn Féin then committed itself to certain principles of democracy and non-violence known as the 'Mitchell Principles'. These principles were named after George Mitchell, a US senator who had been appointed by the Irish and UK governments as chairman of an international body charged with reporting on how to handle the 'decommissioning' of paramilitary weapons. The Good Friday Agreement includes the statement:

> Participants recall their agreement in the Procedural Motion adopted on 24 September 1997 'that the resolution of the decommissioning issue is an indispensable part of the process of negotiation'.

The Good Friday Agreement records the fact that all parties to it

> note the progress made by the Independent International Commission on Decommissioning and the Governments in developing schemes which can represent a workable basis for achieving the decommissioning of illegally held arms in the possession of paramilitary groups.

In a controversial section, the Good Friday Agreement also makes reference to 'the total disarmament of all paramilitary organisations' and confirms the commitment of all participants in the agreement

> to continue to work constructively and in good faith with the Independent Commission, and to use any influence they may have, to achieve the decommissioning of all paramilitary arms within two years following endorsement in referendums North and South of the agreement and in the context of the overall settlement.

It was agreed that 'the Independent Commission will monitor, review and verify progress on decommissioning of illegal arms, and will report to both Governments at regular intervals'.

The Good Friday Agreement was never universally regarded as a perfect solution to all problems. There remained many on both sides who were distrustful of the motives of those who signed up to it on 10 April 1988. Unionists suspected that Sinn Féin was making opportunistic political advances until such time as a strategic decision would be taken yet again to renew IRA violence; and nationalists suspected that the politicians of the majority would water down their commitments to parity of esteem and cross-border co-operation as time passed and peace prevailed on the streets.

No single document could ever settle the dispute that is Northern Ireland. Carved out of the ancient province of Ulster, constituting six of its nine old counties, Northern Ireland was created to protect the interests and aspirations of a Protestant minority on the island of Ireland that wished to remain within the United Kingdom. In the process, a Catholic nationalist minority within Northern Ireland was alienated and abandoned, and subsequently maltreated in various ways. In February 1922, when the House of Commons was considering the Irish Free State Bill, Winston Churchill referred to the effect of the Great War (1914–18) on people's thinking and observed: 'As the deluge subsides and the waters fall, we see the dreary steeples of Fermanagh and Tyrone emerging once again.' He added: 'The integrity of their quarrel is one of the few institutions that have been unaltered in the cataclysm which has swept the world.' The inability of the two sides to hammer out a workable compromise can be exceptionally tedious for those who are not directly involved in daily life in Northern Ireland. It can be fatal for those who are.

The British public and their elected representatives had little inclination or need to take much interest in Northern Ireland after its foundation and left the province to fester. Westminster yielded an amount of absolute control to local unionists, who discriminated against Catholics and nationalists, thus ensuring that trouble would continue to erupt, as it did, most notably from the late 1960s onwards. For their part, the public and the politicians of the Republic of Ireland paid lip service to caring about 'the fourth green field' of Ireland that was still under British control. However, as time passed, that part of the fourth Irish province that is Northern Ireland benefited from British expenditure and from the facilities of the UK welfare state. The cost of absorbing Northern Ireland into the Republic, even if that had been a realistic political possibility in the twentieth century, was regarded as prohibitive. Few in the Republic had the stomach for such expenditure or for the political turmoil that might ensue if unification was attempted. In the closing decades of the century, as the Republic of Ireland strengthened economically and then boomed, even the aspirational political rhetoric about unity subsided.

People were relieved and genuinely delighted when the Good Friday Agreement appeared to provide a framework within which the problem of Northern Ireland might disappear. Claims of sovereignty over Northern Ireland contained in Articles 2 and 3 of the Republic's written Constitution of 1937 had offended many unionists, and the people of the Republic abandoned them when, on 22 May 1998, they voted in a referendum to accept the Good Friday Agreement. A whopping 94.39 per cent of the electorate were in favour of altering the Constitution. Within Northern Ireland, enthusiasm for the agreement was more constrained but still substantial, with 71.12 per cent voting yes. However, nationalist voters were considerably more enthusiastic than unionist voters. The reservations and suspicions of unionists were not to be quickly allayed, as the IRA has proven reluctant to decommission its arsenal promptly and as various paramilitaries have continued to engage occasionally in violence against local alleged criminals and others.

Nevertheless, most people on the island of Ireland took the opportunity of the referenda on the Good Friday Agreement to register the fact that their thinking on the political future of the island of Ireland had mellowed during the last quarter of the twentieth century. The fact that progress in respect of the institutions envisaged under the agreement has been painfully slow, and that there has been a subsequent polarisation of electoral support within Northern Ireland, cannot take away from the great achievement of 10 April 1998.

IMMIGRANTS

Drinagh Business Park, Co. Wexford, 8 December 2001

It was a shocking moment, not only for the unfortunate families of the victims and for the driver who found them, but also for the people of Ireland in general. It was a moment when the human beings at the centre of discussions about immigration became all too visible. Irish politicians have struggled to find ways of welcoming migrants who are an asset to the economy or who deserve political asylum, while simultaneously limiting the influx of economic migrants who impose a burden on the State or who upset voters in other ways. Economic buoyancy has allowed us to bake a bigger pie, and others now want a slice of it.

The container of furniture from Milan had arrived on a ferry from Zeebrugge into the port at Belview, Co. Waterford, before being driven on to Drinagh Business Park in Co. Wexford. When the doors of the container were opened, they revealed an awful sight. Inside it lay thirteen people, eight of whom were dead. The victims included three young children. Those who were still alive were rushed to hospital in a critical condition, but they survived. Most or all of the victims were Turkish nationals.

The immigrants had entered the container at a truck stop outside Brussels. They had spent more than four days and nights inside it, possessing between them for refreshment just eighteen bottles of mineral water and some cheese. The container was ventilated by four small apertures, measuring two inches by six inches. One by one, the victims died of a lack of oxygen. Their deaths were all the more poignant because the victims did not even know, when they boarded the container, that they were bound for Ireland. They had been informed that they were going to Dover in England and that their journey would last about three hours. Desperation in search of opportunity had met disaster.

Details of what had happened to the immigrants emerged subsequently in Belgium at the trial of six men charged with human trafficking and manslaughter. It transpired that the immigrants were the victims of an Albanian gang whom they had paid and who were believed to have been responsible for smuggling hundreds of people into Britain. Members of the gang had taken the immigrants by taxi from the centre of Brussels to a truck stop outside the city on the morning of 4 December 2001. There, they entered the container.

Once inside the hold of the Dutch *Navigator*, the immigrants found themselves in total darkness. The fact that the container happened to be near the ship's engine made it very warm. The hold itself was shut tightly because of a fierce gale, which also meant the ship took longer than usual to make the crossing. Its frightened human cargo banged on the walls of the container, and one tried to force open its door. But it was all in vain. Their ordeal did not end when the ship docked, because another day passed before the container was collected at the harbour.

Irish people were disgusted by news of the deaths. Taoiseach Bertie Ahern promised that 'every possible effort' would be made to bring those responsible to justice. He added, 'The criminals involved in this cruel trade of trafficking in human beings have perpetrated yet another atrocity on the victims of their greed.' One member of the European Parliament who is from the Wexford area, Avril Doyle, observed: 'Refugee and illegal entry into Ireland has become a big issue in this country and is a new phenomenon.' One year later, a religious ceremony was held at Drinagh Business Park in remembrance of the victims. Four of the five survivors were still in Ireland fourteen months after their ordeal. Two of these were said to be unemployed and two working in kitchen jobs. None travelled to Belgium to give evidence in the trial of those charged with their trafficking and with the manslaughter of their companions.

The eight deaths discovered at Drinagh were certainly not unprecedented, even in Ireland. Less than four months earlier, staff at

Belview had found the body of an African when unloading animal feed. At Dover, in June 2000, dozens of Chinese people were found dead in a container.

During the late 1990s and early 2000s, the arrival of unprecedented numbers of immigrants in Ireland led to a tightening of migration procedures. Many people, especially from Nigeria and Romania, sought refugee status. Those immigrants who gave birth here strengthened their chances of being able to stay. The Irish government put in place a new system to cope with the influx, including an Office of the Refugee Applications Commissioner. During 2004, that office published its third annual report. It stated that the number of applications received in 2003 (7,900) was 32 per cent lower than in 2002 (11,634). This and other factors resulted in a reduction in the backlog of claims. Various measures making it more difficult for migrants to reach Ireland, or to stay once they arrived, were clearly having an effect. Of particular significance was the Supreme Court's decision in the 'L and O' case, where it was held that the parents of a child born in Ireland, who were not themselves Irish, no longer had an automatic right to reside here. It had been alleged that many women were arriving in Ireland at a late stage of pregnancy in order to give birth here and then claim the right to remain.

All babies born in the island of Ireland enjoyed a Constitutional right to Irish citizenship from 1999, following the adoption of the Good Friday Agreement, until 2004. Politicians pointed out that this was unusual compared to the situation in other European countries, and that the Good Friday Agreement had been negotiated within a particular historical context. In a referendum on 11 June 2004, Irish citizens voted, by a majority of approximately 4:1, to confine the automatic right of citizenship to children of people with an Irish background, or as the wording of the referendum put it:

> Notwithstanding any other provision of this Constitution, a person born in the island of Ireland, which includes its islands and seas, who does not have, at the time of the birth of that person, at least one parent who is an Irish citizen or entitled to be an Irish citizen is not entitled to Irish citizenship or nationality, unless provided for by law.

The Office of the Refugee Applications Commissioner rejects the vast majority of applications for refugee status. A higher percentage of applicants are successful upon appeal. Applicants are provided with accommodation and meals and are given small amounts of spending money, pending a final decision on their future.

Immigrants of various colours and cultures come to Ireland. The presence of Chinese, Nigerians, Polish, Romanians and other eastern Europeans has caused most comment. Their arrival in substantial numbers has changed the appearance of the country and added greater variety to our daily lives. It has also sparked some resentment, hostility and racism.

Growing immigration has created cultural and social challenges that are being addressed politically. While the Irish government has pleaded with that of the United States for generosity towards Irish people wishing to work in America, or already illegally present there, it has sought to tighten our own laws on migration and to limit the rights of people who come here. For example, many immigrants are permitted to work only for a particular employer and enter into a kind of dependent service that few Irish people would find tolerable in any but the most extreme circumstances. Some have been badly paid and otherwise exploited.

The complexity of the immigration issue, and of the public's response to it, was underlined in March 2005 when dozens of Nigerians were rounded up and deported by air to Lagos following the failure of their applications to remain in Ireland. Some had been attending school here, for years, and the manner of their arrest and deportation evoked considerable sympathy for their predicament. Olukunle Elukanlo, a twenty-year old who had been preparing for the Leaving Certificate at Palmerstown Community School in Co. Dublin, received such extensive publicity that the Minister for Justice, Michael McDowell, quickly agreed to reverse his deportation.

In a global environment where cultures are quickly polarised, even to the point of 'ethnic cleansing', immigration is a great political challenge. It has changed Ireland. No longer is it a matter of facilitating just two main traditions on this island, or of attempting to reconcile settled people with the Travellers. We live today, increasingly, in a multicultural State.

Society

Even if aggression whets the knife,
a calm mastery has a keener edge.
Consume me in searching out the golden apple
but don't urge the prick of jealousy,
tame in me that wildest beast.

MICHEAL O'SIADHAIL, 'Three Charms: Against Jealousy'
FROM *Hail! Madam Jazz*, 1992

HI MAC!

Cork, 24 November 1980

Some call it 'foreign direct investment', or FDI for short; others prefer to describe it as 'inward investment'. Its arrival has been a major factor in the transformation of Ireland's industrial and economic landscape during the past forty years. The level of foreign direct investment in the Republic of Ireland, relative to the size of our economy, is one of the highest in the world. Employment has soared by over 50 per cent and labour productivity has grown in leaps and bounds. During the late 1990s, Ireland became the most successful economy in the OECD region.

More than 1,100 companies have come from abroad and built up their businesses here. Between them they generate combined annual exports of goods and services worth at least €60 billion. Among the best-known arrivals have been Apple in Co. Cork, and Intel in Co. Kildare. For its part, by the end of 2004, Intel alone had invested €5 billion in its Irish operations at Leixlip and was continuing to expand. Inward investment was sustained even when the Irish economy experienced difficulties. Other prominent investors in recent decades have included Microsoft, Dell, Hewlett-Packard, IBM, Pfizer, Abbott Laboratories and Wyeth Biopharma. Various international call centres have also been established. The Internet company, Google, has been one of a number of companies locating their European headquarters in Ireland. By 2001, the rate of unemployment was below 4 per cent, and Ireland was experiencing a rush of immigration to take up the many jobs on offer.

Ireland benefited early from the process of globalisation, and few people objected when the government actively sought to take advantage of our position as an English-speaking member of the European Union, located conveniently between Britain and the United States. For decades, the new State had languished in the economic shadow of Britain. When dedicated politicians such as Seán Lemass and public servants such as T. K. Whitaker set out to devise strategies for growth in Ireland, their efforts created the opportunity for new generations of Irish people to enjoy levels of financial prosperity and social welfare that were unimaginable as late as 1960.

The introduction of favourable tax incentives for big business has also helped to attract the attention of investors from abroad, as has the State's creation of a proactive Industrial Development Authority (IDA). By 1975, the IDA had secured more than 450 foreign-owned industrial projects which, already, between them accounted for two-thirds of Ireland's total industrial output. As new industries began to locate operations in Ireland, people from small farms adapted early and remarkably well to the routine of life at their local multinational and welcomed the opportunity to supplement their agricultural income with a job at the factory. They and many others took advantage of the new opportunities presented by foreign investment. Foreign employers generally expressed satisfaction with the standard of education in Ireland. At least until recently, Irish labour costs were considered 'competitive'.

Since the 1970s, the Irish State and the IDA have constantly sought to adapt to change. Electronic manufacturers were followed by those involved in 'life science' and software. Information technology companies, financial services, research and development operations, biopharmaceutical companies and 'e-business' are all among the activities whose international promoters have found a welcome in Ireland. Investors from the United States have played a particularly important role in the development of contemporary Ireland.

For its part, Apple's Cork experience reflects the ups and downs of inward investment during the past three decades, and illustrates how one of Ireland's few older multinational industries, Ford, was supplanted in a community's daily life by the force of new technology. In the late 1970s, Apple decided to locate its European manufacturing headquarters in Cork. The plant opened on 24 November 1980. As time went by, the manufacturing model increased in its sophistication and a full printed circuit board (PCB) manufacturing facility was located on the Cork site.

The people of Cork found work at Apple in large numbers. Its force of employees grew gradually to 1,500. This generated welcome revenue for a city where Ford Motors had once been a major employer but had gone into decline and closed. As Apple grew in the 1980s and into the 1990s, it created further employment among subcontractors who manufactured both PCBs and systems. This helped to keep down Apple's labour costs in Ireland, when compared to those in other countries. However, vendors in the Far East and eastern Europe were gradually coming to compete effectively in respect of both the scale and cost of manufacturing in Ireland.

In 1998, things took a turn for the worse at Apple in Cork. Following a strategic assessment of its operations, the company relocated the manufacturing of its PCBs to Indonesia, and its portable product manufacturing to Taiwan. Other work went to the Czech Republic. These changes underlined the increasingly vigorous competition between countries when it comes to attracting what seems to be ever more mobile capital. Irish labour costs and state aids are two big carrots dangled in front of potential investors, leading some critics to claim that Ireland is selling its soul to foreign capitalists.

The changes at Apple in 1998 and 1999 looked like the beginning of a withdrawal from Ireland, as the number employed in Cork dropped by two-thirds, from 1,500 to 500. However, at this same moment, management at the Irish plant also re-marketed the advantages of Ireland to Apple, 'this time within the context of engaging in higher value added activities', as Joe Gantly, the company's senior director of European operations has pointed out. In the IDA's *Business Ireland* newsletter of summer 2003, Gantly wrote:

> The principal messages that were communicated to the corporate headquarters were:
>
> 1. Smart, well-educated and flexible workforce.
> 2. English-speaking but with major language capabilities.
> 3. Competitive telecoms infrastructure reflected in huge growth in technical support, call centre and shared services activity.
> 4. Very effective tax structure with global implications.

5. e commerce infrastructure growing rapidly.
6. Major government investment in education to improve skills availability.

Management's strategy paid off. Cork became Apple's European operations headquarters and its number of employees rose again. This reflects the fact that Ireland has been 'retooling' its workforce to bring specialist skills to the market in search of fresh inward investment. Competition from countries in eastern Europe and from India remains intense, with the enlargement of the EU in 2004 bringing its own challenges.

The IDA's efforts have been assisted by the government allowing generous tax breaks for investors. One particular use of tax breaks involved the rebuilding of a whole section of Dublin. Located in what was formerly a neglected docklands area, near the old Customs House, the gleaming new buildings of the International Financial Services Centre (IFSC, established in 1987) have become a world-class location for a wide range of internationally traded financial services and their ancillary functions. Some 12,000 people are employed directly there. The creation of what is partly a tax haven has been criticised by some people within Ireland and beyond, but most citizens appear to be unconcerned about that aspect of the operation and welcome whatever additional revenue the IFSC brings to the State.

Some international companies that were already operating in Ireland relocated to the IFSC. One of these was Citigroup. By the time it had built its own new office block, the largest in the IFSC quarter, its employee numbers in Ireland had soared from 80 to 1,200. It became the fourth largest in the European Citigroup network of operations. That this growth may have been at the expense of other locations or communities was not something about which those Irish who benefited became sentimental.

Overall, Irish people are too familiar with the history of deprivation, poverty and emigration from Ireland not to welcome a ride on the pig's back when the animal runs through our yard. The pride which many feel in our recovery from economic hardship, and our success in sustaining growth even through difficult times in the last two decades, is reflected in the kind of language used by the IDA in its recent little promotional book, *Ireland: Knowledge is Our Nature.*

The IDA has actually registered that phrase as a trade mark and sees it as its current marketing message: 'The new Ireland brand message is designed to tell the story and highlight the characteristics that define Ireland and its people', according to IDA chief executive, Seán Dorgan, in late 2003.

The IDA declares in its book's preface:

> Fifteen hundred years ago, Ireland was recognised as one of the great centres of knowledge in the civilised world. This innate creative imagination survived centuries of oppression and adversity and, in recent years, has provided the impetus for Ireland's sparkling accomplishments.
>
> This book explores some of the many facets of the special Irish combination of surging vision, pragmatic problem-solving and can-do confidence. It tells the story of some remarkable Irish people who have contributed to Ireland and the world. It shows the Irish flair in scientific innovation, literature, the arts, entertainment and business enterprise, above all. This book highlights Ireland's inspired achievement in building a modern economy by forging partnerships with the leaders and pacesetters among global corporations.

Rattling off a list of authors such as James Joyce and Oscar Wilde, the book notes: 'Irish writers have been lateral thinkers, long before the phrase was popularised.' It asks:

> Could it be that the centuries-old Irish genius for creative communication, the basis of literature, provided the catalyst that has propelled Ireland into the knowledge society and made it one of today's leading software producers?

This 'Waiting for Microsoft' version of Irish cultural history supports a national self-identity that sees, for example, the Limerick facility of Analog Devices Inc., *Riverdance* and Ireland's participation in the World Cup as integrated aspects of one process. And, sure enough, *Riverdance* finds its place in the IDA's recent book on Ireland, because the 'show has achieved iconic status, a dramatic metaphor for the flair, creativity, confidence and international outlook of modern Ireland that has taken the world by storm.'

The perseverance of the Irish in their struggle for independence and prosperity appeals to the entrepreneurial spirit of some investors. Michael Dell, chairman and chief executive officer of Dell, sums up the relationship:

> I believe there is a connection between Ireland and Dell that goes beyond our business partnership. In many ways, Ireland and Dell are kindred spirits.
>
> At the heart of both the Irish and Dell character is big dreams, a passion for building and re-building, and the tenacity to adapt to challenging circumstances. There's a link between a country that works hard to become a technology powerhouse and a small company that does the same. There's a bond among groups of people who have overcome great challenges and great odds to achieve what they dared to dream.

———

As we Irish changed our ways to facilitate foreign direct investment, the new industries that arrived on our shores changed us even more. We dared to believe that we could, after all, succeed in our material ambitions for Irish society. That success was based no longer on a narrow nationalist dream of 'ourselves alone', but on a new model of international exchange and interdependence. Whatever the price we have paid for that change, it appears that most people find it acceptable.

PARTNERSHIP

Arigna, Co. Roscommon, 1 January 1987

Life for the average Irish worker changed significantly, and for the better, on 1 January 1987. That was the moment when the first national agreement on fiscal, social, economic and competitiveness policies came into effect. It had an impact on every family in Ireland. Employers, unions and the farming organisations all supported the Programme for National Recovery. These interest groups, known as the three 'pillars', had been coaxed by the government into finding a new way of working together for wage restraint, taxation reform, industrial growth and greater social justice. Earlier national pay agreements were less ambitious than the Programme for National Recovery of 1987–1990.

Since 1987, and the emergence of a social partnership in Ireland, most Irish people have seen a steady and significant rise in their living standards. Before 1987, many had worried increasingly about losing their jobs, about their children not finding work in Ireland, and about not being able to afford even the basic necessities of modern life. However, after 1987 such concerns steadily receded in the minds of most citizens and were slowly replaced by anxieties about the problems of prosperity, including the daily hassle of commuting to work on crowded roads. Compared to his or her counterparts before 1987, the average worker now 'eats out' more often, has longer holidays in more exotic places, lives in a bigger dwelling and drives a finer car. Their better-educated children may not be able to afford a home of their own, as prices soar, or their offspring may not find pensionable jobs, but few would wish to return to the way of negotiating wages and policies that prevailed before 1987. It was, quite simply, less fruitful.

Certainly, some citizens have benefited far more than others from the fruits of social partnership. There is still a big divide between the richest and poorest in Ireland. One measure of Ireland's future development will be the State's ability to distribute the benefits of growth equitably, especially to communities in places like Arigna on the borders of counties Leitrim and Roscommon. Since 1 January 1987, as it happens, Arigna has been devastated by the closure of traditional industries such as the Arigna coal mines and Ballinamore Textiles. The social partners are now among those who have founded the Arigna Leader Company to initiate a community-led response to the problems of rural decline and depopulation.

Older Irish people remember just how short of cash most people once were on this island. Even into the 1960s, Ireland was still a poor country. Its inhabitants were not starving, as many of them had been in earlier centuries, but emigration was a constant drain on the vitality of the State. Today, younger people may have some difficulty believing that 'eating out' was once a really rare treat, not a regular occurrence. Buying a car, especially a brand new one, was once a very big event in a family's life. Going abroad for recreation was most unusual. Clothing was unexciting but sturdy, and it was expected to last a long time and could be handed down to others until it was no longer serviceable. When people are strapped for cash today, it is often because their expectations or demands have risen rapidly and remarkably, and because their way of living is much more elaborate than it needs to be.

The economic transformation was not instant; nor did it begin suddenly. As the Republic of Ireland slowly built up an industrial base from the 1950s, its workforce at every level also became better educated. Membership of the European Economic Community encouraged people to look outwards and to imagine how they might take advantage of wider markets to benefit the Irish economy and their own pockets. A growing awareness of what might be possible economically was underpinned by a sense that the more we developed the more we stood to lose by confrontation and by sterile recriminations in the social and economic spheres.

Before agreement was first reached in 1987, Ireland's economy had been heading into some very stormy waters. Ireland borrowed heavily during a period of international recession, and the national deficit began to climb steeply. Following the ending of national pay agreements in 1982, bargaining had reverted to being decentralised and there was a wages free-for-all. There was a recession from 1980 to 1987, during which living standards fell. Unemployment soared in ten years, from 7 per cent in 1979 to nearly 18 per cent in 1987. Inflation and the growth in unemployment saw emigration return as a common option for young people. It was a real crisis, with national insolvency looming. A Fianna Fáil government had engaged in reckless spending and the national debt was spiralling out of control. Now, another Fianna Fáil government attempted to rein in economic expectations, while arguing that sacrifices would lay the foundation for growth in the longer term.

In 1987, the government succeeded in fostering agreement between the employers, unions and farming organisations on a series of important matters relating to pay and working conditions. The 'Programme for National Recovery' (PNR), as this agreement was called, immediately became the basis for social and economic progress from 1987 to 1990, and had lasting effects. It constituted a binding agreement reached in advance on wage levels in the public and private sector for three years. It also involved trade union support for a tightening of public expenditure in return for maintaining the value of social welfare payments and reforming the income tax system. The ordinary public whose taxation was deducted at source from their salaries (Pay As You Earn) had begun to take to the streets to object both to the level of taxation and to widespread tax evasion by the self-employed.

The Programme for National Recovery was regarded as so successful that all the parties involved agreed to adopt the principle of partnership throughout the 1990s. Their agreement is believed by many economists and others to have laid the foundation for the phenomenal boom in Ireland's fortunes that transformed the Republic of Ireland into the 'Celtic Tiger'. Irish people may have tired of the State's new nickname, but they did not tire of the spoils that the beast brought home.

The Programme for National Recovery of 1987 was based substantially on the 'Strategy for Development' that had been produced earlier by the National Economic and Social Council (NESC). Each of the subsequent agreements was also based on a similar 'framework' devised under the auspices of the NESC. The NESC had been established in 1973 to advise the government on the development of the national economy and on the achievement of social justice. Its membership is drawn from across society, including farming, employer, union and voluntary organisations. The fact that these organisations worked so successfully together at the end of the twentieth century marked a maturing of Ireland's economic relationships, as well as the dawning of an awareness that we are all in the same boat when it comes to the economy, even if we do not all travel first class. The community and voluntary sector had not been formally recognised in the first three agreements as one of the pillars of social partnership, but this was rectified with their inclusion in negotiations thereafter.

When the Programme for National Recovery expired in December 1990, it was immediately succeeded by the 'Programme for Economic and Social Progress' (PESP) between 1991 and 1993, and then came the 'Programme for Competitiveness and Work' (PCW) from 1994 to 1996. After that there was 'Partnership 2000' from 1997, followed by the 'Programme for Prosperity and Fairness' (PPF) from 2000 to 2002. After that, 'Sustaining Progress' was agreed between the social partners to run from 2003 until 2005. These names were used regularly in newspaper articles and heard often on radio and TV, and their invocation became the soothing background music of continuing economic prosperity for most people.

The later agreements built on the initial breakthrough of 1987, with the cornerstone of each being the control of wage increases. Such restraint by workers would not have been possible, were the partners not also in a position to agree on a range of policy changes relating to taxation reform and social inequality, among other matters.

Some economists and other critics argue about the merits of such pay agreements, but the deals became associated in the public mind with industrial tranquillity and personal prosperity. There were employers who deeply resented the trade unions having a direct say in the determination of how business might or might not be conducted, while some workers thought that the unions were being 'co-opted' into an economic model founded on conservative principles. Some voluntary organisations suspected that the deals were better for workers in employment, including trade union officials, than for the marginalised and unemployed. Groups interested in global issues have worried that Ireland is simply throwing in its lot with the rich countries of the European Union, sharing wealth rather than redistributing it across the world.

However, most Irish people have been very happy to see average real economic growth during the last fifteen years, notwithstanding a downturn in the world economy in the early 1990s and other problems. They accept that there are still poor people in Ireland, but they feel that everyone has somehow benefited from the fruits of successive partnership deals. They see the unprecedented phenomenon of immigration to Ireland from poorer countries as evidence of the fact that industrial stability has bred wealth. Noticeable effects of the deals have been a great reduction in days lost due to strikes and a growing ability to resolve industrial disputes peacefully.

The Irish government points out that during the period of the first four programmes alone, between 1987 and 2000, economic growth was greater than twice the EU average, inflation fell to one of the lowest rates in the EU, and employment in the private non-agricultural sector showed an annual average growth of about 2.5 per cent. Budgetary consolidation measures linked to the programmes gave Ireland's government one of the lowest financial deficits in the EU. However, notwithstanding Ireland's quite recent experiences of hard times, it must also be said that there is evidence of considerable careless spending now that we have money, with roads being just one of the areas where insufficient cost controls have resulted in wastage that we may come to regret.

The ability to repeat and sustain national pay agreements into the future cannot be taken for granted. Those negotiating them have ideological critics to the left and right, and the decision to grant public servants in 2003/4 certain additional increases based on unclear benchmarks of productivity severely strained the patience of workers and employers in the private sector. As Ireland approaches the twentieth anniversary of its first collective pay deal, it is worth recalling that the title of the first deal was 'Programme for National

Recovery'. The government and the people whom it represents cannot afford to get carried away by the success of agreements between the social partners to such an extent that the State is tempted to engage in the sort of extravagance from which it was necessary to recover in the first place. To do so would be a shameful reversal of changes for the better.

MAD COWS AND FARMERS

Co. Cavan, 25 January 1989

It was a bad day for Irish farmers, and a worrying one for the public. On 25 January 1989, the first case of BSE was diagnosed in an Irish herd. 'Mad Cow Disease' had arrived, and any hope that it was a peculiarly British phenomenon was dashed. Its outbreak threatened the reputation of Irish food and helped to puncture the economic euphoria surrounding a sector that had benefited greatly from Ireland's EU membership. Steps were taken immediately to contain the outbreak and its effects. Since then, BSE has hit Ireland far less severely than Britain, but it is still taken very seriously by both the public and the farming community alike. The Irish Department of Agriculture stresses that Irish beef is recognised as a good product, produced in a clean environment under good conditions:

> Ireland's cattle production is predominantly grass based and is based on a largely self-contained national herd. Having regard to the fact that BSE (Bovine Spongiform Encephalopathy) is generally regarded to have been caused by the recycling through meat and bonemeal of infected sheep and cattle tissue feed, it should be noted that there is an extremely low incidence of sheep scrapie (which is also a notifiable disease) in Ireland. The ratio between its sheep and cattle population (approximately 1:1) also reduces the risk factor to BSE.

> In view of the criteria adopted by the Office International des Epizooties (OIE), Ireland can claim, for the purposes of international trade, the status of a country with a low incidence of BSE.

This is good news for both consumers and for those farmers who own any of the 138,000 herds of cattle in Ireland, containing more than 7 million beasts. A total of 1.5m cattle are slaughtered each year in Ireland, with nine out of every ten carcasses destined for export. However, some of the evidence given to the public inquiry into the beef sector, in respect of companies associated with Larry Goodman's operations, suggested that such meat has not always been of as high a standard as the Department of Agriculture might wish. In November 2004, it was learnt that a young man at a Dublin hospital was suffering from the first indigenous case of VCJD. He had never donated blood or had an operation, so it was assumed that he had contracted the disease from eating meat contaminated by BSE.

Since joining the EU (then the EEC) most Irish farmers have experienced more ups than downs in their sector. Under the European Common Agricultural Policy (CAP), financing has been made available for structural and rural development measures and, in some cases, for market supports and direct payments. This investment has provided an enormous boost for Irish farmers whose families, just a few decades before we joined the EEC, had suffered on the frontline of de Valera's 'economic war' with England. Once inside the European Community, rural life prospered in many ways and the old dependence on English markets eased.

At first the CAP meant fixing prices above world market levels in order to secure stable supplies of food at a time of insufficiency. Subsequently, this approach, together with technological breakthroughs, gave rise to surpluses in many products. The CAP was regarded by some critics as a reckless means of supporting farmers who overproduced and failed to innovate or diversify. So-called 'butter mountains' or 'wine lakes' became the symbols of a policy which was thought to support inertia in the agricultural sector, and to benefit farmers at the expense of European consumers and producers outside the EU.

With growing pressure on the CAP from consumers and from those European member states whose economies were less reliant on subsidised farming, it was clear that the sector would come under increasing pressure to rationalise, reduce surpluses and become self-sufficient. As the Irish Department of Agriculture puts it:

> The cost of these surpluses, the external trading environment, concerns about food safety and animal welfare and a growing awareness of environmental issues led to successive reforms. In the 1980s the reforms were targeted at specific sectors. Subsequent reforms were more broadly based.

In any event, it was proving difficult to keep people on the land, as sons and daughters of farmers chose regular jobs over irregular hours spent tending crops and animals. The availability of cheaper produce outside the EU, and the control of internal markets by middle-men and women, also kept down prices for local producers and saw traders in the middle exploiting the CAP. There was a growing sense of foreboding about the future of farming in Europe. In that context, continuing health scares about food quality and production have added to the woes of those who work in agriculture.

Animal health scares are not new. Indeed, the failure of the Irish farming sector and the Department of Agriculture to eradicate bovine TB (tuberculosis) became a scandal. Year in and year out, public money was poured into the eradication scheme. Vets prospered while herds continued to be infected. Moreover, from the 1980s onwards, animal growth was stimulated by the use of hormones which posed a hazard to human health and which were banned by the authorities. It may be that only a minority of farmers have used 'Angel Dust' or other banned products, but too little was done by their peers to ostracise them quickly and to condemn such practices. The public came to suspect that the agricultural sector was not very concerned about what people were eating. Only a few culprits were eventually convicted.

Given modern agricultural methods, the public was not entirely surprised to learn of the circumstances in which BSE had arisen in Britain as a threat to animal and human life. It transpired that cattle's brains had been infected after the beasts had been fed ground-up parts of dead animals. This practice defied cattle's natural inclination to be vegetarian. People were disgusted and their worst fears about what they themselves might be consuming were exacerbated. BSE was recognised in the UK for the first time in 1985. During 1987, the number of reported cases of BSE in England began to rise dramatically. At first, Irish farmers hoped the problem might be confined to Britain. Those hopes were dashed in the Republic of Ireland on 25 January 1989. The first case was in a mixed dairy and suckler herd of 83 Friesians in Co. Cavan. The Department of Agriculture declines to reveal the location more precisely.

In 1990, the feeding of meat and bone meal to ruminant animals, either directly or through feeding stuffs, was banned. Since 1 January 2001, the feeding of meat and bone meal has been banned for all farm animals intended for human consumption. Nevertheless, since then, there has been a small number of cases of younger cows still being diagnosed as having BSE. In July 2004, one such animal was discovered in Co. Cavan, the very place where BSE was first found in the Republic of Ireland.

During the 1990s, concerns about the meat industry were considerably heightened by the publicity surrounding Larry Goodman and his beef processing business. Some people have stopped eating beef altogether, especially since it became known that human beings could and have contracted Variant Creutzfeld-Jacob Disease (VCJD), a human form of BSE, from eating infected meat. The British introduced controls too slowly and then botched their research programme relating to the disease. Forecasting the course of such illnesses is difficult because there is a long typical incubation period of four to five years. However, it is hoped that the consequences will be confined to just a few unfortunate victims. It seems sometimes that British authorities fear a possible epidemic.

Other Irish animal health scares in the past two decades have included those relating to the radiation of sheep on high ground following a fire at the Chernobyl nuclear power plant in the Ukraine in 1986, concerns about the incidence of disease among 'battery' chickens, and reports of an increased level of carcinogens in farmed salmon. In respect of genetically modified crops, Irish people have tended to wait and see what the outcome of arguments elsewhere will be.

During 2001, farmers in the Republic of Ireland had a narrow escape when, with one exception involving sheep in Co. Louth in March, Foot and Mouth Disease was kept outside our borders. Much credit for this success went to the government which, once the seriousness of the outbreak in England became clear, moved promptly with the help of the Gardaí and the defence forces to stop and inspect traffic as it entered the State. The disease had reached Northern Ireland in February, in a batch of sheep imported to Meigh in south Armagh. Nevertheless, Northern Ireland was also fortunate to escape relatively lightly when compared to England.

Reforms of the CAP and regular animal health scares have caused many farmers to worry about the future. The early decades of EU membership now seem golden compared to what may lie ahead, and old farming families wonder if they can survive on the land at the current level of income available to them. Farming is now a much less significant part of Irish society than it used to be not so long ago. In October 1966, Rickard Deasy, president of the NFA (later the IFA), led farmers on a march to Dublin, demanding better living conditions and laying siege to the Department of Agriculture in a successful battle for recognition of their association's representative role. The protesters wanted a fair share of the fruits of Ireland's incipient economic growth, and their protests ensured that they benefited when Ireland joined the EEC. However, in January 2003, those farmers who converged on Dublin in their 'tractorcade' protest seemed relatively chastened, as though they recognised that many of their fellow countrymen sympathised with their plight but could do little to control global economic realities in the sphere of agriculture. Between the dates of those two demonstrations, the number of farmers had declined steadily and the relative importance of farming to the Irish economy had diminished considerably. In 1971, there were 279,450 farms in the Republic of Ireland. By 2002, there were just 141,527.

Nevertheless, the situation is certainly not one of total despair. According to the Department of Agriculture and Food's *Annual Review and Outlook, 2003/2004*, the agri-food sector continues to make a significant contribution to Ireland's economy, accounting for 9 per cent of both gross domestic product and employment, and over 8 per cent of exports. Indeed, when adjustments are made for outflows associated with importing materials and the repatriation of profits by multinational corporations, the agri-food sector accounted for 20 per cent of net foreign earnings. During 2003, aggregate farm incomes rose by 5 per cent, with the department paying out over €1.6 billion in direct payments to farmers, accounting for 63 per cent of aggregate farm income. Moreover, the review states:

> Contrary to the adage of '80% of payments going to the top 20% of producers' — analysis of 2002 direct payments show that 39% went to the top 20% of Irish farmers and 9% to the bottom 20% of farmers.

On 7 January 2005, Taoiseach Bertie Ahern explicitly rejected pessimistic forecasts about the future of farming. He said he had heard doomsday warnings before and added:

> The fact is if you look back now over fifteen years these things have not come to pass; so, of course, there's always fears, there's always concerns, but I agree with the President [of the IFA] that we have to be working in a proactive way to try and get the best deal at home and abroad for farming.

The age profile of Irish farmers is younger than the average in western European countries. However, the proportion of women owning farms in Ireland, 11 per cent, is below the average in western Europe.

———

Where farmers have decided to try and stay on the land, they are looking now to new ideas for future development which can enhance existing activities. Ireland's position as a prime location for organic agriculture has not been fully exploited and there is a growing awareness that our environment is an asset which can be marketed to tourists and to consumers by way of access to unspoilt countryside and by means of the marketing of pure Irish produce.

COMPO

Eyre Square, Galway, 16 July 1997

In 1987, just thirteen members or former members of the Irish Army had sued the State because, as they claimed, their hearing was permanently damaged by loud noises to which they had been unreasonably exposed in the course of their military work. Those noises included gunfire and explosions. As the cases reached the courts and settlements were concluded on the basis of legal and medical advice, it became clear that these were thirteen precedents upon which many future claims would be launched. By 2004, approximately 17,000 compensation claims had been lodged in relation to the impairment of hearing of members of Ireland's armed forces, and the total cost to the public of losing or settling these claims was expected to reach around €300 million.

The avalanche of claims for army deafness contributed to a growing public awareness of the increasing incidence and cost of legal actions for personal injuries that were being taken against State-owned and private companies. It must be assumed that those army deafness claims were all well founded on hard medical evidence and on actual damage, and that the State never settled without a good reason. However, not every personal injury claim is honest.

The fact that people sue in circumstances where their parents might not have done so is not necessarily because they are dishonest or malicious. Today, there are higher social expectations, new consumer rights and easier access to lawyers; besides which, most businesses have insurance policies, and insurance companies appear to be more inclined to settle than to fight. Companies forced to settle such actions for personal injuries are also more likely to talk about the high cost of insurance premiums and to hint at fraud rather than accept any need on their part to invest their money in greater safety precautions. In 2000, the Insurance Industry Federation admitted: 'Because insurance fraud is, by its nature, a clandestine activity, there is no way of quantifying the actual extent of the problem in Ireland.' Because of Ireland's strict libel laws, which themselves give rise to some compensation claims that would be thrown out in other jurisdictions, it is difficult for people who are the victims of scams to discuss them openly in the absence of hard evidence, and it is difficult for the media to report them.

Individual plaintiffs were creating a 'compo culture' which permeated even the lowest social classes. Meanwhile, big companies were resorting as never before to judicial review proceedings and to claims for compensation when their plans for expansion were thwarted by decisions of state agencies or of other official bodies.

In one particular action dismissed by the president of the Circuit Court, Mr Justice Esmond Smyth, a woman who sprained her ankle in a nightclub at the Red Cow Inn in Dublin sought damages from its owners. She failed when staff at the club gave evidence of hearing a male friend of the woman say to her, 'There's money here. Tell them you fell on wet steps and that you only had two drinks.' He was also alleged to have said, 'You will get that kitchen you always wanted', and remarked, 'I feel a holiday coming on.'

During 2000, the Small Firms Association held a conference entitled, 'Compo culture — Don't get ripped off'. The association estimated that the compensation culture was, by then, annually costing small businesses more than three-quarters of a billion euro. Many people blamed lawyers for encouraging people to sue over the merest grievance or the slightest accident. An incentive of 'no foal, no fee', offered by some lawyers, reduced the element of risk for litigants. In February 2003, the chairperson of the Motor Insurance Advisory Board, Dorothea Dowling, said publicly: 'We . . . need to change the culture whereby solicitors have misled people into thinking that alleging an injury — whether it is genuine or not — will automatically give rise to compensation.' A large slice of the money paid to settle compensation claims was going to lawyers. If plaintiffs were impecunious, then defendants had to weigh the cost of fighting and winning but still having to pay their own lawyers against the cost of paying the plaintiff to go away. Some lawyers blamed the medical profession. One told a meeting of the Irish Medical Organisation that some doctors were acting in a 'semi-political, sly way, rather than squaring up to the client'.

One claim that collapsed spectacularly, when the plaintiff was confronted with video evidence of his wrongdoing, related to events at a branch of Supermac's in Eyre Square, Galway, on 16 July 1997. The event was to prompt the founding of the Alliance for Insurance Reform, a business organisation. A young man and his friends went to the washroom of the fast-food restaurant and proceeded to splash water from the hand basins on to the floor. Later, when some members of the public entered toilet cubicles, the same young man fell to the ground and began to groan. The alarm was raised and an ambulance crew took the future plaintiff away in a cervical collar and on a stretcher. He subsequently lodged a claim against Supermac's for £30,000, alleging that he had been knocked unconscious and had suffered back pains as a result of his fall. It was only on the eve of the hearing in the High Court that the plaintiff learnt that there was a complete video recording of his behaviour in the washroom, including his practising how to fall, whereupon he withdrew the claim. In Seanad Éireann on 5 December 2001, Fianna Fáil's Eddie Bohan spoke about the Supermac's case. Himself a former president of the Vintners' Federation of Ireland, Bohan said:

> There are 111 cases pending against 47 Supermac's stores and the owner believes that 75% of these are fraudulent. It happens every day in my trade, the pub trade, that people trip over carpets and so on, and it seems that all they have to do is go to a solicitor and with the 'no foal, no fee' provision those solicitors are falling over themselves to take the cases.

Gradually, the courts have become somewhat more resistant or sceptical in respect of compensation claims. For example, the State had feared an epidemic of actions relating to the presence of asbestos in public buildings, similar to the army deafness outbreak. In the High Court, a worker was awarded damages for the psychological impact of having been exposed to asbestos in the course of removing lagging ı pipes in the basement of Leinster House, seat of Dáil Éireann. ever, in February 2003 the Supreme Court upheld an appeal against the Leinster House judgment, with Chief Justice Ronan Keane speaking of plaintiffs' 'irrational fear of contracting a disease because of their negligent exposure to health risks by their employers, where their risk is characterised by their medical advisers as very remote'. Although there was no reason to doubt the plaintiff's good faith and sincerity in bringing the action, the court awarded costs against him. The State then decided to set about recouping legal costs from almost 500 other asbestos claimants.

The Civil Liability (Assessment of Hearing Injury) Act 1998 had obliged the courts to take judicial notice of an official report on the assessment of hearing disability. In a judgment of December 1999, the Supreme Court agreed in general that this formula was a fair way of assessing hearing impairment. An early settlement scheme further reduced legal costs. Initially, the average award or settlement per hearing had been about €30,000, but by 2002 that dropped to €10,000 or less. The State managed to keep down the cost of settlements in army deafness claims to about one-third of the €1 billion that it once feared it might have to pay. On 5 February 2004, the Minister for Defence told Dáil Éireann that savings on deafness claims had funded the purchase of a Learjet.

Among cases that have received media attention because of the judge's scepticism was one in which, in 2002, a woman failed to get damages from Dunnes Stores. She had fallen on an escalator while carrying up to eight bags of shopping and attempting to control a buggy and child. An emergency team was called to release her hair from the mechanism of the escalator. In his judgment, the president of the Circuit Court, Mr Justice Esmond Smyth, said: 'The plaintiff is one of a number of people suffering from a disease . . . the symptoms of which are concoction and exaggeration', and added that the file for the case could be made available to the Director of Public Prosecutions if it were requested. Smyth also commented: 'The courts are aware of the fact there are an increasing number of fraudulent or exaggerated claims being made and judges scrutinise with great care such cases.' He added: 'It seems that the happening of an accident leads inevitably to the hope for compensation whether it be as a result of negligence on the part of a defendant or not.'

Tralee Aqua Dome won what it regarded as a landmark case and had costs awarded in its favour against a customer who cut his foot while in the swimming pool and who returned to the Aqua Dome the day after he was injured demanding money. The judge requested that the claimant be investigated by the Gardaí. CIÉ had a series of cases dismissed where it had anticipated from past experience that the judge might rule in favour of the plaintiff. Judge Desmond Hogan dismissed one case against Bus Éireann, remarking that a particular plaintiff was 'extremely accident prone'. The man had alleged that certain back injuries had been exacerbated by his being jolted forward in his bus seat on his way from Sligo to Donegal, but admitted that he had also been injured in other accidents which included walking into a plank and falling in a restaurant.

On 29 March 2004, almost seven years after he had staged the fall in Supermac's of Galway, Ronan Quinlivan (23) was prosecuted for making two claims under false pretences. The District Court was told he had been motivated 'by greed and jealousy' after a friend of his had successfully sued for damages against another company

The government pressed ahead in the face of opposition from members of the legal profession and established a Personal Injuries Assessment Board to streamline the claims procedure. Announcing details of the reform of the law relating to civil liability, Minister for Justice, Equality and Law Reform Michael McDowell, said on 4 July 2003:

> Put simply, we have developed in this country a 'compensation culture' which has encouraged people to engage in litigation to recover damages for personal injury while we have a system for delivering compensation that is too costly. The result of this is that both the business and personal sectors are under an excessive burden in insuring themselves against possible claims. This has very negative knock-on effects for the whole of society.

The law was also changed to inhibit lawyers from advertising for business on a 'no foal, no fee' basis, and a Bill was introduced to allow the courts to penalise those who deliberately make false claims. Nevertheless, some cases have continued to surprise defendants. On 19 December 2003, a man who had climbed a wall on a steep bank and trespassed on to a railway line in Offaly, in the middle of the night and while very drunk, was awarded €111,081 for the loss of his leg after he was hit by a train while asleep with a friend on the ground. Mr Justice Diarmuid O'Donovan of the High Court held that the drunk was only 85 per cent negligent! The judge described the apportionment of these damages against Iarnród Éireann as 'small'. He thought the company should have done more to prevent access to the line. However, on 21 January 2005 and in apparent contrast to that decision, the Supreme Court overturned a High Court award of €84,000 to a woman who was injured when she fell down a Donegal cliff while watching the sun set. The woman had suffered certain injuries and it was not suggested by the court that her claim was in any way insincere. Nevertheless, Mr Justice Hugh Geoghegan observed that a person sitting down near a cliff 'must be prepared for oddities in the cliff's structure or in the structure of the ground adjacent to the cliff', and acts at their own risk unless there were exceptional and unusual features that might reasonably require a warning notice. The Supreme Court's decision was warmly welcomed by the Irish Farmers' Association.

AMERICAN OAK STAIRS

Carrickmines, Co. Dublin, 24 April 1999

Between 1994 and the end of the twentieth century, the average price of a house in Ireland more than doubled in real terms. The rising cost of accommodation became a predictable topic of conversation at social events. People who already owned property took pleasure in the soaring value of their homes: it was a pleasure offset by a growing awareness of the difficulties being created for their children in the future. People who did not own property worried that they might never be able to afford a home or that their straitened financial circumstances would be worsened as landlords increased their rents.

When it came to the inflation of house prices, Dublin set an international record during the 1990s. In fact, throughout Ireland, it became much more expensive to buy a house. The average price of an Irish house was €76,000 in 1994, but €220,000 by 2004. Those figures conceal the fact that people living in some parts of Ireland pay far more for their homes than others do. Property in Dublin is especially expensive.

On 24 April 1999, the first development of new houses in Dublin to cost £1m each went on the market. They were snapped up. Located off Brennanstown Road in Carrickmines, Co. Dublin, each had five bedrooms and was detached. Unsurprisingly, at that price, they were well finished and had good gardens. The houses were fitted with American oak staircases in high entrance halls, with overhead windows and solid oak doors.

A remarkable property barrier was breached in spring 2002 when David Doyle, of the well-known hotelier family, paid €10m for a house on Shrewsbury Road, Dublin 4. It was purchased solely as a residence and had no further development value. Until then, the highest price known to have been paid for an urban Irish residence was on Raglan Road, Ballsbridge, by Denis O'Brien, the communications millionaire. Just six years earlier, in 1996, Des McEvaddy reportedly paid what was then the record price of £1.55m for a large detached house on Shrewsbury Road, albeit in need of total refurbishment.

In June 2004, again, a house in Dartry with no obvious development potential went for €10m. By then, the average asking price of a second-hand house in Dublin was over €500,000, ranging from an average of nearly €250,000 in Ballyfermot to an average of more than €750,000 in Dublin 4 or Dublin 6.

The rise in house prices has been fuelled by various factors, including greater wealth, a growing population, high employment, immigration, income tax cuts, investment incentives, easy lending by financial institutions, and low interest rates. Before 1994, the rate of increase in house prices had largely kept pace with inflation in other areas. Only in the last decade has a marked acceleration in property values occurred.

The economic recovery of independent Ireland during the second half of the twentieth century is reflected in the fact that almost twice as many dwellings are occupied within the State as were occupied sixty years ago. Since the foundation of the State, Irish people have sought to own their own homes. There is a common belief that historical insecurity of tenure stiffened the determination of families to acquire their own property once that opportunity arose. Whatever the actual reasons, the fact is that Ireland now enjoys one of the highest levels of home ownership in Europe. Four out of every five families are said to own their own home.

Only Spain and Greece among other European countries have a level of home ownership as high as our 80 per cent, while Germany's rate is half that. However, there is not as wide a gap between us and all other countries as is sometimes thought, with Italy, Belgium,

Luxemburg and Britain, for example, having a level of about 70 per cent. Furthermore, proportionately, we also have one of the highest numbers of mortgaged homes in Europe.

The fact that property prices have risen sharply, coupled with a perception that fewer jobs are now permanent or even long-term, has fuelled anxieties that young people may not be able in due course to afford to buy their own homes and that those who take the plunge are being saddled with long-term mortgages which could become crippling in the future. It has also given rise to fears that tenants in rented accommodation are more vulnerable than ever to big hikes in what they must pay landlords.

However, the level of home ownership has not decreased even during the past decade of great inflation in property prices. There has been a building boom in recent years and the overwhelming majority of new houses and apartments built have been for the private market. Even among those people on low incomes, three out of every five poorer families own their own homes. This phenomenon has been facilitated by local authority schemes that permit tenants to purchase their homes.

During 2004, a report by members of the ESRI for the Institute of Public Administration and the Combat Poverty Agency played down fears about house prices and suggested that soaring house prices had not created the sort of serious problem that table gossip might suggest. The authors of *Housing, Poverty and Wealth in Ireland* (Tony Fahey, Brian Nolan and Bertrand Maître) found that aggregate measures of affordability show only moderate worsening during the 1990s. They discovered that, by 2000 and 2001, at the peak of the house price rise, the combination of falling interest rates and rising after-tax incomes meant that the repayment burden was somewhat worse than in the mid-1990s but was still reasonably low by historical standards.

The authors acknowledged that many people are vulnerable to any significant rise in interest rates, and pointed out that low-income householders who are not home owners may be further disadvantaged by rising property values, especially if living in the high-rent private rented sector. The 2004 report is essential reading for those who wish to understand the state of the housing market in Ireland today.

However, critics discern underlying trends that are alarming.

Speaking in Dáil Éireann on 17 December 2002, Labour's Eamon Gilmore castigated the government for laying the seeds of future social problems. He claimed:

> Ireland is now facing its worst housing crisis since the foundation of the State having regard to the fact that new house prices have increased by almost 100% (more than four times the rate of inflation) since the election of the Fianna Fáil-Progressive Democrats Government in 1997; that the numbers on the local authority waiting lists have increased from 26,000 to 48,000; and that homelessness has increased to 6,000.

Gilmore added:

> In Dublin the average price of a new house has increased from €124,000 to more than €300,000 in the five and a half years of the Fianna Fáil-Progressive Democrats Government. That is not all. As average prices have increased, the average size of a new house has diminished. . . . In other words . . . the house buyer is paying more than twice the price for a much smaller dwelling.

The Labour TD rounded on Minister Cullen, pointing out that there had been a 'dramatic' increase in private renting:

> In 1997 there were approximately 135,000 private rented tenancies. Today there are about 200,000. Like house prices, rents have also shot up. There are no official figures for rent levels, but most commentators agree that a family-sized unit which would have been rented for €500 to €600 per month in 1997 would now cost between €1,200 and €1,500 per month.

Gilmore noted that Martin Cullen, Minister for the Environment and Local Government (with responsibility for public housing policy), had recently drawn attention to the norm on the European mainland where people rent rather than buy their homes. He said that the minister had omitted to state that in other European countries tenants enjoy legal rights and security of tenure which do not apply here.

Where approximately one in every three homes being built in the

1970s was part of the 'social housing' stock, only one in ten houses today are being constructed for those who cannot afford to buy their own homes or to rent at commercial rates. This is a change which may simply reflect the fact that Ireland's economic boom has resulted in a greater share of the population being in employment and buying more houses, but it can also be seen as an indicator that people are expected now to fend for themselves in the housing market rather than wait for the State to provide accommodation. Meanwhile, house prices have continued to rise. While the rise during the twelve months to January 2005 was down to 8.5 per cent from 13.3 per cent one year earlier, the rate of increase is still well ahead of general inflation and of growth in personal income.

Between 1971 and 2002, the number of occupied private households (including apartments) in the Republic of Ireland rose from 726,363 to 1,287,958. This surge of 77.3 per cent was due partly to the population increasing by 31.5 per cent during the same period, but also reflects the fact that growing prosperity and family planning resulted in a decline in the average number of persons living in each private household, from 3.94 in 1971 to 2.95 in 2002. A considerable number of Irish people now also own second houses or apartments either within Ireland or abroad. The overall increase in private housing is remarkable, especially for anyone old enough to remember the boarded-up homes of people who were forced to emigrate and who could not find a buyer at a price worth taking.

Despite the reassuring tone of that 2004 ESRI report, there remains a nagging doubt about increases in house prices and their ultimate impact on society in general, and on younger families and the poor in particular. In so far as the property boom has changed us, it has made us more aware of our attachment to home ownership and even more obviously a people who like to take pleasure in the nominal value of our property. It has led to some very tedious table-talk about the price of houses.

BREATHE IN

Ballytruckle, Co. Waterford, 29 March 2004

We stopped smoking in pubs and restaurants. In hospitals, factories, offices and trains, there was to be no more puffing on tobacco. Even seats in vehicles used for work were deemed non-smoking zones. On 29 March 2004, Ireland became the first country in the world to enforce such a complete ban. There were just a few minor exceptions, including hotel guest rooms (though not the lobby or the bar), cells in prisons, nursing homes and some wards in psychiatric hospitals.

The ease with which the ban was generally accepted in Ireland astonished those who had predicted it would not work. Some had campaigned vigorously against the prohibition. They said that the number of people visiting public houses would decline as a result of the ban and that their businesses would suffer. They were unconvinced by arguments that clean air in pubs might actually attract new customers. Some claimed that the government was being hypocritical in banning smoking in public places for health reasons while continuing to enjoy excise revenue from the sale of tobacco, which was not banned.

Among the ban's opponents were fifty Waterford publicans who had met at Garvey's of Ballytruckle and voted to defy the ban whenever it was introduced, describing it as 'unworkable' and objecting to the fact that they could be prosecuted for the transgressions of their customers. According to the *Waterford News and Star* (17 October 2003), Michael Fitzgerald, local chairman of the Vintners' Federation of Ireland, said: 'While we don't want to end up in court or in jail, we are prepared to face the consequences of our actions because we have no other choice.' Publicans in other counties were also defiant. However, in Ballytruckle as elsewhere, by the end of March 2004, objecting vintners had to face the fact that the law had changed, thanks largely to the determination of the Minister for Health, Micheál Martin. When Fianna Fáil fared poorly in the local elections of June 2004, some members of that party suggested that the smoking ban had been partly to blame for their misfortunes. This tempted one publican in Galway to defy the ban that summer but, having received much publicity, the owner of Fibber Magee's backed down in the face of a threat of legal action.

The smoking ban is a sign of the Irish State's awareness of the health needs of its citizens. Almost one in three Irish people smoke and it is estimated that, each year in Ireland, 7,000 people die as a direct result of illnesses related to direct or passive smoking. The main target of the new ban was passive smoking, where people inhale smoke from someone else's cigarettes even though they themselves are not smoking. Passive smoking is believed to increase significantly the risk of lung cancer.

During the four decades prior to the introduction of the smoking ban, Ireland's health services underwent a gradual transformation. One key moment was the passing of the Health Act 1970, which established health boards for the administration of the health services. They replaced local authorities in fulfilling this role and helped to place our health services on a professional footing as both medicine and society became more complex. The State's health services before then have been usefully considered in Ruth Barrington's *Health, Medicine and Politics in Ireland 1900–1970* (IPA: Dublin, 1987). The regime after 1970 has been described from time to time in various editions of Brendan Hensey's *The Health Services of Ireland* (IPA: Dublin).

From 1970, the health boards issued medical cards to those financially eligible, and the cards allowed many citizens access to certain services and benefits of a kind that their ancestors did not enjoy. However, deficiencies have remained in the overall system of health care in Ireland, especially for those just above the income level that qualifies one for a medical card. Recurrent news stories about waiting lists and about ill people left on trolleys in hospital corridors for many hours have sounded a reproach to governments that struggled during the past two decades to match expenditure to changing needs and expectations. Irish people in general, especially the Travellers, live shorter lives than do citizens in some other EU countries.

A medical card normally covers the eligible person together with any dependent spouse and child dependants. While eligibility for those aged under 70 is based on a means test, everyone over 70 and normally resident in Ireland is now entitled to a medical card, regardless of means. The card entitles one to free GP (family doctor) services; prescribed drugs and medicines (with some exceptions); in-patient public hospital services; out-patient services; dental, optical and aural services; medical appliances; and maternity and infant care services. People are free to choose a GP from a panel of participating doctors. Medical card-holders may also be exempt from paying school transport charges.

Ireland annually spends vast amounts on its health services, including a 'free drugs' scheme. Many citizens also have additional private health insurance, particularly through various VHI and BUPA schemes. However, Irish expenditure on its health services, as a share of the State's Gross Domestic Product and in comparison with other EU countries, declined after 1980. The system was severely affected by financial cutbacks. Critics also claim that much money has been wasted on an inefficient system of management.

Even as the Irish State experienced an economic boom at the end of the twentieth century, and some people made fortunes, there was a political outcry about public patients being treated differently from those who could afford private treatment. The opposition complained that the gap between services available to the rich and poor was widening, and that the waiting lists for certain services were far too long and had been exacerbated by cutbacks in public expenditure. Vested interests, including church proprietors of hospitals as well as medical consultants who have both public and private practices, made it difficult to implement some desirable reforms. Some pharmacists and others have made fortunes from the system and economists claim that it could have been administered far more efficiently. A major reorganisation of the health services began at the end of 2004.

Critics say that tax cuts and tax incentives for the wealthy have been financed at the expense of the welfare of poor people and that a two-tier health service has been fostered, one for those who can afford to pay and one for those who cannot. The Blackrock Clinic and other expensive new private hospitals are a sign of that division, and an indication of Ireland's growing affluence. In her critique of the system, *Unhealthy State: Anatomy of a Sick Society* (New Island: Dublin, 2003), Maev-Ann Wren laments the fact that, ultimately and in too many cases, 'Ireland has retained a shameful system in which access to care is determined by means not needs.'

The new affluence itself causes certain medical problems. Irish people eat more and the incidence of both obesity and diabetes appears to be rising. People take more holidays and the risk of skin cancer increases as they lie in the sun. There are more chemicals and other pollutants in the environment, partly because we drive many cars, expect cheap or perfectly formed food and consume so many manufactured luxuries. We may have stopped smoking in pubs but we certainly have not stopped drinking, and both alcohol and drug abuse are serious problems. Some of these 'optional' lifestyle illnesses were not a hazard for many of our ancestors. They would have been very glad indeed to enjoy the range of medical and pharmaceutical benefits that are now available.

The evident complexity of the health system makes its performance difficult to assess objectively, and a great deal has been spoken and written in recent years about whether or not it is value for money in economic and social terms. Medical professionals sometimes sound overwhelmed by the burdens that they bear on a daily basis, but perhaps they are no more or less burdened than their predecessors were.

Discussions about the health service are sometimes highly emotive, which is not surprising when so many lives and so much money are at stake. For example, in January 2004, Mary Kelly spoke on RTÉ about the plight of her son, aged 19, who had been seriously injured in a car crash and who was on a life-support machine in Mayo, waiting for a bed in Beaumont Hospital, Dublin, in order to receive a neurological assessment. She complained that millions were being spent renovating O'Connell Street in Dublin when money was badly needed for equipment in some hospitals. 'They should get their priorities right', she argued.

Financial considerations loom large at the Department of Health, as it struggles to provide the level of care that politicians promise but do not necessarily finance. Despite growing public expenditure on health services, many patients are still being kept too long on hospital trolleys and waiting lists. Doctors, nurses and social workers on the ground are overstretched. Faced with shortfalls, health officials struggle to make ends meet but fail to please everyone. On 7 March 2005, a report by John Travers for the Minister for Health, Mary Harney, pointed out that for decades old people in nursing homes had been charged for certain services that ought by law to have been provided free of charge. These charges generated revenue for the health services, and successive governments turned a blind eye. When Travers revealed that the Department of Health had failed to stop the practice, even after it had reason to believe that it was legally indefensible and might incur massive liabilities on the part of the State, there was a public outcry and the secretary general of the Department of Health was transferred to another position.

What is clear is that, overall, our health services have certainly improved since the passing of the Health Act 1970 and the introduction of medical cards. What is equally clear is that they have some distance to go before they are as good as they might be.

Lifestyle

The old live on, wait out their stay
of execution in small granny flats,
thrifty thin-lipped men, grim pious wives . . .

Sudden as an impulse holiday, the wind
has changed direction, strewing a whiff
of barbecue fuel across summer lawns.

Tonight, the babe on short-term
contract from the German parent
will partner you at the sponsors' concert.

Time now, however, for the lunch-break
orders to be faxed. Make yours hummus
on black olive bread. An Evian.

DENNIS O'DRISCOLL, 'The Celtic Tiger'
FROM *Weather Permitting*, 1999

PHONE HOME

Athlone, Co. Westmeath, 27 January 1982

It is less than twenty years since the last manual telephone exchange in Ireland finally closed down, on 28 May 1987. Located at Mountshannon, Co. Clare, its closure brought to an end the era of personal service when members of the public depended on the efficiency of local operators to connect their calls to the world outside their communities. Already, the country's first digital exchange had been officially opened in Athlone. Its opening was a development that heralded the remarkable transformation of Ireland's telecommunications system. Today, we are among Europe's heaviest users of mobile phones and many regard email and the web as intrinsic parts of their daily lives.

As late as 1965 there were still about 900 manual exchanges around Ireland. They were generally operated by the local postmaster or postmistress, many of whom doubled as local shopkeepers. You lifted the receiver at your home or place of work and wound a handle at the side of the set. This alerted the operator to the fact that service was required. Confidentiality then depended upon operators not eavesdropping, or upon their discretion in not repeating what they overheard or knew about connections. Incoming calls were put through to your home by the operator, and some people had to share a party line where a certain number of rings on the phone identified which particular party was wanted. If others subsequently lifted their receivers, they could hear their neighbour on the phone. There was no dial or numbers on the front of sets that were connected to manual exchanges and, in the late 1950s, most manual exchanges served fewer than twenty lines.

From 1957, automatic 'crossbar' exchanges gradually began to replace manual ones. By 1965 there were 200 of them. However, the pace of economic development put increasing pressure on the entire system and foreign industries coming to Ireland demanded improved services.

The Irish telephone service was modernised in leaps and bounds. Government ministers who oversaw substantially increased investment included Labour's Conor Cruise O'Brien and Fianna Fáil's Albert Reynolds. On 4 December 1973, O'Brien announced that his department intended to spend on the phone service over the following five years an amount exceeding all total previous capital expenditure on phones since the foundation of the State. In 1974, the first international telephone exchange in the Republic of Ireland opened in Dublin. Telecom Éireann would later recall:

> For historical reasons, Ireland was rather unique in western Europe in that telephone calls to and from the Continent were switched through London. In 1974, the Irish International Exchange, using the crossbar system, was opened. Coming on the heels of Ireland's accession to the EEC, it greatly facilitated communication with the other members and with the rest of the world, particularly North America. (Telecom Éireann, *ReCalling: The Telephone in Ireland and How it Began* (Dublin [1988] p. 18))

In 1977, the new Fianna Fáil government of Jack Lynch granted Irish pensioners living alone a special entitlement to free telephone line rental. This social policy was a concrete assertion of the principle of universal access to services and it was to be enjoyed by growing numbers. Fewer than 10,000 people had availed of the entitlement by 1979, but more than 114,000 were benefiting twenty years later.

In 1979, an accelerated telecommunications development programme was announced following the publication of a key report by the Posts and Telegraphs Review Group under the chairmanship of M. J. Dargan. Within two years of its publication, the first digital telephone exchange was officially opened at Roslevin, Athlone, Co. Westmeath, on 27 January 1982. At that time, Ireland's telephone service was still the responsibility of a government department that long gloried in styling itself rather quaintly, 'the Department of Posts & Telegraphs'. There were growing complaints about the time it took to get new lines installed for tens of thousands of eager applicants, with some people waiting for longer than a year to get what they had requested. Charges were also criticised. A high proportion of 'trunk' (long-distance) calls failed. The service was undercapitalised, the network was underdeveloped and industrial unrest made the system worse. Nevertheless, the decision to introduce digital technology into the network was shrewd and meant that Ireland could avoid the expensive and time-consuming step of expanding analogue and switching systems.

It gradually became clear that the future progression of the telecommunications sector was intrinsically bound up with new technological developments such as cable, wireless and internet connections. Powerful local and international commercial forces began to lobby to ensure that the role of central government in providing such services would be supplanted by that of private enterprise. While politicians across Europe continued to affirm the importance of universal access to communications systems, they also prepared the ground for the eventual privatisation of the telephone service and for the introduction of commercial competition within it. Some welcomed these developments as creating an opportunity to put the consumer in the driving seat when it came to future options, but critics worried that the maintenance of the Universal Service Obligation (USO) would be jeopardised and that the poor or isolated would be marginalised when it came to new technologies.

One very early indication of the interest of private investors in Ireland's telephone services had been the arrival of the *Golden Pages*. This annual directory of businesses and services was first published in Ireland in May 1969 by a company of which my own father, Michael B. Kenny, was one of the first directors. He was invited to join the board because of his long experience in selling the advertising space in Ireland's State-published telephone directory, which was a simple affair in the days when the number of telephones was quite limited. I recall my father bringing his work on the old directory home from our family's advertising agency in Dublin, glad of the additional if modest revenue that it earned when economic times were hard in the late 1950s and early 60s.

In the Republic of Ireland, one important step towards telecommunications privatisation was the creation of Telecom Éireann, a State-owned company which took over from the Department of Posts & Telegraphs the responsibility of operating the national phone service. On 1 January 1984, Telecom Éireann came into existence. It succeeded both operationally and financially, cutting waiting lists and making enough profit to reduce previous debts. Its success made it very attractive to potential investors, who were encouraged by European legal and political developments to regard the field of telecommunications as fruitful territory.

Moves to privatise Telecom Éireann were stalled in 1991 when a controversial land deal involving both its property and its chairman, Michael Smurfit, led to the latter's resignation. However, this was a temporary diversion from the government's developing strategy of using the privatisation of Telecom as a planned precedent for privatising various national assets. In July 1999, Telecom Éireann was floated on the stock market and hundreds of thousands of Irish citizens bought shares in the privatised company, which was thenceforth to be known as Eircom. The privatisation was to prove a bad idea for small investors, being followed by a collapse in the company's valuation that was attributable only in part to an international recession in telecommunications. Recriminations flew between the company's chief executive, Alfie Kane, and Tánaiste Mary O'Rourke, who had eagerly promoted privatisation on behalf of the government and whom some citizens blamed for misleading them into losing a substantial part of their investment.

The government has also attempted to adopt policies that keep Ireland abreast of the latest telecommunications developments, establishing an Information Society Commission to assist in the process. Eircom has continued to dominate the Irish telephone market, although its new competitors have slowly gained a foothold. Its continuing dominance has been the subject of criticism by employers and others, especially as both cost and access factors have contributed to Ireland's take-up of broadband lagging behind that of some other countries with which we compete for business. It would be ironic if privatisation turned out to have effectively slowed the progress of telecommunications modernisation in the Republic of Ireland.

Meanwhile, responsibility for regulation of the market passed from the civil service to the Office of the Director of Telecommunications Regulation (ODTR), which on 1 December 2002 underwent a statutory metamorphosis and became the Commission for Communications Regulation (COMREG). Comreg's website is a useful resource but is not for the faint-hearted.

In 1971, there were only 248,000 telephone subscribers in the Republic. However, that number had doubled by 1981 and quadrupled by 1991. Today, in addition to at least one phone line in almost every house, and many extensions off those lines, we constantly chatter on mobiles and exchange emails and text messages. Irish people spend more than other Europeans on mobile phone conversations, but whether this is because we talk more or are charged more (or even both) is contested. During 2004, in Ireland, the average revenue earned by Vodafone from each of its mobile customers was €602 (almost twice that from Germans), while the income for O_2 from each of their Irish customers was €564. Not surprisingly, there is now scarcely a place where a harassed employee can long escape the e-mail, text or telephonic reach of her or his employer. Many people regard these changes as, at best, a mixed blessing for society, but most would not wish to abandon the new and improved services. Our appetite for them has been a boon to telecommunications companies. We are truly hooked.

MICARUS

Irish airspace, 25 November 1988

Icarus tried to fly on wings of wax, but the sun melted them and he fell to his death. He should have flown Ryanair. It goes from strength to strength, on a wing and a prayer, under the guidance of Mick O'Leary.

Today, for Irish people a trip to Europe is almost a commonplace event. That is thanks in large part to the provision of low airfares by Ryanair, and to Ryanair's impact on its competitors' services.

For those Irish who work long-term in Britain, the days of having to pay top rates for Aer Lingus flights or else make tedious journeys on train and boat services of indifferent quality are gone, and they can return home with a frequency never enjoyed by earlier generations of emigrants. Policy decisions that loosened the official regulation of international air travel, as well as growing prosperity in Ireland, have helped to fuel Ryanair's growth.

Ryanair was founded in 1985 by the Irish businessman, Tony Ryan. It did not immediately assume the low-cost format with which it is now identified by airline passengers. Indeed, at first it lost money on its regular air services. However, Ryanair's profile changed after Michael O'Leary was recruited by Tony Ryan, an acquaintance of his, to join the company. On 25 November 1988, O'Leary became a director of Ryanair. His involvement was not to be confined to the boardroom. The airline really began to take off after he was appointed its deputy chief executive in 1991. He became chief operating officer from June 1993 to December 1993, and chief executive from 1 January 1994. Having been given a share in the company's future, O'Leary went on to be appointed the chief executive of Ryanair Holdings on 21 April 1997. He is, today, one of Ireland's wealthiest businessmen.

The disdain which O'Leary generates in certain quarters was wonderfully expressed in a *Financial Times* profile on 20 June 2003. A senior but anonymous British air industry official told the *FT*: 'He [O'Leary] is not regarded as very lovely. He is a bully. He will have his run but he will almost certainly disappear in a puff of smoke. These people always do.' No doubt, in January 2003, this official was gratified when the European Commission decided that Ryanair's deal with Charleroi Airport in Belgium had breached certain rules on state aids to private industry. Its decision forced up airfares, as well as Ryanair's costs.

However, even if O'Leary and Ryanair do disappear in a puff of smoke, which seems unlikely at present, their legacy of cheap airfares to and from Ireland will remain. That change has facilitated other changes by helping people to go abroad more easily and to reach beyond Britain.

Tony Ryan was educated by the Christian Brothers, while O'Leary had a more privileged Jesuit education. Yet Ryan is seen as polite and urbane while O'Leary is regarded in certain circles as a bit of rough stuff, notwithstanding his comfortable family background, immense wealth and ownership of a fine country mansion, Gigginstown House, near Mullingar, Co. Westmeath. O'Leary attended Trinity College Dublin, before acquiring a number of newsagents shops in the city.

O'Leary was described in that *Financial Times* profile as 'controversial, reviled and one of the most important people in world aviation today'. It is a description with which few would disagree, especially given Ryanair's long-standing refusal to recognise trade unions and O'Leary's frequent public use of foul language and his reputation for indifference to customers' complaints.

He has cultivated a populist image of informality that some find repellent, wearing blue jeans and an open-neck shirt on occasions when other businessmen dress in suits and ties, and swearing during media interviews. He has often and stridently abused governments, national airlines, airport authorities, unions and travel agents, among others, and not always without good reason. Ryanair's advertisements, when deliberately provocative, have caused offence as well as generating publicity. They are sometimes aimed personally at politicians who have not acted as swiftly as O'Leary would like when it comes to matters involving deregulation and competition. Following the appearance of some such ads in May 2004, Taoiseach Bertie Ahern accused him of bullying. An exasperated Ahern told *The Irish Times* (1 June 2004): 'It is impossible for me to keep Michael O'Leary happy.'

O'Leary appears to enjoy stamping on the sensibilities of those who expect more from his airline than it is prepared to deliver. He told Graham Bowley, author of that *FT* profile, 'We don't fall all over ourselves if they . . . say my granny fell ill. What part of no refund don't you understand? You are not getting a refund, so fuck off.' Bowley commented dryly, 'Fuck off, granny, is not the standard spiel you expect from your regular company executive.'

But Ryanair never set out to be regular. It set out to shake up the airline business and, in the process, to make air travel an easier option for those on just about any level of income. It has done so by a mixture of confrontation and imagination, which has seen O'Leary tussle in the media and the courts with State agencies and unions, while utilising the facilities of small but ambitious airports across Europe that had hitherto been neglected by other airlines. Although these airports may be more than an hour's drive away from cities such as Paris, Frankfurt or Barcelona, there are plenty of customers willing to fly to them.

Ryanair also pioneered the use of the Internet for online booking, spurring Aer Lingus and others to introduce their own low fares and ticket-less web services. The Irish public are proud of the way Aer Lingus has flown the flag for Ireland, and many travellers have felt at home from the moment they stepped on to a green and white 'EI' aircraft in Boston or Berlin. However, travellers' loyalty was sorely tested in more recent years by high airfares. Affection for Aer Lingus has not stopped people voting with their feet when it comes to Ryanair. Aer Lingus survived a crisis in 2001, brought on by competition and industrial unrest, among other factors.

The founder of Ryanair, Tony Ryan, was himself for many years a former senior employee of Aer Lingus. In 1975, he left the national airline and founded Guinness Peat Aviation (GPA), an aircraft leasing company that became a major international success before collapsing dramatically after a failed flotation in 1992. By that time, Ryan had also founded Ryanair with his sons Declan, Cathal and Shane as its dominant shareholders. In 1995, he joined the board of Ryanair and later became its non-executive chairman.

Before Ryanair was founded, Irish people had long availed of charter flights, most commonly on offer to holiday destinations just once a week and in the summer, and these charters paved the way for Ryanair's more regular low-cost services. The new company learnt from low-cost ventures abroad, especially Southwest Airlines in the United States. It became associated with the personality and driving force of one individual, as had Freddie Laker's Laker, Richard Branson's Virgin and Herb Kelleher's Southwest.

Just twenty years ago, Ryanair started out with a fifteen-seater turbo prop flying between Waterford in the south-east of Ireland and London (Gatwick). It was to be no overnight success and as late as 1990/91 was losing money. This propelled its shareholders into relaunching it as a 'low fares/no frills' airline. The transformation was remarkable. By its tenth birthday, in 1995, the company had become the biggest passenger carrier on the Dublin–London route and claimed to be the largest Irish airline on every route it operated. Then, as the EU deregulated what had formerly been a heavily restricted international air business, Ryanair was able to open new routes beyond Ireland and Britain.

Not even the awful events in New York on 11 September 2001 stopped Ryanair's advance, although other airlines suffered badly as a result of the hijackings and murders. In 2002, Ryanair announced a long-term partnership with Boeing, which involved the anticipated acquisition of up to 150 new Boeing 737-800 series aircraft over an eight-year period from 2002 to 2010. In 2003, the Irish company took over the low-fares airline Buzz from KLM and continued to expand its bases across Europe. O'Leary had turned his small Irish company into one of the biggest in Europe. Its market capitalisation of around $5 billion was said to be higher than Lufthansa and almost a third higher than that of British Airways.

Reflecting on the changes in travel abroad from Ireland, in an article in *The Irish Times* on 3 January 2004, Garret FitzGerald deduced from an analysis of recent data that more than two million actual holiday visits are now made each year by Irish people to mainland Europe. The former Taoiseach, and also former employee of the Irish national airline, recalled that when he joined Aer Lingus in 1947, its only direct link with mainland Europe was a thrice-weekly flight to Paris by a 21-seat DC3 — 'which would have brought no more than 2,000 Irish people to the Continent each year'.

Today, many people fly cheaply to Europe and beyond. It is quite common for young men and women to spend up to a year travelling the world. The middle-aged go for a weekend to Brussels as their parents might once have gone to Bundoran. Business contacts are renewed and maintained with relative ease. Families can afford to see European countries while leaving the car at home, rather than making a long journey by ferry to the coast of France. Michael O'Leary has helped greatly to make those changes possible.

DRIVING OURSELVES MAD

West-Link, Co. Dublin, 15 March 1990

Everyday, on average, the tolls of the West-Link are used by drivers more than 80,000 times. Here, vehicles cross the Liffey on a pair of charmless but functional bridges. It is a new part of Ireland, an extension in mid-air that spans the river at the Strawberry Beds. It was created precisely to help people to be somewhere else as quickly as possible. Yet, already the tolls are unable to cope adequately with the volume of traffic that now snakes around Dublin on the M50 motorway. Each day, especially during rush hours, traffic is backed up as drivers wait to pay for the privilege of crossing, thereby avoiding city routes that are even more clogged than the M50. We are driving as never before.

Opened on 11 March 1990, the first West-Link bridge is one aspect of a number of major new road developments throughout Ireland that have been made necessary and possible by Ireland's economic boom of the late twentieth century. The only earlier toll project in Ireland in the twentieth century was the East-Link bridge, which was opened across the Liffey at Irishtown in 1984. The increasing imposition of tolls has been accepted in practice by Irish motorists who are prepared to pay to get somewhere quicker.

Speaking at the official opening of the West-Link in 1990, Taoiseach Charles Haughey praised 'the soaring simplicity of this bridge'. He described it as 'a spectacular landmark in the history of road and bridge building in Ireland'. Finance for the project had included the first ever loan from the European Investment Bank for an Irish infrastructural project undertaken by the private sector.

In September 2003, the second West-Link bridge opened. For nearly two decades, the M50 has taken shape on both sides of the West-Link through countryside that is being quickly swamped by the city's sprawling suburbs. A court battle over ancient remains at Carrickmines delayed its completion, while the ownership of some lands through which it passes has been investigated by an official tribunal.

Speaking in 1990, Haughey pointed out that the government had embarked on 'the most ambitious and sustained road development programme ever undertaken' in the State. This was particularly necessary because, he said:

> The transport costs borne by Irish exporters to Europe are approximately twice those incurred by Community countries trading with one another on the European mainland. These high costs are mainly due to the deficient state of our national roads and the access roads to the principal ports and airports.

Since 1990, economic and population growth and the rapidly rising number of cars on our roads have meant that earlier projections of Ireland's traffic and commuting needs were overtaken. Further evidence of this fact may be found in the heavy demands on the intercity and DART (Dublin Area Rapid Transit) suburban train services and in the scramble by government to provide a light rail system (Luas) in the capital. An absence of comprehensive long-term planning, coupled with corruption in the planning process and a lack of commitment to public transportation and environmental protection, has helped to make suburban living and commuting in our cities, especially in Dublin, a frustrating and unpleasant experience for many people. A particularly sore point for drivers is the roundabout above the M50 exit for Cork and Limerick, close to the Red Cow Inn. The 'Red Cow roundabout' has been popularly dubbed the 'Mad Cow roundabout' because of its general layout, and particularly because of a subsequent decision by city planners to incorporate Luas crossings into its already complex design.

In 1994, there were 1,202,000 vehicles licensed in the Republic of Ireland. Of this number, 939,000 were private cars. Within just eight years, by 2002, that total rose by more than an astonishing 50 per cent to 1,850,100 vehicles licensed. Of these, 1,447,000 were private cars. In the Dublin area the increase was proportionately the same as the rest of the country, even if it feels worse when one drives in the capital. In 2004, IBEC, the employers' organisation, reported that companies in Dublin were being adversely affected by worsening gridlock and were dissatisfied with official responses to the problem. A promised dedicated traffic corps was still awaited.

A further sign of affluence is that the age of the Irish car fleet has also been reduced. In 1994, 71 per cent of private cars were over four years old. In 2002, only 55 per cent of private cars were over four years old. The introduction of number-plates showing the year of manufacture of each car may have spurred people to change their cars more frequently for the sake of appearances. In 2000, a new legislative requirement for a National Car Test certainly accelerated the disappearance of older cars. The NCT conducts more than half a million car tests per annum. It has faced criticism from people who claim that some of the testing equipment is unreliable. Among the new cars on Irish roads, it is now unremarkable to see Mercedes, BMW and Lexus vehicles, where once such makes were quite rare.

According to the Automobile Association (AA), the main problem for Dublin is not so much car ownership as car usage and population growth. Despite the recent surge, vehicle numbers are in the region of 450 cars per 1,000 population. The AA says:

> This proportion is quite typical of northern Europe. Cities like Amsterdam, Munich or Copenhagen are similar yet they do not suffer anything like Dublin's level of congestion. The main problem for us is car *usage*. We are an extremely car-dependent city. This is caused primarily by a lack of good quality public transport. The AA is therefore strongly in favour of investments in and development of public transport.

However, with significant EU assistance, the government has engaged in an unprecedented programme of road development in recent years. Various towns on major routes have been bypassed. There is, at last, a fine motorway running north of Dublin to

Dundalk, and due to be extended as far as the border. For decades, notwithstanding the stated ambition of the Republic of Ireland to be united with Northern Ireland, the road towards Belfast was a succession of obstacles and delays for anyone trying to drive between Ireland's two biggest cities. Other major developments include tunnels serving the ports of Cork and Dublin, taking heavy traffic away from those cities' centres.

Not everyone is happy with the State's policy and practice when it comes to building roads. During 2004, the Comptroller and Auditor General reported that the actual cost of building planned roads had more than doubled since 1999, partly because the National Roads Authority (NRA) originally lacked sufficient cost-control expertise, and partly because consultants were being rewarded with percentage payments regardless of cost overruns. Some of our finest stretches of new road had cost €16 million for every single mile built. The NRA was created as an independent statutory body under the Roads Act 1993, with effect from 1 January 1994. This marked a point of change, when the government accepted that national roads needed to be planned on a long-term and co-ordinated basis. However, another decade passed before the government finally agreed to provide the NRA with a multi-annual budget and did not simply continue to fund it from year to year.

Environmentalists and others believe that public transport has been seriously underfunded for decades and fear that bigger roads simply encourage greater use of the motor vehicle. Nevertheless, despite such concerns and despite some evidence of profiteering by certain people in relation to the acquisition of lands for roads, the general public is impatient with traffic jams and supports most of the activities of the NRA. The State's reliance on roads for carrying passenger and goods traffic has been one of the highest in the EU. The replacement of leaded by unleaded petrol has helped somewhat to restrain the related growth in pollution, as have developments in car engine design.

The rising number of cars on our roads has heightened public awareness of safety issues, with recurrent campaigns against speeding and against drinking alcohol while in charge of a vehicle. Penalty points have been introduced as a disincentive for those who might otherwise break the law. Governments continue to pledge to improve public transport, even if the pace of improvement has been painfully slow.

The design of the Luas, Dublin's new tram system, has been controversial. The first two Luas lines built are not connected, and their construction caused great disruption to traders in central Dublin. Plans for extensions, or for a Dublin underground, that might include direct rail access to Dublin Airport have been under discussion for years. The DART system has been extended in fits and starts to cater for the large increase in the number of people using it. Many builders have constructed apartments and houses in the vicinity of DART stations without having to contribute financially to a publicly funded facility that enhances their value. DART trains that have been added to the service are less comfortable and contain fewer seats than those originally acquired, and there is a perception that the State is not prepared to invest sufficiently in the DART to maintain the level of comfort that helped to make it such an immediate success.

Better planning and greater expenditure could have helped Irish people to adjust better to the growth in population and transportation needs during recent decades. Inadequate planning and unforeseen levels of growth means that driving and commuting for many citizens in modern Ireland, especially for younger people who live far from the centres of towns and cities in sprawling suburbs, is now a frustrating experience.

SHOP UNTIL YOU DROP

The Square, Tallaght, 23 October 1990

Long into the twentieth century, Alex Findlater's & Co. was the nearest thing that Ireland had to a chain of food stores. Shopping was staid. Local grocers stood behind big counters serving customers individually. But then came self-service and the creation of supermarkets, including Powers and H. Williams & Co. In 1960, Feargal Quinn opened his first store in Dundalk. In 1970, he renamed this and other outlets Superquinn, summing up in one new word the merger of big convenience shopping and the Irish entrepreneurial spirit. Quinn later became a senator and was appointed by the government to chair the national postal service, now known as An Post. He was not the only Irish business person to recognise the future direction of retailing. Other innovators included Pat Quinn of Quinnsworth, and Ben Dunne Sr and his children of Dunnes Stores.

In 1961, background taped music was introduced into Irish shops. This was just one of the small but significant ways in which our experience of shopping has changed. Shop fronts are now brighter. Promotion, variety and creativity have come to seem almost as important as the quality of the produce. In 1969, Findlater's finally shut down after 146 years in business. The company had been unable to adapt sufficiently to survive the new world of consumerism.

Irish shops and shopping centres have continued to get bigger, with new malls being built across Ireland from Waterford to Westport, and from Douglas to Derry. People spend increasing amounts of their time and money in the pursuit of products and services. We drive to shop where once we only walked, and this both tempts and allows us to purchase larger quantities every time. The introduction of credit cards, ATMS and 'easy' financing has made instant gratification more possible than ever. Great growth in the Irish retail market has sparked interest from abroad. Names widely seen on English high streets, including Boots, Tesco and Marks & Spencer, now appear around Ireland. In March 1997, Tesco took over the former Quinnsworth/Crazy Prices chain. Now, Tesco and Dunnes Stores are Ireland's two biggest multiples, with Superquinn in third position.

Irish traders have responded to the challenges of inward investment by opening their own outlets overseas, including Dunnes Stores and O'Brien's Irish Sandwich Bars. The latter are a relatively wholesome riposte to the international fast-food industry, which has visited on Ireland franchises such as McDonald's and Kentucky Fried Chicken (KFC). Brands including Pizza Hut and Eddie Rocket's seek to please our palettes. We have also developed our own fast-food chains, including the very successful Abrakebabra and Supermac's. There are new 'food courts', offering a multiple choice of styles of fast food, ostensibly based on recipes from every part of the globe. 'Superpubs' have mushroomed to cater for our seemingly insatiable thirst, pushing some smaller establishments of character to the brink of financial ruin or beyond.

Our willingness to embrace massive shopping developments, no matter what the reservations of some town planners and environmentalists, has found expression most notably among the sprawling suburbs of Co. Dublin. On 23 October 1990, a shopping centre on a new scale opened its doors in Tallaght. Topped by a pyramid-shaped roof, this was The Square. In the absence of proper town planning, it doubled as a privatised town centre for a transformed Tallaght. The size of the entire site, internal and external, is 1.7 million square feet. On 14 October 1998, the massive Liffey Valley Shopping Centre opened to the public. Before long, more than ninety leading retailers from Ireland and the United Kingdom were trading there. According to Liffey Valley Management Ltd:

> Over 580,000 concrete blocks, 22,000 cubic metres of concrete, 7,000 square metres of marble flooring and 2,860 square metres of glass were used in the construction — nearly 100% of the construction work was undertaken by Irish contractors.

A vast car park was created across 23 acres to cater for customers at Liffey Valley, taking full advantage of the new M50 around Dublin and acting as a magnet for traffic. Of the three anchor stores that opened in this development, only one, Dunnes, was Irish. The others were Marks & Spencer (its first out of town store in Ireland) and Boots (its largest store in the Republic). As in The Square at Tallaght, the presence of a multiplex cinema increases the pull of the location. Then, on 3 March 2005, the first phase of the Republic of Ireland's biggest shopping complex opened at Dundrum town centre in south Dublin. Yet another multiscreen cinema, as well as a new theatre, are also being built there.

New multiplex cinemas have reversed the decline in the numbers watching films. Our appetite for electronic stimuli has been further fed by video and DVD outlets that include Xtravision and Chartbusters. At Golden Discs, Virgin, HMV or Tower Records, among other stores, massive quantities of recorded music are sold and tickets for concerts are bought at high prices. Ireland is now a part of the tour circuit for international pop celebrities, and their expensive concerts at Slane and elsewhere are part of a way of life for many Irish people.

The great increase in the number of new households at the end of the twentieth century has supported a whole burgeoning furniture sector. Navan, Co. Meath, developed the largest concentration of bedding and furniture warehouses in Ireland, but it now has many competitors. Chains such as Atlantic Homecare, PC World, Power City, Roches Stores, Curry's, Motor World and Woodies also feature prominently in the everyday world of Irish householders. However, notwithstanding a trend towards ever bigger shopping centres, the independent and family trader has managed to survive and still holds a very substantial share of national business. Indeed, the Irish grocery trade is said to be unique in western Europe because the Irish independent sector retains almost half of the market. Some independent traders run sizeable local supermarkets and supermarket chains, while others operate single convenience stores on the corner, and still more have cashed in on our willingness to buy food when buying petrol by creating and expanding their shops on garage forecourts. According to Michael Campbell of the Retail Grocery, Dairy and Allied Trades' Association (RGDATA):

> Whether shoppers live in Killenaule, Killinick or Killiney, there is a modern grocery shop with top class standards within walking distance. It may be a symbol group-shop like Centra or Spar, or a non-group retailer.

The Centra and SuperValu franchises, under the parentage of the Musgrave Group in Cork, as well as Spar and ADM Londis, have helped to maintain independents and to sustain healthy competition in the grocery trade. This has prevented the narrower concentration of ownership that some fear is the ultimate fate of the retail sector. The Irish shopping market has become even livelier with the more recent arrival of Aldi and Lidl from Germany. Arguments about the permitted size and location of supermarkets, as well as about such controversial issues as below-cost selling, rumble on.

At weekends, the roads of our towns and cities are now cluttered with drivers making their way to shopping centres, sometimes for essential purchases but as often as not for a kind of recreational browsing. Irish shops remain open for long hours, including Sundays in many cases. Buffeted by ubiquitous advertising and the battle of the brands, we spend money in ways that our ancestors could never have envisaged. Not only are we relatively wealthier, but the range of products on the market has never been wider. And while we support a fast-food and low-cost retail sector, we also enjoy looking for special quality items when we can afford them. A range of Irish outlets for fine goods, including Kilkenny Design, Avoca Handweavers and Blarney Woollen Mills, have grown up alongside established traders such as Waterford Glass. Irish fashion designers such as John Rocha are widely respected. Meanwhile, Dubray Books is just one of a number of new outlets that have helped enormously to sustain a healthy new trade in Irish books. Galleries dot our streets, evidence that many artists can at least hope to sell their work in a manner and to an extent that was once beyond the expectation of Irish painters and sculptors. Our ancestors kept fit by working in the fields, but many of us now pay for the privilege of working out in new gyms.

We also eat out as never before. From Temple Bar to Tralee and from Kinsale to Killybegs, there are new restaurants across Ireland that do a brisk trade, despite the fact that many are quite expensive by comparison with those in some other European countries. Darina Allen and Conrad Gallagher are among those who have helped to make Irish cookery and cuisine respected internationally. Supermarkets stock a range of products unknown to our ancestors, and our eating and drinking habits have changed accordingly. It is said that, in 1964, actor Micheál Mac Liammóir opened Ireland's first specialist wine shop, the Bacchus Wine Centre. Since then the volume of wine bought in Ireland has increased progressively and substantially. At the end of the century, a sharp rise in immigration resulted in the opening of specialist African, Asian and eastern European outlets that are frequented also by native Irish people. On-line shopping allows us to instantly summon up books or other items from almost anywhere on the globe. Irish traders too benefit from the Internet, with Kenny's Bookshop in Galway being one of many businesses that have notably used new technology to bridge the seas between Ireland and other countries.

If we feel guilty about the level of our consumption (and we certainly have come a long way in Ireland from the shortages of the Great Famine), then we have managed to assuage that guilt in one unique way. Thus, the Irish government ostentatiously engaged in environmental protection by banning the provision of free plastic bags for groceries. It reckoned that some 1.2 billion plastic shopping bags were being provided free of charge to customers in retail outlets annually. Since 4 March 2002, a levy of fifteen cent has been imposed on shoppers who buy a bag instead of bringing a carrier of their own. This measure is said to have led to a sharp reduction in the overall number of plastic bags and in the amount of plastic rubbish in the countryside. However, bags are still allowed for certain items, including meat, and manufacturers continue to use excessive plastic packaging on products. One of the least attractive aspects of the growth in our consumption as a nation is the resultant mountain of domestic refuse that is posing an environmental threat and strengthening the case for the construction of incinerators.

LOTTO LOOT

Bailieborough, Co. Cavan, 2 November 1996

It was a moment that made Mary and Paddy Kelly of Bailieborough, Co. Cavan, very happy. In fact, they were on the pig's back. On 2 November 1996, their Lotto numbers came up and they split the prize money of £7,486,025 (€9,505,290). The other half went to a consortium of seven people in Co. Meath.

Not that Mary and Paddy were the first or last Lotto millionaires. The first had been Rita Power. Her family was bursting with excitement when, on 6 May 1989, Rita, from Portumna, Co. Galway, won £1,200,937. However, the person who has pocketed the most so far bought the winning ticket in Cork in 1997 and remained anonymous. That Cork windfall was €7,892,753.

And in August 2004, an Irish person also won the biggest ever prize in the United Kingdom's Camelot draw. Iris Jeffrey from Belfast only checked her ticket when she happened to hear that the jackpot of £20m had not been claimed.

The Republic of Ireland's National Lottery was launched in 1987 and has changed the nation's betting and shopping habits. With tickets being sold at thousands of special terminals in newsagents and post offices up and down the country, queues now form whenever there is a big prize to be won. Even those who should know better have a flutter. Perhaps some people have become mildly addicted to the lottery, and others might spend what little money they have more wisely. But most people who play enjoy the remote chance of overnight wealth. Besides, Ireland is a small country and many citizens know of someone who has won or they shop at a place where a winning ticket has been sold. As the company's own promotional release puts it, 'National Lottery games have become a normal part of everyday life.'

In October 1984, the government undertook to prepare a White Paper with a view to establishing a national lottery. The name of that discussion document, 'Building on Reality', seems paradoxical in the circumstances. What are the chances of your numbers ever coming up, in 'reality'? They are very slim, but that never stopped the purchaser of a Lotto ticket building castles in the air. 'Building on unReality' might have been more appropriate! Irish Saturdays have never been quite the same since the Lotto draws began.

In 1986, the National Lottery Act was passed. A competitive tender resulted in An Post, the State-owned national postal authority, being franchised to run the lottery. On 22 March 1987, the National Lottery itself was launched at the Royal Hospital, Kilmainham. The 'Instant 3' scratch card was its first game and its sales had topped £34 million by the end of May. The following month, the first Grand Prize Game was televised on RTÉ's *Late Late Show*, with the top prize of £25,000 going to a Limerick player. The Lotto itself was launched one year later, in April 1988. A big fireworks display was held in the Phoenix Park, Dublin, attended by tens of thousands of people and also televised on the *Late Late Show*. The very first Lotto winner was Bridget McGrath from Letterkenny, Co. Donegal, who won an amount equivalent to €186,726 on 16 April 1988.

The popularity of the Lotto has normalised the practice of betting in a way that is not to everyone's liking, especially given the growth of other forms of gambling such as online betting via the Internet. Moreover, not everyone agrees about the worthiness of some of the 'good causes' that have benefited from the distribution of National Lottery funds. However, its administration and its financial affairs are far more transparent than ever were those of the Irish Hospitals Sweepstake, which many regard as the forerunner of the National Lottery. For years, people purchased Sweep tickets without knowing what proportion of the takings of the privately funded venture actually ended up in the Irish health services and without being aware that criminal elements on both sides of the Atlantic were making money from the operation. During the 1970s, an RTÉ investigative documentary about the Sweep was suppressed while in the course of production, following pressure from the government and elsewhere.

The early popularity of the Lotto was such that, during 1990, an additional mid-week draw was introduced. That year also saw the launch of 'Winning Streak', an instant lottery game with an associated television game show hosted then by Mike Murphy, a well-known broadcaster. The TV show became a big hit with viewers. Five years later, Marty Whelan became the presenter of *Millionaire*, the first National Lottery summer TV game show. Later came *Tellybingo*.

As the National Lottery strove to keep up the momentum of public interest, it sponsored or supported major events such as Pavarotti's visit to Dublin (when the capital was designated European City of Culture in 1991) and the National Lottery Congress Centenary Carnival celebrating the centenary of the Irish Congress of Trade Unions in 1994. It also ran some ingenious and amusing advertising campaigns, and developed a variety of instant games and other subsidiary products.

In almost two decades since its foundation, the National Lottery has distributed well over €1 billion in prize money, turning more than 250 people into millionaires in the process. The government has also given almost €2 billion of lottery revenue to various projects. Difficult as it may be to believe, jackpots totalling approximately €10 million remained unclaimed. These included a number of jackpots worth more than €1 million each. Some people either threw away or never checked their tickets. They seem unlikely to have been members of one of the many syndicates that regularly buy tickets, and all of whose members presumably keep an eye on how their numbers do. Then again, perhaps each member of some syndicate has mistakenly assumed that someone else in the group had checked to see if they had won!

Some people put checking the results on the long finger, or else are just backward about coming forward. None has been slower than the winner of €1,639,685 on 18 September 2002. Almost ninety days passed before that jackpot was claimed on 17 December. Some win only to find that they must share the jackpot with quite a few others, and none more so than the twenty winners in November 1991, who ended up with just £119,842 each, instead of the sum of more than £2 million that a single winning ticket would have netted.

During the first fifteen years of the National Lottery's existence, from 1987 to 2002, the government gave the biggest slice of National Lottery income to Youth, Sport, Recreation and Amenities, and the second biggest to Health and Welfare. It gave less to Arts, Culture and National Heritage and to the Irish language. The amounts distributed were:

Youth, Sport, Recreation and Amenities	€681.90m
Health and Welfare	€676.20m
Arts, Culture and National Heritage	€390.20m
Irish Language	€100.44m

Among the beneficiaries have been the Higher Education Authority, Institúid Teangeolaíochta Éireann, the Irish Red Cross and various sporting bodies. The National Lottery's *Annual Report* gives only general headings, for the most part, and those wishing to discover exactly what organisations benefit from the money will not find in it the information they seek. Critics point out that much National Lottery funding is directed to activities that were formerly funded by the Exchequer, and is not spent on creating special new schemes or facilities.

———

The United Kingdom followed in Ireland's footsteps by introducing its own national lottery, for which the first draw was held by Camelot in November 1994.

Culture

Is chualathas mo chéile ag rá ina theanga féin
'Ná fiafraigh d'fhile cá bhfuil an bóthar go Baghdad.
Léimfidh a samhlaíocht thar íor na spéire
is raghaidh tú amú sa phortach.'

Admhaím go raibh an tsiúlóid achrannach,
is an talamh fliuch
is gur chuaigh cuid againn síos go hioscadaibh
ins an bhféith bhog.

And my husband was heard to remark in his own tongue,
'Don't ask a poet the way
to Baghdad for among
the bogs and bog-holes she'll lead you astray.'

I admit that the going was a bit
heavy and the ground so damp
that some of us were up to our armpits
in the swamp.

NUALA NÍ DHOMHNAILL, 'Loch a' Dúin'
TRANSLATED BY PAUL MULDOON
FROM *The Astrakhan Cloak*, 1992

AMONGST HIS PEOPLE

Foxfield, Co. Leitrim, Easter 1974

It was a homecoming and a healing. In the 1960s, John McGahern had left Ireland in unhappy circumstances. By writing honestly, he had forfeited his job as a teacher and saw no way of earning a living on this side of the Irish Sea. Going to England, he worked for a very short period with his brother-in-law on building sites before finding employment as a teacher again, in Waltham Forest. He subsequently resided in Spain and in the United States. Now, in 1974, he was back to live on a farm near where he was born in Co. Leitrim. McGahern's departure had served as a catalyst that hastened public recognition of the persecution of some writers in Ireland, and his return symbolised Ireland's changing relationship with the arts.

Throughout the decades following Independence, the new State certainly had among its citizens vibrant artists and interesting writers. However, a stifling blend of nationalism and conservative Catholicism made it increasingly difficult for many to express themselves freely or to work in ways that they believed to be moral and necessary. A paralysing form of Irish censorship resulted in good books and films being banned or otherwise censored, including works by anthropologists such as Margaret Meade. In 1942, even a simple account by Eric Cross of the daily life and tales of an old couple who lived in west Cork, namely the tailor Buckley and his wife Ansty, was banned and then condemned publicly by members of Seanad Éireann in the most heartless and personal fashion.

It almost became an insult to one's artistic integrity not to have had works banned. The censorship of publications and films continued into the 1960s, albeit not quite as extremely or extensively as earlier. When RTÉ started its television service, one of the first speakers to appear was Cardinal D'Alton, the Catholic primate. On that first night, 31 December 1961, viewers learnt from him that he had already had a word with the chairman of the new RTÉ Authority, broadcaster Eamonn Andrews. Dressed in full episcopal regalia, the cardinal looked viewers in the eye and said of Andrews:

> He made it clear that he would be a very unhappy man if he sponsored anything that would be either corrupting or might be a cause of scandal. I am sure that he, (Mr Andrews I may say), on this occasion as in all others has been on the sides of the angels. I am sure that he and the director-general, Mr Roth, can be depended upon to provide programmes that will be enlightening, entertaining, reflecting high ideas, and not presenting us with the caricature of Irish life such as we have had from some of our writers in recent years.

Television programmes from Britain were being received by a growing number of Irish households, and this allowed RTÉ to argue that it must compete by producing programmes of a similar type or range. Higher levels of education and greater opportunities to travel were also opening people to a broader view of reality. Yet, I had to wait until I visited Belfast in the mid-1960s before I could purchase a copy of George Orwell's *1984*. In 1965, John McGahern's *The Dark* fell foul of the censor and was banned. Such works were clearly of literary merit, but the minds that steered Ireland's censorship policies through the early decades of this State's existence were hostile to any form of enquiry or expression that did not reflect their narrow consensus. Artists and writers were suspected of moral and political subversion of some uncertain kind. In 1978, I reported and scripted a documentary for RTÉ about *The Tailor and Ansty* episode of 1942. A man aged 102, who had attended the tailor's wedding, said that he knew no good reason for all the fuss. Three priests had gone to the tailor's remote cottage in Gougane Barra and had forced the octogenarian to kneel down and burn his own copy of the book in the fire. The youngest and only surviving priest told me that times had been different then. By 1978, I could find nobody to defend the banning or to explain precisely what in the book had been considered so objectionable.

An important moment in the development of the State's attitude towards the arts was the passing of the Finance Act 1969, which included a provision (section 2) exempting writers and others from any liability for income tax that would otherwise arise in respect of works having cultural or artistic merit. Such works might include a book or certain other writings, a play, a musical composition, a painting or other like picture, or a sculpture. Credit for this imaginative provision went to the Minister for Finance and future Taoiseach, Charles J. Haughey. The benefits of the exemption from taxation were available to any resident of the State and not just to its citizens. As a result, a number of writers from other countries moved to Ireland. Critics pointed out that some of these foreigners were already wealthy, but that many Irish artists had incomes too small to benefit from tax exemption. Nevertheless, by accident or inspiration, the provision has stimulated the creative life of Ireland. It has remained in force, notwithstanding occasional criticism. For example, in Dáil Éireann on 30 January 2003, Tommy Broughan of the Labour Party noted: '. . . artists and writers have done well in this State. To be an artist or a writer is an honourable profession, just like any other job, and perhaps everyone should pay his or her fair share.'

While Haughey allowed writers and artists a tax break, successive ministers for justice presided over a rapid loosening of the binds of censorship from 1967 onwards. By the end of the century, explicit sexual magazines were widely on sale. Creative freedom was given further impetus by the introduction of tax breaks for film and television programme makers (known first as 'section 35' and later as 'section 481'). The level of film production in the State increased significantly. Along with the Arts Council and other public bodies, a new Film Board became a source of unprecedented financial support for the creative community. The Arts Council itself, which had been founded back in 1951, had its budget boosted by successive governments. This, in turn, helped to make possible a string of regional arts centres and theatres throughout Ireland.

In 1983, a special body was created under the auspices of the Arts Council to honour some of those born in Ireland who are most active in the fields of literature, music and the visual arts. This body, Aosdána, meets annually in a general assembly. Its members include Louis Le Brocquy, whose canvas entitled 'The Family' (1951) was originally offered to the Municipal Gallery in Dublin but was rejected. It is a sign of changed times that, in 2002, Mr and Mrs Lochlann Quinn donated the same work to the National Gallery of Ireland, which gladly accepted it. Such patronage by Ireland's wealthy is now unremarkable.

Aosdána also includes some former social irritants such as Mannix Flynn and Edna O'Brien, and even one formerly outrageous writer from Leitrim called John McGahern. Indeed, in 2003, the government appointed McGahern a member of the Arts Council itself. Aosdána is a self-perpetuating body of up to 250 members, who are eligible to apply for a means-tested stipend of €12,089. It may further honour artists, writers or musicians by elevating them to the status of *saoi*. The latter title is for life, and there may be no more than five *saoi* at any one time. The current *saoi* are Anthony Cronin, Seamus Heaney, Benedict Kiely and Louis Le Brocquy. Earlier *saoi* were Patrick Collins, Samuel Beckett, Mary Lavin, Seán O'Faoláin, Tony O'Malley and Francis Stuart. In 1996, the election of Francis Stuart as a *saoi* proved controversial because of his involvement with Nazi Germany. No musician has been made a *saoi*.

Irish people are not entirely lacking in a sense of irony about some of these developments. Citizens take Aosdána with a large pinch of salt and are sceptical of the ultimate value of some works granted tax exemption or exhibited at the IMMA and elsewhere. However, in general, citizens are tolerant and proud of official policy when it is actively supportive of the arts. Once, Joyce and Beckett and others felt they had to go abroad to survive creatively. Today, leading politicians such as Mary Harney, Ireland's Tánaiste (deputy prime minister) and leader of the Progressive Democrats, are eager to display their appreciation of the arts. On 3 November 1998, at the *Sunday Independent*/Ford 'Spirit of Life' arts awards in Dublin's exclusive Berkeley Court Hotel, Harney said:

> People normally associate me or pigeon-hole me with economic issues of major importance. . . . It is therefore a special night in my

calendar of events to be with people — artists, poets, actors, playwrights and more, who have a special place in my life. This might be a little-known place but [it is] a special one none the less.

There is nothing I like better than the opening night of a new play or film or exhibition of paintings . . . I did have the honour earlier in the year of officiating at the opening of an exhibition of paintings by my good friend Geraldine Hone when I was in Brussels on official business. Those who know me well are aware that I like to buy the occasional painting or piece of sculpture when I have a few pounds to spare. For those that do not know me that well, there is nothing I treasure more than a present of an artistic work, from the simplest piece of pottery to filling an empty space on my wall with a Jack Yeats.

The creative is pivotal to the cultural spirit of a nation. At the core of the cultural spirit of Ireland is the productive labour of artists, artists in the broadest sense — painters, sculptors, musicians, authors, actors, cinematographers. In recent times Irish artists have been demonstrating a growing sophistication in terms of expression and communication, a fact which reflects the dynamic changes that have been occurring in contemporary Ireland. Their creative energy makes a highly significant contribution to the richness of all our lives and to the health and prosperity of our society. . . . creative accomplishments should be generously rewarded.

Official Ireland has come a long way from the days when it imposed a stifling apparatus of censorship, and treated its creative community with great suspicion. Today, it tends to smother it with kindness.

FIELD DAY

(London)Derry, 23 September 1980

It was well intended and well received. The play was a success by any normal theatrical standards. Beyond that, it helped to change the way in which nationalist Ireland imagined its relationship with the majority of people living in Northern Ireland.

The opening of *Translations* at the Guildhall in Derry on 23 September 1980 was a feel-good event for those who were present, including unionist members of the local council. It was the first flower of Field Day, an ad hoc group formed principally by playwright Brian Friel and actor Stephen Rea. Before long, Field Day came to be regarded as a powerful cultural force.

The founders of Field Day wanted to help bring theatre to people who do not usually see plays. Certainly, the Guildhall in Derry was an unusual venue for a professional production. The city had suffered heavily during the continuing troubles and the Guildhall itself was a favourite target of the IRA. It was regarded by many nationalists as a symbol of unionist oppression and domination. On 23 September 1980, it became the site of a standing ovation, led by the Unionist mayor, Marlene Jefferson, who was reported to have described *Translations* as 'fantastic'. She and most of the audience deemed the play a success. Her city council had given considerable assistance to the producers, including a grant for equipment.

Friel and Rea were soon joined in the Field Day enterprise by Seamus Heaney, David Hammond, Séamus Deane and Tom Paulin.

Together, these six constituted its first board of directors.

The Field Day project has been represented as a creative space in which people from both of the main traditions in Northern Ireland came together and invented a new way of seeing themselves. It is more accurate to say that Field Day brought together some disaffected people from both traditions who helped nationalists, in particular, to edge away from a narrow form of self-identity. Citizens of the Republic of Ireland, in particular, were happy to interpret *Translations* in a manner that reaffirmed their determination not to go to war over the divisions among Irish people, but to offer the hand of friendship to northern unionists.

Translations is set in Donegal in the 1830s and is a play about change. It marks the point at which Britain and Ireland were being minutely mapped for the first time, in a scheme executed by the soldiers of the Ordnance Survey of the United Kingdom. Potato blight is in the air, although the Great Famine is still some years away. The Irish language is in continuing decline, and the Ordnance Survey has begun the process of officially recording many placenames in an Anglicised form of their Gaelic original.

On the day the play opened, the *Derry Journal* wrote:

> The main characters, English and Irish, stand at a moment of cultural transition, and the play explores their response to this crisis in their personal lives and its effect on the historical life of the community.
>
> The play deals with the meeting of two cultures, and specifically of two languages, 'and the translations which follow — linguistic, psychological and social,' says Friel. He declines to be drawn on present-day parallels.
>
> 'The play has a great deal of political resonance,' says [Stephen] Rea. 'If we put it on in a place like Dublin's Abbey Theatre, its energy would be contained within the theatre and its clientele. But its energy is bound to spread much more profoundly through a place like Derry.'

The main Irish character in the play is a poor schoolmaster and scholar, played in the Guildhall by Ray McAnally. He is associated with the tradition of 'hedge schools', a tradition which is thought to have originated with the suppression of Catholicism under the penal laws. Apart from any other achievements, these schools are reputed to have imparted to generations of Irish people a smattering of classical learning. The schoolmaster recognises the decline of indigenous Gaelic culture and has taken to drink. His son Owen was played by Stephen Rea. Other actors included Liam Neeson.

One of the leading English characters is a military captain who patronises those who speak no English but who himself is quite uneducated. However, the Ordnance Survey party also includes as its orthographer a young and cultured lieutenant. He falls in love with Ireland and with an Irish girl and wants to remain in Donegal. He even tries to learn Irish. Friel plays with the tensions within and between both sides in this encounter of cultures.

While these ingredients could have become the recipe for a pure melodrama, Friel was already an established playwright and avoided professional disaster. *Philadelphia, Here I Come!* and other successes were behind him. Now, *Translations* succeeded in engaging the audience even as tragedy loomed over a romantic and complex set of relationships. The play received critical acclaim both north and south of the border, and in Britain, and was described immediately as 'a watershed in Irish theatre' (*Irish Press*, 25 September 1980). On the opening night, John Hume, leader of the SDLP and a future joint winner of the Nobel Peace Prize, said that he felt Brian Friel had made a marvellous gesture to the local people. Others who attended that first performance included Tom Murphy, the playwright, and Cyril Cusack, the actor.

For the *Derry Journal* of 26 September 1980, Noel McCartney reported:

> Underlining the whole play is the strong sense of identity which the hedge school community has arising from the Irish speaking culture, while the British army survey is out to destroy this. And indeed, as one person commented afterwards, 'They were speaking in different languages then and are still speaking in different languages now.'

McCartney noted that the audience 'is in the fortunate position that the actors playing the part of the hedge school community speak in English when they are supposed to be speaking in Irish.'

After five nights at the Guildhall, *Translations* moved to Belfast for a week at the Opera House. Then it went to Dublin's Gate Theatre for a fortnight, before returning north for a series of one-night performances in various towns. Field Day had received sponsorship from the Arts Council of Northern Ireland and a smaller grant from the Arts Council in the Republic. *Translations* has gone on to be performed very many times, at venues that include Dublin's Abbey Theatre.

As history, *Translations* is misleading. Its references to hedge schools are idealised. There is evidence that some later hedge schoolmasters actually encouraged the speaking of English and violently discouraged Irish speaking. Friel's representation of the Ordnance Survey is somewhat inaccurate and even unfair. It was a peaceful and quite indulgent venture that employed certain great Irish scholars, albeit on a project beneficial to those planning imperial intrusions or military control as well as to others. Even as Friel encouraged people to consider how they related to those of a different tradition, he reinforced certain stereotypes or myths about the past. Such paradoxes and contradictions are considered by Marilynn Richtarik in an engaging study of the Field Day Theatre Company and Irish cultural politics from 1980 to 1984 (*Acting Between the Lines*, Oxford, 1994).

Friel jokingly invented history at will when he went on stage at the end of the first performance of *Translations*. In a short speech at the Guildhall, he informed the capacity audience that the play had fulfilled yet another of those prophecies of the local saint, Colmcille. According to the *Derry Journal* of 26 September 1980:

> He said that while living in Iona the Saint prophesised that the town of the Oaks ['Derry' is from the Irish word for an oak tree] would in the second half of the 20th century host the Field Day Theatre Company. Amid laughter, he said that this had begun six weeks previously when they had come there to rehearse. Then, in three languages, aptly reflecting those dealt with in the play, he said 'Thank you' to the audience in Latin, Irish and English, in that order.

Translations, and Field Day itself, ultimately came to be seen as less important by the unionist tradition than it was by nationalists.

Field Day remained a loose affiliation of intelligent minds, producing various works and initiatives. Simultaneously and independently, its six directors pursued their individual careers. In October 1995, Seamus Heaney won the Nobel Prize for Literature. Announcing the award, the Swedish Academy referred to, among other matters, the fact that in 1990 Heaney had published *The Cure at Troy* (Faber and Faber, London). This was a version of Sophocles' *Philoctetes*, 'from the point of view of composition the most modern of the classical dramas'. The academy noted that Heaney's play had received a positive reception when staged by Field Day that same year. US President Bill Clinton quoted certain lines from *The Cure at Troy* on a number of occasions during his presidency. One such occasion was his visit to the Guildhall in Derry on 30 November 1995:

> History says, *Don't hope*
> *On this side of the grave.*
> But then, once in a lifetime
> The longed-for tidal wave
> Of justice can rise up,
> And hope and history rhyme.
>
> So hope for a great sea-change
> On the far side of revenge.
> Believe that a further shore
> Is reachable from here.
> Believe in miracles
> And cures and healing wells.

———

Clinton came to Belfast and Derry to support the Peace Process. Field Day, too, has been a part of that process of healing rifts and has helped significantly to bring about a reappraisal of how we see ourselves and each other on this island.

NÍ NEART GO CHUR LE CHEILE

The Point, Dublin, 30 April 1994

Riverdance is not just a musical. It is a national phenomenon. The show burst on to the stage at a time when many Irish people were ready for a cultural expression of their growing sense of achievement, pride and optimism. *Riverdance* was brasher than the Chieftains, more self-confident than the Clancy Brothers, and more self-important than the Dubliners ever were. It rhymed with the changing times as Ireland embraced the world. It had amplified sounds to rival those of U2, as well as the warm glow of tradition. It reached out to emigrants and their descendants, for whom President Mary Robinson kept a beacon lighting in the window of her official residence. The producers of *Riverdance* say their show 'floods the world in a vital joyous riot of celebration'.

Riverdance began as a trickle but became a torrent. What started as a minor seven-minute spot on an international television programme propelled Moya Doherty and John McColgan into the ranks of Ireland's new multimillionaires of entertainment.

In 1994, Moya Doherty was asked by her bosses at RTÉ to take responsibility for the Eurovision Song Contest, an annual spectacle due to be staged that year in Dublin. The contest has a certain recurrent fascination for up to 300 million television viewers who regard it as passable entertainment. National broadcasters know well that critics ridicule the Eurovision Song Contest, but they nevertheless tend to see it also as an opportunity to exhibit their professional skills and to promote their own lands. RTÉ is no exception, and so producer Moya Doherty and her director John McColgan planned something special. In the space that occurs between the last performance of the contestants and the calling in of votes from each participating country, *Riverdance* now exploded. For seven minutes, on 30 April 1994, TV viewers were taken by storm. A kind of Irish dancing never widely seen before burst on to the stage and out across Europe's airwaves. The dancing was choreographed and led by American-born Michael Flatley and Jean Butler. An Irish choir, Anúna, brought to the whole performance an ethereal Celtic air.

By the following morning, it was clear that *Riverdance* had been an instant success. Doherty and McColgan immediately set about exploiting its possibilities in conjunction with RTÉ and their creative team. The team included, most prominently, composer Bill Whelan and choreographer Michael Flatley. Flatley would later part company with *Riverdance* and launch his own successful show, *Lord of the Dance*. Meanwhile, *Riverdance* itself was a meteor about to blaze across the firmament of worldwide entertainment. The original routine was developed into a two-hour stage show.

When a single of *Riverdance* was released it went straight to No. 1 in the Irish charts and stayed there for eighteen weeks. In November 1994, tickets went on sale for the planned stage show. That same year, the original seven-minute version was also staged at the Royal Variety Performance in London, at the invitation of Prince Charles. When the single was released in Britain it reached No. 9 in the UK charts.

On 9 February 1995, the full stage show opened to a euphoric reception at the Point Theatre which is, appropriately for a show called *Riverdance*, located beside the River Liffey in Dublin. The run of five weeks was sold out. In April, the Irish video release went straight into the top position in the Irish charts. In May, the show was performed at the London Coliseum as part of the Royal Gala celebrations of the fiftieth anniversary of Victory in Europe, again at the invitation of Prince Charles. Twenty million television viewers reportedly tuned in. When the video of *Riverdance* was released in the United Kingdom it went straight up the charts and remained in first or second place for seven months. In June, the show opened at the

Labatt's Apollo in Hammersmith, London. It was to break a number of box-office records during its various runs on both sides of the Irish Sea.

In March 1996, *Riverdance* crossed the Atlantic and opened in New York at Radio City Music Hall. The tape went straight into the US video charts while the CD entered the Billboard World Music Chart at NO. 1. By October, *Riverdance* had created two touring companies, called after Irish rivers, the Lee and the Liffey, to cope with American demand. In November the Australian show was sold out in advance to 350,000 people, and *Riverdance* continued its US success by opening in Los Angeles. By the end of the year, almost one million people had seen it in the United States, while back in Britain the *Riverdance* CDs and videos had collectively spent 150 weeks in the UK charts. No Irish production had ever been so commercially successful.

During 1997, the first performance in a non-English speaking country took place in Oberhausen, Germany. On the first day that tickets became available for six Canadian cities, sales amounted to $11 million. By 1998, there was a third *Riverdance* touring company, the Lagan, which first performed in Vancouver. That same year, *Riverdance* became the top grossing variety and family entertainment show in the United States. What was the secret of its success? On 3 November 1999, Jeff Kearns reviewed it for *The Cupertino Courier* in California:

> The stage show itself is an odd phenomenon, as if ancient Celtic art forms took a wrong turn and wound up in Vegas. And it's indebted to both — which might explain its popularity and broad appeal. It's as if the Irish, hardly the Vegas types, are piping up after hundreds of years and speaking in neon tongues.

During 1999, the show received a rapturous reception in Tokyo and this underlined its universal as well as its national appeal. Plans were afoot for the Broadway opening which subsequently took place in the Gershwin Theatre on 16 March 2000. The production ran until 26 August 2001. By 5 March 2002, *Riverdance* had been performed 5,000 times throughout the world.

In 2003, *Riverdance* went to China and staged six remarkable performances in the Great Hall of the People, where Mao and other leaders have often addressed the assembled delegates of China's mighty Communist Party. The presidents of Ireland and China both attended the opening night. Some of the audience may have heard echoes of the Chieftains, great Irish traditional musicians who had earlier visited China. These performances of *Riverdance* brought to a close the first Beijing International Drama Festival. Meanwhile, Michael Flatley, the show's former star, had acquired Castlehyde House outside Fermoy and had become embroiled in a lengthy planning wrangle with Cork County Council over his proposed renovations and changes at the mansion and estate.

Irish people, in general, were delighted to bask in the reflected glory of *Riverdance*. Its success could be interpreted as another sign of their State's emergence from insularity and of their own development of a new image of themselves. *Riverdance* was sensual while also being traditional. It allowed one freedom to engage in mythological and romantic fantasies about our Celtic history and nature. The celebratory website of *Riverdance* shamelessly invokes 'our ancestors' and notes that the first half of the performance 'shows them coming to terms with the world and with themselves'.

As dancers flit across stage, the sound of their tapping and thudding is electronically enhanced and the mood swings from gay to sad. One scene features a lament for the great tragic figure of prehistoric Ireland when a lone piper mourns Cú Chulainn, 'the implacable Bronze Age warrior, the great hero of Celtic myth'. This reflective interlude is soon overtaken by a big thunderstorm, full of the fury and energy one might expect from a Celtic Tiger: 'the brute power of elemental forces, beyond human control, beyond human understanding; the defiant courage of those who stand out against these forces, who will not be beaten down'. And so it goes until, suddenly, the story spills beyond the shores of Ireland and encompasses our emigrants. There is a scene entitled 'American wake', which takes its title from the term used to describe the sad domestic farewells for those who were forced by hunger and driven by ambition to board an emigrant ship.

For too long, the Famine was the almost silent undertone of modern Irish discourse, and a nagging pain in the psyche. One of the triumphs of *Riverdance* has been that it has served as a vehicle for the imaginative journey across gulfs of time and space aimed at reconciling emigrants and their descendants with those who stayed 'at home', and that it has done so by means of a dynamic celebration of traditional culture. The note struck by the creators of *Riverdance* is consciously optimistic. 'Lift the wings', a scene which follows 'American wake', does not give in to despair:

> The music and dance that forged a sense of identity are now exposed to new and unfamiliar cultures. Ultimately, in the blending and fusion that follows, the emigrants find that the totality of human experience and expression is greater even than the sum of its many diverse parts.

Through this narrative device, the creators of *Riverdance* feel free to incorporate in their show many other dancing traditions, even those of places to which few Irish emigrated. These include Harlem, Andalucia and Russia. Thus, the show builds up to its great finale and its producers explain the ultimate message of that finale:

> We are one kind. We are one people now, our voices blended, our music a great world in which we can feel everywhere at home. *Ní neart go chur le cheile*: together we are strong.

Is it any wonder that standing ovations are usual when *Riverdance* ends? The thunder of hard shoes on stage may drive up the heartbeat of audiences in their seats, but it is the underlying sense of euphoria that truly intoxicates. We can do it. We have done it. The Irish have survived. Make our dream your dream. At the dawn of the twenty-first century, *Riverdance*, rather than 'A Soldier's Song', may be regarded, at least unofficially, as the national anthem of an ostensibly multicultural, outward-looking and largely prosperous Irish State.

SÚIL EILE

Baile na hAbhann, Co. Galway, 31 October 1996

It was dark outside, on a night of the year that was once widely celebrated in Ireland as the Celtic festival of *Samhain*. Inside the brightly lit Connemara Coast Hotel, 500 guests gathered to enjoy a reception hosted by RTÉ. We were there, on Hallowe'en 1996, to celebrate the launch of a new television station, one for which campaigners had fought hard and long. As fireworks lit up the sky over Galway Bay, *Teilifís na Gaeilge* (TnaG) went on air from its studios down the road in Baile na hAbhann. Fluent speakers of the Irish language, along with many others, welcomed the arrival of TNAG (later to be rebranded as TG4).

The first programme broadcast on TnaG was a one-hour 'extravaganza' of music and dance, incorporating panoramic views from around the country and brief greetings from President Mary Robinson and Taoiseach John Bruton. Ireland's Olympic swimming champion, Michelle Smith, also spoke. The theme of the first programme was 'lighting up', a theme that reflected not only the glare of TV lights but also the flames of *Samhain* (Hallowe'en) bonfires. References to our prehistoric past, as well as participation in the programme by the Galway street-theatre group Macnas, were indicative of a contemporary taste for Celtic motifs that were sufficiently vague to be stripped of any problematic elements that may have been part of actual Celtic practices. The opening programme was immediately followed by a drama specially commissioned for TnaG, and written by and starring the popular actor Gabriel Byrne.

Behind the celebrations of 1996 lay a harsh historical and social reality. The independent Irish State had not only failed to revive the Irish language; its policy, arguably, had even assisted in its decline. No amount of bluster or blarney could hide the fact that *Teilifís na Gaeilge* copperfastened our abandonment of an old aspiration. We had moved from revival and restoration to preservation and consolation.

The foundation of *Teilifís na Gaeilge* effectively marked a moment when we accepted that the Irish language would never again be the first national language, but agreed that it might be indefinitely maintained on a life-support system for the sake of diversity. The station's motto, *Súil eile*, meaning 'another eye' or figuratively 'another way of seeing', was ironically appropriate: for behind the romantic language of politicians such as Charles J. Haughey or Michael D. Higgins, who had both helped to create the station, lay a further shift in the emphasis of State policy on Irish from one of revival to one of survival.

The Constitution of Ireland, adopted in 1937, still proclaims boldly: 'The Irish language as the national language is the first official language' (Article 8), despite the fact that most official business has long been conducted in English. By 1996, when TnaG went on air, official efforts to force people to speak Irish, or to entice them to do so with material benefits, had come to be regarded by many, but not all citizens, as a disastrous failure, one for which no government has ever accounted.

Nationally, there is still considerable affection for Irish, far more indeed than there is an ability to speak it generally. A number of new schools have been founded in recent years (*gaelscoileanna*) for those who wish to see their children educated through Irish. The Good Friday Agreement affirmed its significance.

Most Irish people seem quite happy to respect the aspirations of Irish speakers and to honour the memory of generations for whom Irish was their first language. Most are happy to weave the old language into the particular tapestry of our heritage which we are fashioning for a new age and which is now on show for foreign investors and visitors at the dawn of the twenty-first century. Writing from Baile na hAbhann in that first week of TnaG, I observed in the *Sunday Independent*:

> TnaG is part of that confident modern Ireland which is very much in evidence as you drive west from Galway. Unlike the average employee of TnaG, those who are old enough to remember what this area was like even a couple of decades ago cannot but be struck by the changes. Expensive and comfortable modern housing abounds in a Galway which is bursting at the seams with business and trade.

Much of the programming on *Teilifís na Gaeilge* was intended to be in Irish. When it was launched, its promotional publicity contained this statement:

> The crucial role for TnaG is as a medium, a facilitator, a[n] enabler, a stage where we can tell our own stories in our own language. This vibrant young service is not being established as a preacher, teacher or axe-grinder. Rather it is the Irish illustration of Marshall McLuhan's axiom that the medium is the message.
>
> This will be a very different sort of TV service to what has gone before: it will tackle different challenges, address different agendas. It will project a vibrant vision of a changed Ireland in a new Europe.
>
> It will, in short, be another way of seeing.

There was broad political support for the establishment of TnaG. Murmurs of discontent in the media were not echoed by politicians, who recognised that the Irish language is an emotive topic on which it was still safer to say nothing that might be construed as hostile. Many who do not strongly support language revival tend to be indifferent rather than engaged against it. There is a broad acceptance of the culturally schizophrenic notion that Irish is 'our own language' (as the TnaG statement has it) when, in fact, the vast majority of us do not speak it coherently. Embedded in this fantasy are all kinds of dubious assumptions about nationhood, self and identity.

Prior to the opening of TnaG, there had been a long and sometimes acrimonious debate about the broader role of Irish in broadcasting. Among those who expressed themselves passionately on the subject were Bob Quinn, Donncha Ó hÉallaithe, Muiris Mac Conghail, Proinsías Mac Aonghusa and myself. In 1990 and 1991, when I was invited by RTÉ to produce independently two special TV programmes on issues in broadcasting (called 'What's in the Box?'), I gave to the Irish television lobby its first extended opportunity to explain its case in English on national television, and I was personally thanked for doing so by Proinsías Mac Aonghusa and others.

Early in March 1991, I wrote in *Playback* magazine: 'It is the track record of individual audiovisual professionals which demands a serious response to the proposals for an Irish language service.' I pointed out that responsibility for Irish language policy currently lay with the Taoiseach's department and noted that, 'one hears many complaints about how shoddily the proposal for an Irish language channel has been treated by the Taoiseach'. No sooner were my words in print than Taoiseach Charles Haughey surprised everybody (although I take no credit for this!). On 9 March 1991, he told his party's annual Ard Fheis: '. . . *is féidir liom a rá libh anocht go mbunófar an tseirbhís [teilifís trí Gaeilge] an bhliain seo chugainn*' (I can tell you tonight that the [Irish language television] service will be established next year.) The following day, Haughey elaborated on his commitment during a radio interview on RTÉ's *This Week*.

By Christmas, Haughey was still promising to deliver the station. He failed to do so. However, the momentum for its creation was continued by two ministers who were successively responsible for the project and both of whom represented the West Galway constituency in which *Teilifís na Gaeilge* was eventually built, and where a substantial number of Irish speakers lived. These ministers were Máire Geoghegan-Quinn of Fianna Fáil and Michael D. Higgins of Labour.

Higgins pressed the idea for an Irish language channel so hard that he got approval from the Cabinet to go ahead without there being any establishing legislation in place. It was decided to create the service as a subsidiary of RTÉ. Only in 2001 was statutory provision finally made for TnaG's possible separation from RTÉ. By then, TnaG had been rebranded as TG4. From the outset, Higgins 'requested' RTÉ to provide one hour of programming in Irish each day to TnaG, hours which he repeatedly insisted on describing as 'free', despite the fact that, each year, RTÉ has spent millions producing them ever since. In 2003 alone, TG4 cost RTÉ nearly €12m. The partly-Irish language station has also received an annual grant from the Minister for Finance (approximately €24m in 2004) on a grace and favour basis, with implicit consequences for its editorial independence. Between grants and the licence fee revenue that RTÉ spends on it, TnaG receives about 19 per cent of all public monies spent on broadcasting in the Republic of Ireland. It has been a welcome new source of business for independent producers.

In 1995, an official Green Paper on broadcasting made a number of assertions about the level of public competency in the Irish language. It stated categorically: 'Up to 350,000 people have good bilingual competence in Irish and English.' However, fewer than one in six of even this group now appear to be tuned into TG4 at any time. The most recent annual audience figures for TG4 show that the vast majority of its most popular programmes are in English. Many are Hollywood movies. These helped to boost its average daily audience in 2004 to about 3 per cent of the total national TV audience.

In March 2004, Ireland's failure in respect of the Irish language was underlined when the EU Commissioner responsible for audiovisual and cultural matters responded to demands that Irish be adopted as an official working language of the European Union. Ms Viviane Reding, herself a citizen of the multilingual State of Luxemburg, said:

> You know what you [Irish] should do in Ireland? Speak Irish, write Irish, be proud of Irish, use Irish in everyday language and show Irish culture to the 24 nations around you. But making it an official language doesn't bring you a thing.

MEDIA MATTERS

Lurgan, Co. Armagh, 28 September 2001

The *Sunday World*, launched on 25 March 1973, was Ireland's first modern tabloid newspaper. It is also the only Irish newspaper to have seen two of its journalists shot in the course of their employment. Both were attacked north of the border by loyalist gangs engaged in criminal and paramilitary activities. In May 1984, the *Sunday World*'s northern editor Jim Campbell was seriously injured but later returned to work. On 28 September 2001, Martin O'Hagan was shot dead in Lurgan, Co. Armagh.

The *Sunday World* has been very successful, both editorially and commercially. It burst on to the Irish media scene as a splash of newsprint colour, within a couple of years of RTÉ switching from black-and-white to colour television. The *Sunday World* mixes gossip, fun and news. From the start, big headlines and short paragraphs were combined with an unprecedented level of editorial interest in what was on TV and with a tendency to flaunt the identity of its columnists and reporters. The brash newcomer disturbed the Sunday newspaper market, which had long been dominated by the *Sunday Independent* and *Sunday Press*. Its slogan, 'We go all the way', was a sexual innuendo that echoed the cheekiness of British tabloids, even if the *Sunday World* itself was actually quite a bit more restrained than some tabloids across the Irish Sea.

The *Sunday World* has helped to change the way we take our media. Just over thirty years ago, when that particular tabloid first appeared, the Irish Press group still existed. At that time, British newspaper proprietors made little allowance for the fact that Ireland was another country, and simply circulated copies of their English editions here. In the Republic of Ireland, only RTÉ was licensed to transmit radio and television services (just one of each). Domestic video recorders and Playstations were still in the future, as was the Internet. Cinema multiplexes were an unknown luxury. Irish weekend newspapers contained no elaborate supplements and the shelves of newsagents stocked far fewer glossy magazines than they do now. Irish publishers were only beginning to capitalise on a growing market for books produced in Ireland.

The *Sunday World* was founded by two businessmen, Hugh McLoughlin and Gerry McGuinness. They were already partners in the Creation group, which successfully produced popular women's magazines. By 1983, they sold their controlling interest in the *Sunday World* to Independent Newspapers. The Independent group also bought into the *Sunday Tribune.* The latter had been launched in 1980, with Hugh McLaughlin again involved. This time, his partners were the Smurfit printing group and the editor-proprietor of *Hibernia* magazine, John Mulcahy. Those who feared that the Independent group might somehow abuse their strong position in the Irish media market became even more worried in 1995, when the Irish Press group collapsed and Ireland lost three titles that had served the State well during the previous half-century. These were the *Irish Press*, the *Evening Press* and the *Sunday Press.* In its final years, the daily *Irish Press* had been redesigned as a tabloid, but neither its readers nor its journalists ever seemed very comfortable with it in that format. This author's own first articles in a national newspaper appeared in the *Sunday Press* in the mid-1970s, when Vincent Jennings was its editor.

Gradually, English newspaper proprietors awoke to the potential of the Irish market. As technology and working practices changed, they began to introduce an increasing element of Irish coverage into special editions for Ireland. However, growing competition from abroad did not prevent the launch of yet another Irish paper, the *Sunday Business Post.* This continues to survive after several changes of ownership and despite the limited appeal of its title. Launched on 26 November 1989, the *Sunday Business Post* was the creation of four journalists: Damien Kiberd, Frank Fitzgibbon, Aileen O'Toole and James Morrissey. Funding came initially from a French investor, Jean-Jacques Servan-Schreiber.

There have also been some launches that failed. In October 1982 the *Sunday Tribune* attempted an unsuccessful *Daily News*. In 1996 the *Evening News* vanished into obscurity. In 2003 the *Dublin Daily* crashed on take-off. During 2001 and 2002 *The Irish Times* also got a fright. As part of its restructuring to recover from considerable overspending, staff were let go by 'The old lady of D'Olier Street'. Nevertheless, despite failures, readers today enjoy a wide choice. At weekends, in particular, papers are fatter than ever, containing supplements and give-aways such as free CDs featuring music compilations.

The newspapers have been to the fore in revealing many aspects of Irish life that were hidden even when the *Sunday World* was first launched. It repeatedly incurred heavy lawyers' bills as it tried to negotiate the choppy waters of Irish libel law. For a few years the *Sunday Independent* adopted a particularly aggressive style of commentary that reached a climax in the columns of Eamon Dunphy, before he parted company with that paper. Debates about libel reform and the need for a press council continue. The *Sunday Independent* continues to be the most widely read broadsheet in Ireland.

Tony O'Reilly, chairman of the Independent group, has asked people not to overlook the threat to Ireland's media from outside the country. On 30 July 1996, O'Reilly wrote to the Taoiseach, John Bruton:

> It must be clear to even the most biased observer that the enemy is not within but without. It is in the person of Rupert Murdoch, whose affection for Ireland is not among his most discerning characteristics. If Ireland is to have an indigenous print industry, it is going to have to have support from every quarter if it is to repulse the long-term efforts of Rupert Murdoch and his lieutenants in Ireland from simply taking over the Irish media through BSkyB, the *Sun*, *The Times*, the *Sunday Times* and the *News Of The World*.

However, while O'Reilly and others, including leftist commentators, lament the growing influence of Rupert Murdoch's media companies in Ireland, many of the Irish public appear to enjoy Murdoch's offerings. Indeed, the following summer, commentators saw reason to worry about O'Reilly's own power.

On 5 June 1997, the day before the general election, the *Irish*

Independent published an editorial column on its front page, rather than inside the paper as usual. Headed, 'For years we have been bled white — now it's pay-back time', this editorial complained about taxation levels and called on voters to support Fianna Fáil. Critics of this editorial noted that the outgoing coalition of Fine Gael and Labour had failed to close down unlicensed TV deflector systems that were seriously interfering with the State's licensed Multipoint Microwave Distribution System (MMDS or 'wireless cable') in which the Independent group had invested heavily. However, suggestions that the editorial had been influenced by narrow corporate considerations were denied.

Independent News & Media itself is a player in other countries, being one of Ireland's most successful companies. Summarising its activities in 2004, Tony O'Reilly said: 'We publish in six countries. Seventy per cent of our business is outside Ireland. We have twenty daily newspapers throughout the world. We print fourteen and a half million papers per week.' It owns the English *Independent* among its other titles.

In radio and television, RTÉ remains the dominant player, although its average share of the total audience is gradually decreasing. Only with the passing of the Radio and Television Act 1988 did Ireland finally join other European countries in allowing private investment in stations. Yet, because of RTÉ's dominance and other factors, it took ten years for the first privately owned TV station to attract sufficient investors to go on air. On 20 September 1998, TV3 was finally launched. Today, it is owned jointly by Canada's CanWest and Britain's Granada Television. TV3 is more popular than RTÉ's second television channel, first aired on 2 November 1978. It also contends with some competition from the bilingual TG4, which went on air on 31 October 1996.

Ireland was one of the countries that faced earliest the reality of transfrontier television, receiving British terrestrial channels by rooftop aerial or cable, and it is now experiencing the impact of satellite broadcasting. Rupert Murdoch's SKY dominates digital television services in Ireland partly because the Irish government failed to deliver an alternative Irish system of 'Digital Terrestrial Television'. New Irish satellite, cable and MMDS programme services are now beginning to come on stream.

We also enjoy a much broader range of radio than we did when the

Sunday World was launched. In May 1979, RTÉ was allowed by the government to respond to the challenge of pirate radio by opening a second national radio service, Radio 2 (now 2FM). Today, there are around three dozen stations broadcasting locally in the Republic, as well as certain other specialist services. Most have been successful, targeting city or county or community audiences, and some have changed hands for large sums of money. Moreover, they have not undermined Ireland's old network of successful and popular local newspapers. In some cases, local newspapers have even invested in local radio. About the same number of people listen to local radio, in general, as listen to RTÉ's national services. Since 1 May 1999, RTÉ has added the very welcome Lyric FM to the national airwaves, broadcasting classical music and other delights.

The one national radio service that is privately owned had a bad start. Century Radio was a commercial catastrophe, at least as much for managerial and technical reasons as for programming ones. This surprised those who hoped that the involvement of entertainment entrepreneur Oliver Barry would guarantee its success. The circumstances of its licensing were also clouded by factors that were later investigated by a tribunal of inquiry. Century collapsed and has been replaced by Today FM, which is commercially a modest success. None of the new stations has significantly challenged RTÉ's role as the most extensive and trusted provider of news coverage or current affairs. Indeed, some provide little news, current affairs or other speech programming of merit. One notable critical success for Today FM was *The Last Word*, when presented by Eamon Dunphy.

In Northern Ireland, the media landscape continues to be dominated by the BBC and Ulster Television, with the latter company now also investing heavily in local radio stations south of the border. In the North, as in the Republic, new and privately owned local radio stations have attracted many listeners. The established *Belfast Telegraph* has survived a number of changes in its ownership and is still the province's leading local broadsheet. During 2005, the *Irish News* had to contend with the arrival of a compact and more nationalist paper, the *Daily Ireland*. Launched on 1 February, *Daily Ireland* was an initiative of the Andersonstown News group in Belfast. Also within Northern Ireland, RTÉ's various television services are now more widely received than hitherto. Increasingly, media buyers here and abroad have been interested in buying media space for advertisers on an all-Ireland basis.

The number of books and magazines published in Ireland has also soared during the past three decades. In the 1970s, Irish books tended to come out one at a time, with each appearance being noted as a special event. Now there is a constant stream of publishing. From novels and local history through to specialist areas such as law or theology, Irish authors appear in print with an ease that was unimaginable during the first three-quarters of the twentieth century. New bookshops have sprung up around the country. This is one of the signs of affluence and confidence in Ireland today. Here, again, one finds that Rupert Murdoch has taken an interest. For example, his publishing firm HarperCollins signed a lucrative deal with the daughter of Taoiseach Bertie Ahern for the publication of Cecilia Ahern's debut novel, *PS. I love you* (Hyperion, 2004).

The names O'Reilly and Murdoch are mentioned frequently in discussions about the power of the media in Ireland. It is a way of personalising concerns about the control and ownership of newspapers and broadcasting organisations, which are of great importance to society today when people depend so heavily on the media for their information. Critics are understandably nervous that proprietors might seek to slant editorial content for their own commercial or ideological reasons. That such possibilities are of more than academic concern has been vividly underlined in Ireland by the murders of Veronica Guerin and Martin O'Hagan, and by the role that the media have played in uncovering political and other scandals. It matters who decides what stories are reported, and how they are covered.

The launch of the *Sunday World* marked a point when Irish people began to enjoy their media in new and different ways. Today, the media are less staid, more daring and varied, generally no less responsible, and arguably more entertaining and informative than ever. Few would wish to turn the media clock back forty years.

MAKING A MARK

Kilmainham, Dublin, 25 May 1991

In 1923, Mainie Jellett sparked critical controversy in Dublin. People were unsure of what to make of her 'Decoration'. It is said to have been the first abstract work exhibited in Ireland by an Irish artist, and some of those who saw it were dismissive.

Almost seven decades before the Irish Museum of Modern Art opened its doors, the newly independent State was being challenged imaginatively by its most creative citizens. Artists such as Jellett, Evie Hone and Jack Yeats were deeply committed to their visions of reality. While the Free State struggled to survive and could ill afford to spend much money on modern art, some of its politicians appreciated what was being attempted. For example, Jack Yeats and Éamon de Valera mutually admired one another. Artists, too, were sometimes embraced for what they contributed to the new sense of identity being forged by a society emerging from centuries of colonialism. Moreover, if some of the avant-garde were misunderstood or misrepresented, there was nothing peculiarly Irish about their experiences.

Ireland has a long history of visual expression, one that has survived times when material support for the visual arts was very limited. During the middle decades of the twentieth century, the Irish Exhibition of Living Art and the Rosc Exhibition were two ways in which Ireland's art world was able to keep in touch with international developments. The challenge was not always easy, and some found it soul-destroying or otherwise ruinous. More recently, in an era of rising prosperity and new ambitions, one man decided that Ireland should have what many still regarded as an extravagant luxury. On 25 May 1991, Taoiseach Charles J. Haughey opened the new Irish Museum of Modern Art (IMMA). It was a very nice sunny day, and guests from both home and abroad gathered at Kilmainham to celebrate the event. Haughey told them: 'At this time there is in Ireland a great artistic vitality, a surge of creativity, with many exciting achievements in different areas of endeavour.'

The IMMA is located in the former Royal Hospital, Kilmainham, a building said to be modelled on Les Invalides in Paris. It once served as a home for old soldiers. Founded in the seventeenth century on the site of an old monastery, the former hospital was renovated by the Irish government before being fitted out for art works. There was some disagreement about its suitability as an exhibition space, and critics speculated about the IMMA's role in relation to existing galleries. However, few people with an interest in culture were entirely negative, and the popular press was provided with a permanent opportunity to express periodically its amazement and outrage at the appearance or cost of particular works of art.

In the *New York Times*, on 18 August 1991, Michael Kimmelman wrote enthusiastically about the IMMA and about another new institution in Frankfurt:

> Yet two more signs of Europe's re-emergence in recent years as a powerhouse in contemporary art have come this summer in the form of new museums. The creation of the Irish Museum of Modern Art in Dublin, under the charge of one of Europe's most charismatic and innovative directors, is an especially remarkable event, coming as it does from a country that has not made much of a mark on the history of the visual arts since the Book of Kells.

The first director of the IMMA was Declan McGonagle and he ensured that those who questioned the need for Ireland's latest gallery were given their answer. His opening exhibition was aptly entitled, 'Inheritance and Transformation'. During its run, McGonagle proclaimed that he saw his institution as

> making an important strategic contribution to the development of the general community, in this case through visual arts

> programming and the associated debates and ideas that go with it. We aim to provide an essential platform for a wider understanding of what contemporary art is all about and a vehicle for Irish artists to meet the world.

Haughey took a personal interest in the arts and was, no doubt, pleased to have a monument such as the IMMA that will be long associated with his period as Taoiseach — just as the new national library in Paris is associated with the presidency of François Mitterand. For years, critics have complained quite fairly that official policy towards the arts in Ireland has been inconsistent and short term. Haughey's decisions to allow tax exemptions for artists and to authorise the opening of the IMMA were undoubtedly somewhat flamboyant and personal gestures, if not even egotistical. However, the man was an astute politician with a keen sense of what was popular, and he judged quite rightly that the people would be proud of his cultural measures. He knew the value of a symbol. Irish people were ready to subscribe to new symbols that cost the Exchequer money but that reflected our reputation as an island of saints and scholars. Today, we have a plethora of arts centres and a multitude of arts administrators that would have been unimaginable in the quite recent past.

The opening of the new museum of modern art expressed and encouraged a change in Irish society. Irish people had become more willing to tolerate and even to enjoy a broad range of art, for various reasons. Some were intellectually engaged as never before, and fired by an enthusiasm for the challenges and insights of contemporary artists. Others simply felt that the trappings of an emergent strong economy and a modern European state must include works of art that could hold their own in comparison with others on the international stage. If that meant spending public money on acquiring works that were every bit as mystifying and provocative as Mainie Jellett's 'Decoration' had once been, then so be it. The fact that the IMMA, its administration and acquisitions have not been above criticism since 1991, is itself a sign of creative and intellectual vibrancy.

Rituals

We have each sobered awake in the abyss of dawn,
Longing for a revelation to overwhelm our futility.

DERMOT BOLGER, 'Two Labouring Men: 1. Matt Talbot, 1856–1925'
FROM *Internal Exiles*, 1986

POPE AND PEOPLE

Knock, Co. Mayo, 30 September 1979

It seems so very different now. In 1979, the Pope's visit to Ireland appeared to herald a confident new phase in the development of Irish Catholicism. Now, it looks more like the end of an era.

Pope John Paul II rose at Galway Racecourse and told the assembled throng of teenagers, slowly and steadily, in his deep Polish timbre, 'Young people of Ireland, I love you.' He spoke movingly of his belief in youth, and sincerely of 'the true greatness of your own humanity'. Little did we know then that others standing near him had reason to take a personal interest in the welfare of youth. The Pope's master of ceremonies for the day, Bishop Eamonn Casey, had a dark secret. Casey had a son in America, supported to some extent materially out of diocesan funds, but supported to no great extent emotionally by the bishop who was his father. The other prominent cheerleader on that big day, the populist Fr Michael Cleary, was also a parent and had a continuing relationship with his children's mother. Singing priest and radio star Cleary made being a priest look easy, and he was not averse to scoffing at those who were critical of the Church.

The Pope was in Ireland especially to honour Knock, Co. Mayo, by officially elevating its modern church to the status of a basilica. The Virgin Mary, St Joseph and St John are said to have appeared at Knock to fifteen witnesses, old and young, on 21 August 1879. Speaking at Knock, the Pope described his visit to the shrine as 'the goal of my visit to Ireland'. He stated that since he had first learnt that the centenary of the shrine was to be celebrated in 1979, he had 'felt a strong desire to come here'. He added, 'I want all of you to know that my devotion to Mary unites me, in a very special way, with the people of Ireland.' He described Mary, mother of God, as 'Queen of Ireland'. For him, as for many Irish Catholics then, the term 'people of Ireland' appeared to be synonymous with 'Irish Catholics'.

Knock is fondly regarded as a place of pilgrimage and as a centre of spiritual and even physical healing. Its many visitors provide a thriving trade for the owners of souvenir stalls and refreshment stands. Public devotion has resulted in that isolated location in the wilds of Mayo becoming a hive of commercial activity. The late Canon James Horan modernised and developed the shrine complex itself. He was a popular man and his life's work was crowned by the arrival of Pope John Paul II. Over time, Knock has become a local tourist industry as well as a place of worship.

I was RTÉ television's enthusiastic reporter at Knock. In my commentary on the Pope's visit, I resisted a skittish temptation to inform viewers of the full verse of the New Testament which contains the words that are found on the gable end of the old chapel at Knock (Mark 11: 17). Those words, 'My house shall be a house of prayer to all nations . . .' also occur in the Hebrew Scriptures at Isaiah 56: 7, and their inscription on the old gable is often said to have been prophetic of Knock's subsequent status as a shrine. However, when Jesus repeated the words (Mark 11: 17), he added another phrase from the Old Testament (Jeremiah 7: 11): '. . . but ye have made it a den of thieves.' Critics of commercialisation at Knock might find the full verse even more prophetic than the present abbreviated version.

RTÉ reporters had been told by RTÉ not to refer to any political or other demonstrations, unless a shot of these had been selected by the director to be shown on screen. RTÉ feared that minor demonstrations might be given disproportionate publicity. The number involved in any protest was likely to be small relative to the many others present. So, when a man at Knock ran forward screaming and the Pope stopped and looked up at him, viewers were not informed by me of what had occurred. No camera showed the ten or more Gardaí who grabbed him from every side and whisked him away, back to a vehicle in which he was then transferred to the mental hospital from which he had been released for the day, as I later learnt.

But if that man was disturbed, most Irish Catholics were elated by the Pope's visit. On arriving above Ireland, the specially decorated Aer Lingus jet had swooped over a massive gathering of the faithful in Dublin's Phoenix Park. He joined that crowd sometime later to celebrate Mass. A massive Cross that was erected for the occasion still marks the spot, not far from the official residence of the President of Ireland.

Thousands swarmed on to the streets of Dublin to see the Pope, and his schedule was allowed to slip. An important meeting with representatives of other Christian Churches was truncated. Some saw this change of schedule as indicative of the reluctance of the Irish Catholic hierarchy to engage to any significant extent in ecumenical dialogue. He also failed to stop in a working-class area where he was expected to meet local people.

The Pope did not cross the Irish border. However, he did travel to Co. Louth, just south of that political divide and home to some people with strongly nationalist views. There, he made a moving plea for peace: 'On my knees, I beg you to turn away from the paths of violence . . . violence only delays the day of justice.' It was the other great message of his tour, the first being his plea to young people in Galway to keep the faith. The evident strength of his appeal for peace, sustained at some length and with no ambiguity, had an incalculable but almost certainly significant impact on attitudes in Ireland towards the continuing political violence in Northern Ireland.

The Pope flew around Ireland in a helicopter, and moved through crowds aboard his specially constructed Popemobile. Older people recalled the Eucharistic Congress of 1932, when crowds had also gathered in the Phoenix Park and when senior political figures threw themselves at the feet of the papal envoy to Ireland. John McCormack's rendition of *Panis Angelicus* at the Eucharistic Congress has echoed down the decades. Pope John Paul specifically recalled the event when he spoke in Dublin: 'We are one in faith and spirit with the vast throng which filled this Phoenix Park on the occasion of the last great Eucharist hosting held on this spot.'

If the Eucharistic Congress was an act of deference by the Irish State, the papal visit felt more like an act of triumphal celebration by Irish Catholics. During centuries of struggle for survival and freedom, most Irish people's religious identities had become intertwined with their national and political loyalties. However, considered today, the papal visit of 1979 looks like the end of a more recent phase in the evolution of the Irish psyche. That phase began, symbolically, with the visit of John F. Kennedy in June 1963. These two events marked a growth in the confidence of the Irish people. The first allowed the Irish to wave US flags while harbouring great ambitions for the indigenous Irish economy. The second permitted them to wave papal flags as a conscious act of free will, rather than supine obedience. It was a free will which, subsequently, came to be exercised ever more independently of the authority of that same Pope and his Irish bishops. The reaction to both visits may be understood by reference to the changes being wrought on the Irish consciousness as a result of people's engagement with the domestic, economic and social reforms spearheaded by Taoiseach Seán Lemass, and with those Church reforms initiated by Pope John XXIII through the Second Vatican Council.

As a boy of 12, I stood near the entrance to the Phoenix Park clutching my small US flag and gazing up at the bronzed and smiling hero who was John F. Kennedy. As his open limousine drove past, he saluted a crowd who regarded him almost mystically as the epitome of Irish success, and whose intense joy can be understood as arising from a sense that if the Kennedys from Wexford could make it big as emigrants, then any Irishman might make it big. Suddenly, the failure of emigration was transformed into a success story. JFK's dynamism and good looks added a sexual undertone to public admiration. Such was the adulation of Kennedy in the public mind that his facial features were later set in mosaic in a side altar of Galway Cathedral, along with those of the leader of the 1916 Rebellion, Patrick Pearse. JFK and his wife Jackie were also to be found flanking Pope John XXIII in a popular triptych which adorned the walls of many Irish guest houses.

But if the reaction to JFK's visit reflected a new mood and attitude among the Irish, it was still not time to throw off old ways. A great debt was owed to the Catholic Church and people had genuine affection for the saintly Pope John XXIII. He encouraged people to think afresh about their faith by means of his great Vatican council. It would take time for people to come to realise that the Catholic Church was not about to change as much as the laity might wish, and for people to begin consciously to distance themselves from it, especially in respect of family planning. That process involved a certain level of guilt, a guilt which was assuaged by the affirmative welcome for Pope John Paul II in 1979. The visit became a hail and farewell to a model of religious organisation that no longer suited a changing and more prosperous nation. The fact that crowds flocked to 'the moving statue' of Mary, at Ballinspittle, in the 1980s, and greeted the relics of St Thérèse of Lisieux, brought around Ireland in 2001, was never likely to reverse the trend towards independence of mind in spiritual matters.

Today, people's divergence from the hierarchy of the Catholic Church is clear, notably in relation to those very matters of sexuality which long preoccupied many of the priests and princes of the Church, even as they so abysmally failed to protect children from being sexually abused. Some citizens have simply given up on the Catholic Church, and even given up religion itself. Significantly, after the death of Pope John Paul II on 2 April 2005, Taoiseach Bertie Ahern decided not to declare a day of national mourning because it might unduly interrupt commercial activities. His decision, which was criticised by some Catholics, was a sign of the changed relationship between Church and State.

During his visit, Pope John Paul II set out to change Irish attitudes towards violence. His heartfelt plea for peace at Drogheda, Co. Louth, may well have succeeded in influencing those attitudes and in facilitating the subsequent 'peace process'. The cathartic or purging effect of the papal celebrations themselves was also considerable. Irish people felt that they had discharged a debt to the Catholic Church and were now free to relate to it in new ways. Despite subsequent disappointments, many still hope that it will continue to play a part in their lives and they in its.

'H' IS FOR 'HUNGER STRIKE'

Long Kesh, Co. Antrim, 5 May 1981

Bobby Sands is remembered in Ireland. But if you ask people to name the other nine men who died on hunger strike in 1981, few could identify even one. Elected while on hunger strike as Sinn Féin member of parliament for Fermanagh-south Tyrone on 20 April 1981, Sands was the 'officer' commanding Provisional IRA members in Long Kesh Prison, which was also known as 'The Maze'.

Not even the most revisionist nationalist or ardent unionist could ignore the impact of 'the dirty protest' and hunger strike. The deaths conferred a dignity on the men's lives, which were typical in many respects of those of poorer Catholics in areas where social injustice was severe and where many nationalists expected little from the State other than hand-outs and oppression. However, the hunger strikers' families were not the only ones to suffer that year. During the seven months of the hunger strike, at least another 69 people died as a result of political violence in Northern Ireland, and some of them were killed by members of the organisations to which the ten hunger strikers belonged.

The hunger strike is an ancient way of shaming your enemies and defeating them by the moral force of your actions. During the twentieth century, a number of Irishmen had starved themselves to death in prison in Britain and Ireland. For example, on 25 October

1920, Terence MacSwiney died on hunger strike after seventy-four days, having been arrested by the British. He was not only a local commander of the IRA, but also a poet and the lord mayor of Cork.

The violence for which IRA and INLA men were imprisoned in the H-blocks of Long Kesh was generally regarded as misguided by the electorate on both sides of the border. Most Irish people saw the IRA at best as a last resort of defence in the event of sectarian attacks. Many feared and resented IRA attempts to impose its will at gunpoint. However, people distinguished between the general objectives of the IRA and the narrower objectives of the hunger strikers in seeking certain prison conditions that would reflect what they claimed to be their rightful status as 'prisoners of war'. One did not have to agree that they were 'prisoners of war' — still less that the illegal IRA had any right to wage 'war' on behalf of the Irish people — to recognise that there was a political dimension to their incarceration or to be disturbed by the attitude of the United Kingdom government towards them. The INLA had even less public support than the IRA, being commonly regarded as an organisation for the most extreme of paramilitary nationalists, or 'mad dogs' as they were dubbed by some.

Little did the architects who designed the H-shaped prison blocks for paramilitaries at Long Kesh envisage that the 'H' might come to symbolise a hunger strike by the inmates that would have traumatic political effects. The hunger strikes galvanised a generation into recognising the high level of alienation and anger that existed in certain Catholic communities. They obliged those who lived on both sides of the border to ask themselves if they had uncaringly washed their hands of nationalist communities in Northern Ireland that had long been subjected to systematic institutional injustice. Later, the IRA atrocity at Enniskillen would similarly force people to examine their consciences for any residual or underlying 'sneaking regard' for terrorists.

IRA prisoners and other 'terrorists' had enjoyed 'special category' status prior to 1 March 1976. When a policy decision was made to withdraw that privilege, new IRA inmates refused to wear prison uniforms and wrapped themselves in prison blankets. It was entirely a matter of principle. The H-blocks themselves were comfortable in comparison with most civilian prison accommodation. The 'blanket protest' became more difficult when attempts were made to oblige the men to go entirely naked in the washrooms and when prisoners responded by refusing to leave their cells. Subsequently, as the confrontation escalated, prisoners began to smear their own excrement on the walls of the cells. This was known as 'the dirty protest' and led on to a thwarted hunger strike in 1980. This was ended in the mistaken belief that certain concessions had been won.

The fatal hunger strike of 1981 was a last resort for the men in Long Kesh. They were determined that they would not submit to a prison regime that had been designed for 'ordinary' criminals. The IRA and the INLA, regardless of the brutality of some of their actions, saw themselves as engaged in a noble struggle for political freedom from Britain. More specifically, their members in jail wanted to be finally recognised as 'special category' prisoners. The ten men who died while on hunger strike were aged between 23 and 30. They were:

Bobby Sands (IRA)
Grew up in north Belfast in a mainly loyalist area. His family was one of many forced to move home when he was a boy, because of sectarian intimidation. He was subsequently intimidated out of a job. He died on 5 May 1981. His solicitor, Pat Finucane, was later murdered by loyalists acting in collusion with members of the UK security forces.

Francis Hughes (IRA)
A first cousin of Thomas McElwee (below), both from Bellaghy, Co. Derry. His parents were small cattle farmers. A very active member of the IRA, who is said to have killed more than a dozen people. He died on 12 May 1981.

Raymond McCreesh (IRA)
Grew up in an area later known as IRA 'bandit-country', in south Armagh, where the British army did not stand on ceremony. He was captured during an attempt by himself and other IRA men to attack an army observation post. The IRA later killed a civilian whom they claimed had assisted in his capture. McCreesh died on 21 May 1981.

Patsy O'Hara (INLA)
From Derry City, he was aged 15 on Bloody Sunday. His parents owned a small pub and grocery shop. An active member of the Irish Republican Socialist Party (the political wing of the INLA), he was jailed for eight years for possession of a hand grenade. He died on 21 May 1981.

Joe McDonnell (IRA)
Born in Belfast's Lower Falls Road area. He and his wife were forced out of their first home by a loyalist mob. Interned for several months in 1972, he later joined the IRA. Fleeing after a firebomb attack on a furniture company, he was captured along with Bobby Sands. In June 1981, while imprisoned, he fell 315 votes short of being elected to the Dáil for the constituency of Sligo/Leitrim. He died on 8 July 1981.

Martin Hurson (IRA)
Born in Cappagh, a very nationalist area of east Tyrone. Said to have not been involved in paramilitary activity prior to 1976, in which year he was arrested and allegedly tortured by the RUC. He was later charged with IRA membership, conspiracy, and possession of a landmine. The judge dismissed medical evidence of ill treatment and sentenced him on the basis of signed admissions to twenty years in jail. During the hunger strike, he failed to be elected for the Longford/Westmeath constituency in the Republic's general election. He died on 13 July 1981.

Kevin Lynch (INLA)
From the Dungiven area of Co. Derry. In 1977 he was sentenced to ten years in jail. He died on 1 August 1981.

Kieran Doherty (IRA)
From Andersonstown in Belfast. His mother was a convert from Protestantism to Catholicism. Two of his grandparents had been chased from their north Belfast homes during the pogroms in Northern Ireland that followed the partition of Ireland. In 1976, he was arrested on an IRA bombing mission in Belfast and sentenced to eighteen years in jail. During the hunger strike he was elected to Dáil Éireann for the Cavan/Monaghan constituency in June 1981. He died on 2 August 1981.

Thomas McElwee (IRA)
A first cousin of Francis Hughes (above). Both from Bellaghy, Co. Derry. An IRA activist from an early age. He participated in bombings of commercial centres. In 1976, he lost an eye in a premature IRA bomb explosion and was subsequently sentenced to twenty years for possession of explosives and for the killing of a woman in a separate

car bomb attack that same day. He died on 8 August 1981.

Michael Devine (INLA)

Born at a former US army base in Derry, which was a slum for Catholic families. His father had served in the British merchant navy but was an unemployed coalman. Michael became active in socialist politics. He was on the Bloody Sunday march. Around then, he took to participating in gun attacks on the British army. He was a founder member of the INLA. In 1977, he was sentenced to twelve years' imprisonment. He died on 20 August 1981.

Among the 69 other people who died during the hunger strike were Joanne Mathers, a Protestant mother who was shot in the head while collecting census returns in Derry. The IRA denied killing her, although the RUC said that the gun involved had been used in previous IRA shootings. Also killed at this time was John Robinson of Armagh, who had left the Ulster Defence Regiment seven years earlier and who was not involved in politics. The IRA murdered him as he drove a works minibus. At the time, a nationalist SDLP councillor described Robinson as 'one of nature's gentlemen'. Others to die included Eric and Desmond Guiney, a father and 14-year-old son, whose milk lorry crashed when stoned by a mob after the death of Bobby Sands. Soldiers and RUC men were blown up and shot down, while Catholics were slain in sectarian attacks by the loyalist UDA/UFF and killed by plastic bullets fired during rioting. No research into the events of 1981 is complete without reviewing the catalogue of carnage reflected in the relevant pages of *Lost Lives: The Stories of the Men, Women and Children who Died as a Result of the Northern Ireland Troubles* (edited by David McKittrick and others, Edinburgh and London, 1999).

The hunger strike itself was called off on 3 October 1981, on the initiative of some families who no longer wanted their relatives to become martyrs for a cause. The hunger-strikers are alleged to have been willing to end their protest earlier, but to have been overruled by IRA commanders outside the H-blocks.

During the hunger strike, black flags were hung and planted at night throughout Ireland in a menacing show of support. The United Kingdom government made only minor concessions, but it had badly mishandled the situation. The IRA gained massive publicity at home and abroad, and Sinn Féin benefited politically from the deaths. Prime Minister Margaret Thatcher had been determined to appear strong in the face of terrorism and threats, but she had handed a propaganda victory to her greatest enemies in Northern Ireland. Three years later, on 12 October 1984, the IRA tried to wipe out Thatcher and her Cabinet when it bombed the Grand Hotel in Brighton during the Conservative Party Conference, murdering five people.

SPORTS FEVER

Genoa, Italy, 25 June 1990

Oh, what sweet moments! People held their breath as Packie Bonner dived. Saved! David O'Leary took the final penalty. Yes! The Republic of Ireland erupted in a celebration of victory over Romania, the score 5-4 after extra time. It had been a tense penalty shoot-out at the end of a tough match in the Luigi Ferraris Stadium in Genoa, Italy. Here and now, on 25 June 1990, this was magic. Ireland qualifying for the World Cup had been remarkable. But getting beyond the second phase of the competition was just amazing. Never mind that Italy would beat us 1-0 in the quarter-finals in the great Olympic Stadium in Rome. We had arrived.

In high spirits, greeting one another excitedly, people poured on to the streets. We had crouched over our TV sets long enough, enjoying the pain and pleasure of following Ireland's soccer team. We were delighted by 'Jack's army', a group of Irishmen and Irish descendants brought together by Englishman Jack Charlton.

Charlton himself once played for England during his home team's most glorious phase. Then, from 1986 to 1995, he was employed by the Football Association of Ireland as its team's manager. His tactic of keeping opponents under constant pressure helped to ensure unprecedented success for 'the boys in green'. He led them to the European Championship finals in 1988, and to the World Cup finals in both 1990 and 1994. Packie Bonner, Ray Houghton, Andy Townsend, Tony Cascarino, Niall Quinn, David O'Leary, Paul

McGrath, Roy Keane and others became heroes on the field, and household names.

Their moments of sporting glory are too numerous to list here. Everyone has her or his own favourite. Mine is Ray Houghton's goal against Italy on 6 June 1994. We watched it with our children in a high-rise hotel room in Vancouver, Canada. God only knows what any other guests thought that day as our room erupted with cheering and laughter. Separated by thousands of miles of land and sea from home, we were united with Ireland through time zones in our focus on the game that was being broadcast live from the Giants Stadium in New Jersey. It seemed like a miracle that Ireland had actually beaten the mighty Italy, especially after our loss in Rome four years earlier. Nor, by any means, was that particular goal Houghton's sole moment of great personal glory. In 1988, during the finals of the European Championship, he had headed the ball past goalkeeper Peter Shilton to give Ireland its first-ever victory against England in a major football competition. The old enemy was finally whipped!

The Irish were not interested in those who moaned about the football team not being 'really' Irish, about the rules being bent to let people play in a green jersey who had never before been to Ireland. Begrudgers complained that many players had a tenuous link to the Emerald Isle through some ancestor of a generation or two ago. So what? Ireland had witnessed wave after wave of emigration, and this was a way of connecting with those emigrants and their descendants. When she was elected President of Ireland in November 1990, Mary Robinson made a big fuss of our great 'diaspora', as she called them, placing a perpetual light in a window of her official residence in order to welcome such people 'home'. At international matches, Irish football fans sang poignant verses of 'The Fields of Athenry', a lament about loss and forced migration that became the team's unofficial anthem. It alternated with the more boisterous if unlikely chant, 'Olé, olé, olé', with its accompanying Mexican wave.

The euphoria that gripped Ireland as Jack's army advanced is linked in many people's minds with a growing sense of national self-confidence, with the birth of the 'Celtic Tiger'. We were certainly proud of 'our' soccer team, as it asserted itself on the international stage, and gratified that 'our' supporters were better behaved and better regarded than those of some other countries, especially England.

Jack's army was the main focus of sporting attention in Ireland at the end of the twentieth century, but its achievements were not the only ones to feature in our new tapestry of national sporting celebrations. Even before the football team began to score its greatest successes, we were enjoying other victories.

On 8 June 1985, boxer Barry McGuigan became the WBA Featherweight Champion of the World. He was the first Irish world champion in more than three decades. He defeated Eusebio Pedroza at Loftus Road, London, to win the title. Known to some as the 'Clones Cyclone', after his home town of Clones in Co. Monaghan, McGuigan went on to defend the title successfully twice, before losing it in difficult circumstances at Las Vegas in June 1986. His successful challenger was a Texan who was better able to cope with the stifling heat. McGuigan subsequently broke up with his manager and mentor, Barney Eastwood. The professional couple were well known to TV audiences nationally, and seeing them split was like watching a divorce.

Although born and bred in Clones, McGuigan had joined the Northern Ireland boxing team for a period and had taken British citizenship. He won a gold medal as a bantamweight in the Commonwealth Games of 1978 in Canada. Although himself reared a Catholic, he married a Protestant and became the object of some sectarian and nationalist venom. 'Barry the Brit' ran one headline in a political paper. He went on to box for the Republic of Ireland. He claimed later to be fighting for all the people of Ireland and he flew neither the Union Jack nor the Tricolour on the night of his World Championship bout. Instead, he bore a blue flag with a white dove of peace. His father, Pat, was a singer who represented Ireland at the Eurovision Song Contest of 1968, when he finished in third place.

Also representing Ireland, when he went to Paris to watch Stephen Roche win the *Tour de France* on 24 July 1987, was Taoiseach Charles J. Haughey. This most demanding of cycling competitions takes riders on a gruelling course that requires of them great energy and fitness. Roche had collapsed at one point, suffering from exhaustion, but managed to stay in the competition and finally win it. Roche's ability to keep going delighted commentators such as Phil Liggett of Channel 4 who, as Roche emerged into view during one particularly tough Alpine stage, shouted excitedly, 'There's someone coming through the mist. It can't be! It is! It's Roche! It's Stephen Roche!'

Haughey, like most of the nation whom he represented, had never been known to exhibit a great deal of interest in cycling. However, he caught the public mood by being at the finishing line to convey the nation's best wishes. Another Irish cyclist who did well internationally was Seán Kelly.

There was more boxing glory for Ireland in 1992 at the Barcelona Olympics. Welterweight Michael Carruth became Ireland's first gold medallist since Ronnie Delany won the 1,500 metres thirty-six years earlier. Bantamweight Wayne McCullough won bronze. On 18 March 1995, boxing fans particularly enjoyed themselves when Steve Collins beat Chris Eubank to take the WBO Super Middleweight title at Millstreet, Co. Cork

It was not just Irish men who could win internationally. Sonia O'Sullivan had broken various Irish track records before coming to the Barcelona Olympics of 1992. There, she just failed to take a bronze medal in the 3,000 metres. By 1995, her many achievements included winning a gold medal at the World Championships in Gothenburg, Sweden. That year, she was designated 'Athlete of the Year' by *Track and Field News*, which was one of the ways in which her talents were by then being recognised abroad. The public believed that she might well win a gold medal for Ireland at the Atlanta Olympics in 1996. At first everything went well in Atlanta and she convincingly won her 5,000 metres heat. Unfortunately, disaster then struck. She fell behind in the finals and eventually dropped out. She also failed to qualify for the 1,500 metres. She was reported to be suffering from diarrhoea, but her condition had been made worse by bickering between the Olympic Council of Ireland and a body representing Irish athletes. She was forced to change her branded clothing immediately before taking part in the 5,000 metres heats, because each of the organisations had a different sponsor.

However, there was an unexpected consolation for Ireland in the astonishing performance of swimmer Michelle Smith. In 1996, she, not Sonia O'Sullivan, made sporting history by becoming the first Irish woman to win an Olympic gold medal. Mary Peters, who had been a gold medallist for Northern Ireland in the pentathlon in 1972, was born in Lancashire. At Atlanta, Smith won not just a single gold medal but three of them, and a bronze also. The only other Irish person ever to win more than one Olympic medal was Pat O'Callaghan, who took gold in 1928 and 1932 for throwing the hammer. In Smith's home village of Rathcoole, Co. Dublin, the community celebrated. Because she spoke Irish fluently, Bord na Gaeilge sponsored her as a symbol of potency in its efforts to encourage people to learn and speak Gaeilge. Suggestions by opponents in Atlanta that her results were too good to be true were rejected by Irish people as mean spirited and malicious. Smith was advised in person by Bill Clinton, President of the United States, to ignore such chatter.

While Michelle Smith was still riding high on the back of her Atlanta victories, Sonia O'Sullivan began to make a magnificent comeback. During 1998, she won the World Cross Country Championships in Morocco, and went on to take gold in the 5,000 and 10,000 metres races of the European Championships in Budapest. Thereafter, Sonia continued to have great successes, although she never fully achieved what many believed was her true potential. The public was thrilled when, on 25 September 2000, she won a silver medal in the 5,000 metres at the Sydney Olympics. She thus became the first Irish woman to win an Olympic medal for a track event. Her success was all the more remarkable because she had given birth to a daughter the previous year.

In 1998, the glorious story of Irish triumphs was tarnished when FINA banned Michelle Smith from competitive swimming for four years. FINA, the international swimming authority, determined that she had tampered with a urine sample demanded from her as part of a routine drugs test. She has continued to deny that she took any banned substance and was never stripped of her Olympic medals. Her husband and coach, a Dutch discus thrower, had earlier received his own doping ban. Ireland, today, does not speak much of Michelle Smith. In the *Sunday Independent* on 23 May 2004, Donal Lynch concluded his profile of her by remarking, 'She was simply too good to be true.'

Also in 1998, a drug scandal damaged the reputation of competitors in the *Tour de France.* That happened to be the year in which, uniquely, the race was held partly in Ireland. The cyclists passed through Bray, Co. Wicklow, and the tour's directors laid a wreath at the nearby memorial to Shay Elliot. Elliott, who died young in 1971, had been the first Irishman to win a yellow jersey in the *Tour de France.*

During 2004, Cian O'Connor's winning of a gold medal for show-jumping at the Athens Olympics, on the horse Waterford Crystal, was also tarnished when tests showed up traces of banned substances in his horse's blood. He was later stripped of the medal.

Nevertheless, sporting achievements have continued to give the Irish pleasure, as they do many people everywhere. If Ken Doherty won at snooker, or Pat Eddery rode a winner, or Paul McGinley sank a vital putt, there was rejoicing. Ireland's defeat of World Cup champions England, which helped us win rugby's Triple Crown in 2004, was another moment to savour. The fact that our rugby squad is drawn from both sides of the Irish border makes any such success all the sweeter.

In September 2002, Paul McGinley provided an abiding image of Irish sporting pride when he sank a long putt to clinch the Ryder Cup for European golfers at the Belfry. A mob of photographers captured the image as he cavorted waist deep in the cold lake that bordered the eighteenth green, draping himself in a wet Irish Tricolour. McGinley, Darren Clarke and Padraig Harrington were the Irish quarter of a European team that upset expectations of a great US victory.

People in many countries experience a sense of national pride when they do well in any international competition. In Ireland, at the end of the twentieth century, that pride seemed special. It was part of believing that we had arrived at some unidentified but desirable destination, of no longer feeling the underdog, of taking our place in the modern world and being able to put others under pressure. But the great public shows of pride betrayed an underlying and continuing insecurity. After all, strategic draws in football games were not really the stunning victories that they sometimes seemed to be at the time. Then there was a hint of anger at Sonia O'Sullivan for 'letting us down' at Atlanta, and more than a hint of displeasure at her earlier decision not to carry the Irish flag during a lap of honour at the World Championships in Sweden. There was the hurrying of Haughey to Paris to bask in the reflected glory of Stephen Roche, and the hitching of the Irish language to Michelle Smith's star, no matter that the Irish State had provided very poor facilities for swimmers and other athletes who harboured sporting ambitions. And there was always a desire to please, to be appreciated as the best football fans, as an island of saints and soccer players. In July 2004, people did not like it when Ray Houghton appeared on *Fantasy Football*, a British comedy TV programme, dressed successively as a leprechaun, a potato and a female member of the cast of *Riverdance*. He did it for a joke, but we were not laughing.

And then there is the GAA. It has bucked the trend towards ever greater commercialisation and professionalisation in sport, by clinging to its admirable affirmation of the value of amateurism. Although it entered into sponsorship deals, it resisted some of the crasser forms of commercialisation that can mar modern sporting occasions. However, it failed to share in the greatest sporting glory of the late 1900s.

During the 1970s and 80s, 'Heffo's army', the Dublin GAA football team that was successfully managed by Kevin Heffernan, captured some of the prevailing mood of sporting jubilation and celebrity. The exploits of Kerry's Páidí Ó Sé and Kilkenny's D. J. Carey, among other managers and players, have been followed with pleasure. Yet, while very many people continue to enjoy GAA football, hurling and camogie, and individual players have had great personal triumphs, the GAA itself somehow lost its place as the great national sporting symbol of Ireland. It yielded, not very gracefully, to a patchwork of other associations and individuals who were prominent internationally. This may have been, at least in part, due to the fact that international events now dominate people's viewing of sport on television. However, it also reflected the manner in which various sporting achievements were interwoven with our changing view of ourselves as potentially successful players on the world stage.

The GAA received generous financial aid from the State for a major reconstruction of Croke Park, but it did not build on its organisational base by opening Ireland's biggest stadium to other sports until 16 April 2005 or by readily dropping its ban on members of the British security forces playing Gaelic games. It had difficulty distinguishing between national pride and nationalist pride.

In his introduction to his book, *A Cut Above the Rest: Irish Sporting Heroes* (Dublin: Town House, 1999), Colm Keane quotes Stephen Roche as saying, 'It is surprising how a country our size can produce so many sporting heroes.' But the public are no longer astonished when Irish people do well at international sporting events. The political defeat of Taoiseach Bertie Ahern's proposals for a new and expensive national stadium at Abbotstown, Co. Dublin (dubbed the

'Bertie Bowl'), reflects the fact that we are not entirely carried away by our continuing enthusiasm for games. Nevertheless, the moments of success which changed our relationship with sport and helped to develop our national self-image, during the past two decades, will be remembered fondly and for many years by those who lived through them.

DRUG SEIZURES

Urlingford, Co. Kilkenny, 8 November 1995

Drug seizures, as well as a series of deaths resulting from drug-taking or drug-dealing, have forced Irish people to recognise the fact that dangerous drugs are a part of Irish society, and have forced citizens to reflect on the extent to which traditional attitudes to consuming alcohol or tobacco are related to the drug problem.

On 8 November 1995, the Gardaí announced what they described as 'the first major drug seizure in Ireland'. They had confiscated 13.5 tonnes of cannabis resin, with an estimated street value of IR£150 million. At first it appeared they had made their seizure near Urlingford, on the Kilkenny-Tipperary border, and the media went there to inspect the scene of the bust. Subsequently, it emerged that the drugs had actually come into the possession of the Gardaí earlier, when an undercover team on board a trawler took delivery of the consignment some 300 miles off the coast of Ireland. The Gardaí then landed the drugs and drove them in a container to the Tipperary-Kilkenny border in the hope of catching members of a criminal gang for whom the consignment was intended. When no criminals turned up, the Gardaí simply announced the seizure as though the consignment had been intercepted on the spot. Customs officials were not amused by the manner in which the matter had been handled. The episode illustrates the complex nature of the fight against drugs.

The Urlingford incident also shows that the sale of cannabis was, already by 1995, big business in Ireland. Some of those who profited from its importation and distribution, or re-exportation, were willing to deal also in harder drugs. During the last quarter of the twentieth century, illegal drugs became a serious problem throughout Ireland.

People had been dabbling in cannabis in Ireland from the 1970s onwards. The type of cannabis then being smoked, usually, was far less potent than some cannabis later sold on the streets. Young people came to believe that warnings about drug abuse were habitually exaggerated or even hysterical, and this made them less inclined than otherwise to heed those who cautioned against substances much more dangerous than pot. By the 1980s, heroin had become a scourge, especially, but not exclusively, in some poorer urban areas. Dublin, in particular, was regarded as a centre of heroin abuse. Those who shared needles came to run a high risk of contracting AIDS from infected blood, especially when some addicts sold their bodies for sex in order to earn the money they needed to buy more drugs.

Anyone who doubted that people at every level of society were taking illegal drugs had their illusions shattered in 1992, when Ben Dunne of Dunnes Stores was arrested, out of his mind on cocaine and balancing on a balcony at his Florida hotel. The terrible way in which heroin, too, could hurt a family of any class was described by Mary Kenny in *Death by Heroin: Recovery by Hope* (New Island, 1999). Her book was written following the death of two of her nephews from drug abuse, within weeks of one another in 1998.

During the 1990s, the drug known as 'ecstasy' became quite attractive to some young people and was associated especially with the clubbing scene. Known as 'E' or 'doves', ecstasy induced a warm glow and allowed its users that drug-induced pleasure of feeling released from everyday worries. A few people died after taking an ecstasy tablet, in some cases their first one ever. Discussion about ecstasy was reminiscent of the debate twenty years earlier about cannabis, in that those who used it argued that the danger from it was exaggerated. They claimed that it did little harm if taken in small quantities and if consumed with plenty of liquids, and they accused the Gardaí and health authorities of hysteria. Ecstasy is still freely available around Ireland at venues that include some nightclubs. It affects the brain long term and is believed to lead to chronic depression.

In 2001, in just one Garda operation on 18 September, fifteen kilogrammes of heroin and 100,000 ecstasy tablets were seized from a car at Lusk, Co. Dublin. The Gardaí estimated that the street value of the drugs seized at Lusk was about €6 million. During 2003, the Gardaí reportedly seized ecstasy worth an estimated €20 million, which was more than the total value of seizures in the previous three years put together. In 2004, they confiscated about one million ecstasy tablets. Research by the National Advisory Committee on Drugs (NACD) suggests that young Irish adults use more ecstasy than their counterparts in some other European countries.

The number of teenage drug abusers is thought to have tripled in Ireland during the 1990s alone. That same decade, there was a reported 50 per cent increase in drug and alcohol addiction in people under the age of 25, and a 50 per cent rise among women.

In August 1999, Dr Catherine Comiskey, commissioned by the Department of Health, estimated that there were in Dublin alone between 10,000 and 14,000 heroin or other opiate users or addicts. She expressed the opinion that one in twenty Dublin males in the 15 to 24-year-old group were using opiates. In 1999, as the century drew to a close, more than 4,000 people were on methadone treatment programmes for drug addiction in the Eastern Health Board area alone. The Gardaí complained about the growing number of crimes being committed by addicts. Further research during 2001 indicated that there were between 14,000 and 15,000 heroin users in Ireland, with all but 2,000 of these in Dublin.

The drug trade has spawned a network of vicious gangs throughout Ireland. These have imported a deadly arsenal of sophisticated weapons, wrapped up as bonuses with their smuggled drugs. The armed gangs threaten the peace and security of the State. From Limerick to Dundalk there have been gang slayings, and the intimidation of witnesses in subsequent trials. When more than six witnesses withdrew their earlier statements during one particular murder trial that collapsed in the Central Criminal Court on 3 November 2003, Mr Justice Paul Carney informed jurors from the bench: 'The likes of what has happened in this case has never, I can assure you, been encountered in this court before.'

The employment of off-duty Gardaí as bouncers at certain venues where ecstasy and other drugs are available has dented confidence in the Gardaí's approach and attitude to the drugs problem.

The widespread availability in Ireland of illegal or dangerous drugs raises questions about our willingness to take action to protect the vulnerable from damaging themselves by abuse, and about our own capacity to be rational when considering the relative dangers of illegal 'soft drugs' and other legal but dangerous substances including tobacco and alcohol. The importation of drugs into Ireland has changed our way of socialising, while at the same time creating serious problems for the Gardaí, the courts and the health services. Drugs also increase the levels of street crime, theft and burglary, as addicts seek ways of paying for their supplies, and drugs bring misery to some of the families of drug-takers. Drug gangs are a cancer that has spread throughout society. When Veronica Guerin was gunned down for reporting on such gangs, politicians vowed that things would change. They did not change extensively or quickly enough to destroy the gangs. Some drugs seized in Ireland were simply *en route* from one foreign country to another, but there remains within the State a large quantity of illegal drugs that are traded by unscrupulous gangs that are making a fortune from their activities.

In 2002, in Dublin alone, nearly 700 new hard drug users went for treatment to the Merchant's Quay centre. And there has been bad news, too, for those who think that soft drugs are harmless. Growing numbers of cannabis users are visiting Irish doctors because of the consequences of taking cannabis long term. In late 2003, the director of Merchant's Quay Ireland (MQI), Tony Geoghegan, said that he was 'greatly concerned by the increased numbers of homeless people and drug users that we are seeing'. The MQI charity offers special services for the homeless and drug users, especially those on heroin. Geoghegan described the situation as 'a clear indication of a failure of government policy to meet the needs of the most marginalised'. But government supporters pointed to the State's increased expenditure on health and social services, including the provision of better treatment facilities for drug abusers throughout Ireland.

About 5,000 of the estimated 14,500 heroin abusers in Ireland are officially recorded as receiving treatment. Others attend doctors who have failed to return long forms to the Health Research Board and some are not getting any treatment. The Health Research Board reports a worrying increase, since 1996, in the proportion of heroin users who inject the highly addictive drug rather than smoke it. This clearly has implications for the spread of HIV/AIDS when users share a needle. While the panic about a possible heroin epidemic in Dublin has peaked and passed, currently available statistics provide no basis for being confident that heroin use in Ireland is in terminal decline. It is associated with the lowest social classes, and is a particular problem for the prison service because many addicts end up there. Ireland did not rate well on a chart of drug use in prison throughout the EU, published in 2003 by the European Monitoring Centre for Drugs and Drug Addiction. On 1 April 2005, having presided in a day over two inquests involving overdoses, the Dublin City Coroner described heroin as 'one of the greatest social problems in our society at the moment'.

Cocaine abuse is on the increase. Crack cocaine, a violence-inducing strain of the drug that is dreaded by Gardaí and health authorities alike, is still quite rarely found. But even ordinary cocaine creates a powerful psychological addiction and is regarded by health authorities as a timebomb waiting to explode.

And anyone not worried by cannabis may be surprised to learn that more than 700 people who were treated for drug-related problems in Ireland in 2000, gave cannabis as their 'main problem drug'. Prolonged use can result in some cases in paranoia and other distressing psychological states, and it is no longer thought that these states are simply uncovered by the drug. Doctors today believe that cannabis itself actually harms some people, and they point out that far more potent strains have come on to the market.

Drug consumption has caused misery to many Irish families, and has bred dangerous gangs. The total value of drugs seized is said to have risen fivefold from 2000 to 2003, when it exceeded €100 million for the first time. During 2004, it again exceeded €100 million. There is a substantial market today for hard drugs. It is one of the unattractive ways in which Ireland has changed.

ETERNAL DOOM?

Christ Church, Dublin, 7 December 1997

It was intended to be a healing moment. President Mary McAleese approached the altar of Christ Church Cathedral and took communion with the other members of a congregation that was largely composed of members of the Church of Ireland. The Roman Catholic Archbishop of Dublin, Desmond Connell, was very displeased by her action and the Irish Catholic hierarchy, in general, let it be known that they did not approve. Father James McEvoy, a professor of philosophy at St Patrick's College, Maynooth, claimed that he would regard it as 'repugnant' if she took communion again at a Church of Ireland ceremony. President McAleese is a Catholic.

Despite decades of ecumenical dialogue and much talk of the need for reconciliation between the two main cultural and religious traditions in Ireland, the Vatican has remained resolutely opposed to Catholics and Protestants sharing the Eucharist as a sign of their common Christian faith. To the authorities in Rome, communion is a sign of union under one Pope. For them, the sharing of the Eucharist must not occur until there is actual union between the different Churches sharing it. In the absence of such unity, intercommunion is currently regarded as 'a sham', as Archbishop Connell later described the President's action at Christ Church.

A significant number of Roman Catholics do not share Rome's view about sharing communion. From theologians to ordinary members of the laity, many Irish people do not agree with their hierarchy that Christians ought to remain divided in this fashion, whatever about their distinctive organisational arrangements. President McAleese warmed the hearts of such people. She herself is not only a committed and practising Catholic but a native of Northern Ireland. There, the two main Christian traditions are especially divided from one another by historical circumstances, and, as children, she and her husband experienced sectarian hatred at first hand. She had been elected as president on a platform that included her strong commitment to building bridges between people, and her decision to take communion at Christ Church was entirely in keeping with that commitment.

President McAleese's active and intelligent form of faith was already a matter of concern to some of the more conservative bishops. These were not reassured by her contact with Buddhists, through her participation in the World Community of Christian Mediation. In 1998, she became the first European Head of State to visit a Buddhist centre when she went to Samye Dzong in Kilmainham, Dublin. That same year, I had the honour of personally conveying a letter from her to His Holiness, the Dalai Lama, which I delivered at an interfaith meeting in Bodh Gaya, India. When he took the envelope from me in a quiet upstairs room of a retreat centre surrounded by fields, he placed his index finger on the embossed harp, the symbol of Ireland, and uttered with a smile the name, 'Frank Aiken'. Aiken had been foreign minister when Ireland became one of only a small number of countries to object strongly to the Chinese invasion of Tibet in the 1950s, and the Tibetans remain grateful for that support.

President McAleese has been discreet and diplomatic about expressing her personal beliefs in public. Following manifestations of the hierarchy's displeasure when she received communion at Christ Church Cathedral, she has not been seen to share communion again with Protestants. Nevertheless, her point was made. It might have appeared unseemly for her as President of Ireland to force a confrontation with the hierarchy of her own Church by flaunting her convictions in the matter and again sharing the Eucharist so publicly.

It is safe to assume that most Irish people approved of what their president did that day in Christ Church. Older citizens recalled a time when their Churches treated each other with contempt and they did not enjoy such memories. Once, Catholics had been forbidden, and were even told it was a sin, to attend ceremonies of another Church, including funerals of their friends or of respected citizens. The *Ne Temere* decree greatly discouraged Protestants from marrying Catholics because of its oppressive imposition of certain conditions in respect of the upbringing of children. The divisions were so petty that even the wording of the English translation of the Lord's Prayer was regarded as significant, with Catholics saying 'Our Father *who* art in Heaven' and Protestants praying 'Our Father *which* art in Heaven'. The laity came to believe that the doctrine of transubstantiation was of crucial importance, with leading Catholics professing to believe that the bread and wine 'really' became the body and blood of Christ, while Protestants supposedly regarded it 'only' as a symbol. In fact, although some clerics fostered black and white pronouncements in the matter, there had actually been from the time of the early Christian Church a wide range of views on the nature of the Eucharist. Modern differences of opinion were fundamentally about the perceived authority of the celebrant, rather than about the dogma of transubstantiation.

In terms of the Irish State's response to such acrimony, a nadir of feebleness had been reached when the first president of Ireland died in July 1949. Douglas Hyde was a scholar and a patriot, but he was also a Protestant. His appointment as a non-partisan president had been intended to send a signal to non-Roman Catholics that the Irish State would not become an exclusive theocracy. However, his funeral was, from a national perspective, a shameful event. Ministers of the interparty government led by John A. Costello, as well as other politicians who were Roman Catholics, were unwilling to enter St Patrick's Cathedral for the service and stayed outside. Inside, near the coffin of Douglas Hyde, was the tomb of Jonathan Swift, political satirist and former dean of St Patrick's. Swift's Latin epitaph suggests that 'savage indignation cannot lacerate his heart' any longer, but his bones must surely have stirred that day. Austin Clarke expressed his own indignation in a poem, 'Burial of an Irish President', that ends with the lines:

Outside.
The hush of Dublin town,
Professors of cap and gown,
Costello, his Cabinet,
In Government cars, hiding

Around the corner, ready
Tall hat in hand, dreading
Our Father in English. Better
Not hear that 'which' for 'who'
And risk eternal doom.

Then, just over 48 years later, Hyde's successor in office wiped away the stain of that memory. Sunday, 7 December 1997, was an important date because President McAleese expressed symbolically the desire of ordinary Irish citizens for reconciliation between the two main Churches in Ireland.

During her first term in office, Mary McAleese and her husband, Martin, devoted much time and effort to building bridges between Catholics and Protestants in Northern Ireland. Unfortunately, three months after she began her second term in October 2004, she made a blunder which alienated some of those Protestants. As she prepared to set out for an official ceremony in Poland to commemorate the sixtieth anniversary of the liberation of Auschwitz concentration camp from the Nazis, she gave a radio interview to RTÉ's *Morning Ireland*, which was transmitted on 27 January 2005. In the course of this, she observed that the Nazis

> gave to their children an irrational hatred of Jews in the same way that people in Northern Ireland transmitted to their children an irrational hatred, for example, of Catholics; in the same way that people give to their children an outrageous and irrational hatred of those who are of different colour and all of those things.

Some Protestants in Northern Ireland immediately reacted angrily, suggesting that she had equated them with Nazis. Despite her use of the qualifying words 'for example' in respect to certain 'people in Northern Ireland', they pointed out that she had not balanced her remarks by also referring to those who bred hatred of Protestants. By the following day, the President realised the full significance of how she had expressed herself and apologised profusely for having spoken 'clumsily'. She acknowledged that she should have 'finished out the example', and her apology was immediately accepted by most of those who had criticised her. However, her words on *Morning Ireland* will not be quickly forgotten in some quarters. They were not untrue in themselves, as she knows only too well from her personal experience growing up in Belfast, but they sounded biased in practice. Had she used the words 'those who are of a different religion', instead of 'Catholic', she could have avoided criticism.

———

Irish Christians have gradually come to understand one another better in the last decades of the twentieth century, due partly to the effects of the Second Vatican Council and to reforms within all the Churches. Ireland itself became a more secular society. A greater number of people than before tend to be intolerant of the intolerant. The long history of denominational education has begun to be considered more critically than hitherto in the Republic of Ireland, with parents themselves founding small but growing numbers of multidenominational schools, and some middle-class Catholics sending their sons and daughters to what had once been exclusively Protestant institutions. In Northern Ireland, the curricula have differed considerably from the schools of one religion to the other, especially in matters of religion and history. However, notwithstanding her choice of words in January 2005, President Mary McAleese demonstrates that it remains possible to be formed within one tradition while coming to appreciate the richness of the other. Her taking of communion at Christ Church was a sign not only of her own maturity, but also of the maturity of the Irish State.

SHOCK AND AWE

New York City, 11 September 2001

'We truly are living the American dream: it's out there, and it's Wal-Mart.'
(Wal-Mart commercial, US television, September 2004)

I am on board a night-flight, rising steadily over New York City and bound for Ireland. As the Continental Airlines Boeing climbs out of Newark, New Jersey, it is impossible not to think of those unfortunate passengers who took off from this same airport, more than three years earlier, only to have their journey end in disaster. Their jet was hijacked and, after a struggle between passengers and hijackers, crashed in Pennsylvania. That same morning, two other hijacked planes ploughed into the Twin Towers of the World Trade Center on Manhattan, while a fourth hit the Pentagon. It was a series of moments that changed not only the United States of America but the whole world.

Since 11 September 2001, Ireland has had to reassess its relationship with the USA, which at present is the sole 'great power' in the world. The Irish State may have shrugged off many of the heavier harnesses of London and the Vatican, but it is restrained today by new political and cultural ties. Maintaining an even course between our US friends and our EU partners is not easy. The Irish government has also had to calculate how to negotiate the growing tensions between Islamic states and western countries, and to keep in favour with rising new powers such as China. We have come to understand better how much we depend on the global economy for continuing economic growth, and how much of that dependence is fuelled especially by US dollars. If the proud independence of this State's early decades was marked by poverty and thrift, the hallmark of our later prosperity has been our growing dependence on a relatively lush lifestyle and on US investment. Culturally, the influence of Rome has gradually been superseded by that of Hollywood.

On a personal level, the events of 11 September 2001 (or '9/11' as they quickly became known colloquially from the US style of dating) have also had a psychological impact on many Irish people. Their sensational nature was especially shocking because the USA had hitherto seemed so distant from most of the troubles that touch the rest of the world, and their impact was amplified by the fact that dreadful images of the attacks were both transmitted live and then repeated innumerable times on television. The attacks on the Twin Towers have reminded us of our vulnerability to the vagaries of politics and ideology, and of our mortality in general. Although Irish people have lived through decades of violence connected to the conflict in Northern Ireland, what happened that day in New York seemed to be in a league of its own. It exposed us, through real time broadcasting, to the realities of a world in which hatred has continued to thrive even while the earth's population expands exponentially. Greater numbers of people than ever before live in proximity to one another, with the remaining distances between them being foreshortened by technology and communications. Where the US government's 'Manhattan Project' had once yielded terrible destruction at Hiroshima and Nagasaki, one felt at least that the concentration of such atomic weaponry in the hands of states was some kind of guarantee against its reckless deployment. Now, however, al-Qaeda's Manhattan project has brought home to people the real possibility of anyone such as Osama bin Laden organising a catastrophic attack on a nuclear power plant, or even using some kind of nuclear, chemical or biological weapon directly against a civilian population. We are living, as the Jewish-American illustrator Art Spiegelman puts it, 'in the shadow of no towers'.

The US response to world affairs since 9/11 has challenged the confidence of those who believe that the prospects of a peaceful world order are best ensured through the deals and admittedly imperfect practices of the United Nations. Down the years since joining it, Ireland has played an enthusiastic role within that organisation, and has participated in many of its peace-keeping operations in places such as the Congo, Cyprus and East Timor. This constructive, secular activism of our armed forces followed a long period when Irish Christian missionaries, in addition to preaching to and converting people in other lands, helped to build up educational and social services abroad. Ireland's reputation in the world has been further enhanced by the charitable activities of aid organisations and prominent individuals in the entertainment industry, most notably the singers Bono of U2 and Bob Geldof, who have helped to raise the level of international awareness about global poverty and inequality. Assistance from the Irish government and donations from private Irish charities to people in need abroad have matched or surpassed those of very many other nations, relative to the size of our economy. However, during 2004, the Irish government appeared to falter in its commitment to foreign aid and seemed set to renege on an earlier long-term target. Some saw this as an indication that Ireland's heart was hardening and worried that we were becoming more selfish, even as we became richer. However, the Irish response to the catastrophic tidal-wave (tsunami) that killed more than 250,000 people in Asia, on 26 December 2004, was spontaneous, generous and heartening.

As the USA dealt brusquely with the United Nations in the aftermath of 9/11, states found themselves under pressure to 'come on side' in Washington. During the years of the Clinton presidency, Irish politicians had enjoyed easy access to the White House, and Bill Clinton took such a warm interest in Ireland that the Irish readily forgave him his personal trespasses. The economy boomed, while Clinton pushed forward the Northern Ireland Peace Process in a way that was over and beyond his normal duties as US President. That comfortable transatlantic relationship was disrupted by the election of a Republican president, George W. Bush, who had little interest in Ireland. It was further upset by the attack on the World Trade Center. As US forces invaded Afghanistan, whose government had long played host to al-Qaeda, an increasing number of US aircraft en route to the war zone refuelled at Shannon. It had long been the practice that US military aircraft were discreetly refuelled at Shannon, notwithstanding Ireland's status as a neutral state, but growing international tension now highlighted the anomalous nature of that practice. With the prospect of an imminent US-led invasion of Iraq, following the conquest of Afghanistan, Irish people took to the streets in large numbers to protest against war. On 15 February 2003, an anti-war protest in Dublin was the largest demonstration of its kind

seen in the capital for decades. It coin
demonstrations around the globe.

On 20 March 2003, the USA and its allie
Iraq, claiming incorrectly that Iraq p
destruction (WMD) and pummelling Ba
in a strategy that Washington had dubbe
earlier, Taoiseach Bertie Ahern tri
simultaneously as anti-war and supportiv
Airport. He resorted to an imaginative interpretation of UN
and Irish precedent to ensure that US investors would not be alienated and that the US government would continue to regard Ireland as relatively friendly. Indeed, during the war in Iraq, it happened to be Ireland's turn to take over the running of the EU Presidency and EU President Bertie Ahern found himself welcoming President George W. Bush to Dromoland Castle for a two-day EU–US summit, on 25 and 26 June 2004. Earlier in June, Ahern as current EU President had flown to the G8 summit on Sea Island, Georgia, USA, in what one local commentator described as 'a very small Irish jet' (actually the official government transport), where his appearance in yellow trousers and light jacket alongside the more soberly clad world leaders elicited some criticism at home.

The onslaught on Iraq seemed calculated not just to impress Iraqis with the power of the United States. Operation 'Shock and Awe' was a clear indication of the fact that those who were considered to pose a threat to the USA faced a range of consequences. That these consequences would not necessarily depend on the approval of any international body, or be consistent with the standard interpretation of international law, became patently clear when US forces abused their prisoners in Iraq and elsewhere. There were even allegations that aircraft carrying such prisoners were refuelled at Shannon. This was deeply depressing for those who had always regarded the USA as ultimately a guarantor of freedom and liberty, whatever that big country's other faults. Coming after the controversial US Supreme Court decision to validate the election of George W. Bush as President, and linked with the new US administration's negative attitude towards environmental and other international agreements, it served to remind us that the world is a volatile place at the start of the twenty-first century. However, complicating concerns about the direction of US policy was a nagging realisation of the potential for serious errorist organisations. That potential was actualised with t when, on 11 March 2004, bombs on board trains in Madrid ered 191 people and seriously injured many more.

s a measure of our anxiety about the future that the anti-war timent evident on the streets of Dublin before the invasion of Iraq did not discernibly become a significant political liability for the Irish government. The Taoiseach may have performed an ungraceful balancing act in sitting on the fence between protesters and people willing to see Shannon used as a refuelling base, but it seems that our fear of the impact of international terrorism and our appreciation of the value of US investment in Ireland ultimately made us ambivalent about protesting too loudly and too long. It is estimated that, since 9/11, more than 400,000 US military personnel have stopped at Shannon on their way to or from their overseas postings. Yet, street protests against globalisation and US foreign policy, occurring outside both the EU enlargement conference at the Phoenix Park, Dublin, on 1 May 2004, and the EU-US summit at Dromoland Castle, the following month, were small and relatively insignificant compared to the huge demonstration during 2003. This was partly because war in Iraq was now an accomplished fact, but it also reflected a widespread appreciation of what was at stake politically and economically. Proclaiming neutrality does not mean that we can remove ourselves from political realities.

Another important factor in the changing political climate has been the continuing, if reduced, influence of London in Irish affairs. Northern Ireland remains fully part of the United Kingdom. Now, as Prime Minister Tony Blair became the most loyal ally of President George W. Bush in western Europe, there was deep concern in Dublin that the government of the Republic of Ireland might suffer a serious reduction in its ability to persuade Washington of any course of action in Northern Ireland that Blair did not first wholly and enthusiastically support. More indirectly, increasing US intolerance of terrorism after 9/11 meant that there was a new level of pressure on the IRA to decommission its weapons and on Sinn Féin to disown the IRA if such decommissioning did not take place. When the robbery of more than UK£24 million from the Northern Bank's headquarters in Belfast, on 20 December 2004, was blamed by both the Irish and UK governments on the IRA, and when Taoiseach Bertie Ahern alleged that some leading members of Sinn Féin knew in advance of that robbery, the delicate fictions and balances that had helped sustain the peace process in its earlier phases no longer seemed tenable. Early in 2005 as growing evidence of serious criminality by members of the IRA emerged, Sinn Féin came under pressure to abandon the IRA or to face a loss of support on both sides of the Atlantic Ocean for its continued inclusion in political dialogue with other parties. US suspicions about Sinn Féin's behaviour had not been allayed by the arrest, and conviction in 2004, of three IRA/Sinn Féin men who had entered Colombia on false passports and who allegedly gave assistance to FARC guerrillas there. While the political influence of Sinn Féin had been growing both north and south of the Irish border during the peace process, the IRA had not gone away. It will be a long time before the other political parties can trust the words of Sinn Féin as much as they had been inclined to do. Those who never trusted Sinn Féin felt vindicated by the revelations of continuing criminality on the part of members of the IRA.

We are now part of an international culture, in a way that seemed inconceivable for much of the twentieth century. Not only have the restraints of cautious censorship long been discarded, allowing us to read books and see films that once would have been banned outright, but people travel abroad as never before. Meanwhile, visitors and migrant workers flow into Ireland in unprecedented numbers. However, while shops selling the produce of China or Nigeria or eastern Europe are found in city streets, the urban landscape has changed more notably in the cultural direction of Britain and the United States. Leading Irish shops have given way to branches of UK outlets, with Main Street in Ireland looking more than ever like High Street in England. New roads, chain stores, fast-food franchises and sprawling housing estates are just some of the manifestations of a continuing transformation, and it seems to my eye that Ireland today more closely resembles the United States than it did when I first visited America in the early 1970s. The cultural influence of US movies and TV series has certainly not diminished, while work practices and lifestyle choices now seem closer to Boston than they previously did. Because of decades of emigration to the United States, Irish people have long had a warm regard for that country and a sense that our people were generally more welcome there than in Britain. Growing wealth at home has allowed us to acquire many of the trappings of affluence that our emigrants found in the USA and that we admired.

From the 1950s onwards, industrialisation attracted US investors and managers to our shores. Our public adulation of Bill Clinton was a manifestation of our love affair with 'the American way of life' that was most innocently evident when JFK 'came home'.

———

We may criticise the USA from time to time, allowing ourselves to believe that we have a culturally superior society, but in the past half-century we have embraced capitalism as an economically and socially liberating force. This embrace has had consequences not only for our neutrality but also for our economy and our environment. No longer do we regard agriculture as the bedrock of our prosperity, having found jobs for many of our workforce in productive industries. Even more recently, we are coming to depend on the services sector for growth. Whether or not it is wise to become removed from our land and reliant on activities that are contingent on wealth being generated elsewhere to support such services is not a question to which most people, at present, care to give a great deal of thought. Nor do most people translate their worries about the impact on the environment of recent developments, including such phenomena as the big increase in the number of vehicles on our roads or the plethora of one-off rural housing, into political policies that result in significant changes of lifestyle. Ireland signed up to the Kyoto Protocol on greenhouse gas emissions but, immediately, proceeded to breach our set targets and make our very own contribution to global warming. We criticise the British for keeping Sellafield open and the Americans for being gas-guzzlers, but deep-seated anxieties about possible environmental catastrophes do not deter us from a lifestyle that is globally unsustainable. We are busy aligning the Irish dream with the American dream, driving our children at weekends to McDonald's or to some shopping mall. It would be no surprise to find one of our major supermarket chains being absorbed overnight into the Wal-Mart retailing empire.

Postscript

Ireland has changed, and the moments that changed us in recent decades were many and varied. Some of the significant moments discussed above were especially important. Our decision to join the European Union, for example, has brought in its train considerable economic, social and other benefits. Our acceptance of the Belfast (Good Friday) Agreement means that, today, at least officially, each of the main traditions on both sides of the border enjoy parity of esteem. Our creation of greater national wealth now attracts foreigners to work in Ireland, while we consciously highlight the positive aspects of new immigration. On formal occasions, one frequently hears diversity and multiculturalism being celebrated.

At the same time, people worry that old ways may simply be abandoned or eradicated regardless of their possible continuing merit. We fear that 'dumbed-down' entertainment and media industries are coarsening the public's aesthetic, ethical and political sensibilities. Moreover, if Irish men and women are asking big questions about the meaning of their lives, many are doing so quietly and privately. For, while insecurities and fears have been mounting internationally during the opening years of the new millennium, in Ireland there has also been a continuing loss of confidence in old forms of religious reassurance. In what is still a predominantly Catholic country, attendance at Mass has been steadily falling for some time and many younger people show little outward sign of any interest in the faith of their fathers and mothers. The main Protestant churches have also had to contend with disenchantment. Furthermore, the scandal of clerical sexual abuse has changed even older Catholics' attitudes towards an institution that had once seemed inseparable from the Irish State. A series of referenda further forced people to make practical decisions about divorce and abortion that conflicted with the advice of Catholic bishops. A steeply declining number of 'vocations' to the priesthood has meant that the structure of the Irish Catholic Church must be radically altered in the near future if it is to continue to function. A large number of people retain an interest in spiritual matters, as reflected in the sales of books of a general spiritual nature, but the power of the Catholic hierarchy in Ireland is unlikely ever again to be what it was for most of the twentieth century. We are still capable of surprising ourselves with our affection for old religious ideas and readings, while at the same time having our feet firmly planted on the ground when it comes to rejecting ecclesiastical influences that were once almost irresistible.

Where many Irish grandparents once ended their nightly Rosary by reciting the *Salve regina*, turning to Mary as the 'poor banished children of Eve', their grandchildren turn on the telly and retreat into a form of electronic consolation. Our hearts may still 'send up our sighs, mourning and weeping, in this valley of tears', but we seem less sure than ever before that anyone is listening to us. Eating the apple of relative prosperity we have become worldly wise, but the world that we see on our television screens and on our streets does not seem to be particularly blessed. Some people welcome the shuffling off of religious trappings, many of which had possibly outlived their usefulness in the forms in which they existed, but others retain nagging doubts about the loss of powerful traditions and alternative sources of personal and communal strength in the face of oppressive forces in the world.

So, was our old religious culture largely a verdant cloak under which we hid our insecurities while harbouring more profane ambitions? Was Beatrice Elvery showing us something about ourselves that we were not ready to see a century ago? In 1907, she painted *Éire*. She did so at a time when the nationalist movement was gathering momentum, when it was supported by a widening range of people including Catholics and Protestants, farmers and industrialists. In her painting, Elvery (sometime Lady Glenavy) depicts Ireland as a seated and hooded woman, 'Kathleen ni

Houlihan', apparently rooted firmly in the past. A dark Celtic cross both supports her back and anchors her, while behind this stands a ghostly crowd of martyrs, patriots, saints and scholars. They are reproachful models of purity and service. At Mother Ireland's feet huddle disproportionately smaller men and women, suggesting in both their nakedness and size the miserable victims of successive Irish famines and war. Éire clearly bears the burden of history. Yet, it is the child on her lap who, above all, catches our attention. He is bathed in a warm light that emanates from a point outside the canvas, ahead of him. That light is reflected onto Mother Ireland's lower face and painted lips, while her eyes remain cast down and shrouded in shadows. The naked babe is larger and more robust than any of the wretched, cowering figures at his mother's feet. He is stretching his right hand and body towards us, in a gesture that is assertive and acquisitive, pert and precocious. This painting may appear at first to be a pastiche of images of the Virgin and Child from earlier times but Éire's infant is scarcely the humble baby Jesus. Although his genitals are discreetly out of sight, he seems about to leap forward fearlessly and seize the future. If one were to associate the spirit of any animal with this infant, who is presumably young Ireland, it would surely be that of the tiger.

Notwithstanding the fact that a life-force evidently courses through the veins of Elvery's male creature, her 'rather banal and sentimental picture' (as she herself described it) elicited a desire for self-sacrifice in some quarters. The painting was purchased by Maud Gonne and donated to St Enda's, which was Patrick Pearse's school in Dublin. This was the same Pearse who would lose his life in the rebellion of 1916, but who earlier showed a keen grasp of practical details when he wrote letters to my grandfather, a Dublin advertising agent, listing local merchants whom he believed could be persuaded to buy space in his school's magazine. Elvery was later horrified when one of the overwrought pupils at St Enda's declared that the painting inspired him 'to die for Ireland', through some peculiar conflation of its divergent elements.*

While the new State partly owed its existence to the self-sacrifice of Pearse and others who died fighting for political freedom, it later came to depend on less clearly heroic activities for its growth and

* Beatrice Lady Glenavy, '*Today we will only gossip*' (Constable: London, 1964), p. 91.

prosperity. Like Elvery's blond child, the Irish were eventually to leap from the page of history and grasp the moment in all its glory. We now enjoy the fruits of material progress that we harvested as a people in the last decades of the twentieth century, even as we have abandoned old certainties. We recoil when an attack such as '9/11' reminds us of our mortality and vulnerability. We cannot find ease or rest in older and formulaic explanations of the human condition, if ever we did.

It seems appropriate to discover that Beatrice Elvery was a friend and neighbour of the young Samuel Beckett, who modelled as a kneeling child for her sister, Dorothy.* Like young Beckett, during the twentieth century, Ireland lost its cultural innocence. However, we did not all share Beckett's courage in literally and metaphorically joining the resistance to new forms of oppression and inauthenticity. Many of us have settled simply for pleasures in life that our ancestors never enjoyed, even as we suspect that they had consolations and delights of a kind that may escape us in our frequently overwrought existences: and we are not so removed from our past that we are unable to fear for the future of our children in a world that is scarcely less materialist or aggressive than it ever was.

Yet, few of us would choose to turn the clock back. We feel that, for all of its imperfections, the Republic of Ireland has achieved at least some of the potential that this State's founders believed awaited it. A tree of economic growth was planted and nurtured slowly in the decades after World War II, following an earlier period of trial and error. Within ten year's of the State publishing its 'First Programme for Economic Expansion', in 1958, it was evident that Ireland was already changing radically. The 1960s soon came to be regarded as a pivotal period in modern Ireland. In *The Best of Decades: Ireland in the 1960s* (Gill & Macmillan: Dublin, 1984), Fergal Tobin later wrote that, 'Ireland had learned a lot about itself in ten years. It had emerged from the secure childhood of the Gaelic myth into the noisy adult world of cosmopolitan consumer capitalism.' We are still working through the consequences of our shift in national and personal identities, and the moments that changed us since 1970 have frequently reflected that fact.

* ibid., p. 48 and opposite p. 160 for the photograph of Beckett, kneeling by his mother's knee, that Dorothy took, from which she worked for two paintings (see Dorothy Kay, *The Elvery family: a memory*, ed. Marjorie Reynolds (Carrefour Press: Cape Town, 1991), pp. 37, 40–41 for 'Twins' and 'Child at prayer').

We even dare to believe that, notwithstanding setbacks, the people of Northern Ireland are now embarked on a course of action that will ultimately transcend the worst moments of recent rivalry and allow both of the main traditions to co-exist more constructively than before.

We recognise that we may never be free of new types of venality and selfishness, which are recurrent features of the human condition, but we are confident that Irish society has really improved. While suffering and injustice take new forms in every generation, and poverty has not been eliminated, Ireland generally seems to have changed for the better in our lifetimes.

We do not expect the island to be predominantly Irish-speaking anytime soon, but we respect the place of the Irish language in the complex web of our island's identity. We welcome the diversity that immigration brings, while not wishing to open our borders to anyone and everyone who desires to share our recent good fortune. We enjoy the fruits of this State's new wealth, while knowing that many inhabitants of the world have far less than us. We are not guaranteed the impossibility of returning one day to the sorts of hardship and frugality with which most of our ancestors were very familiar, but embrace our good fortune while it lasts.

It may be said, with some justification, that the moments that changed us during the past few decades have made us more sure of ourselves while, at the same time, leaving us somewhat less sure of who we are.

Take heed lest you forget the Lord your God, by not keeping his commandments and his ordinances and his statutes, which I command you this day: lest, when you have eaten and are full, and have built goodly houses and live in them, and when your herds and flocks multiply, and your silver and gold is multiplied, and all that you have is multiplied, then your heart be lifted up, and you forget the Lord your God, who brought you out of the land of Egypt, out of the house of bondage, who led you through the great and terrible wilderness, with its fiery serpents and scorpions and thirsty ground where there was no water, who brought you water out of the flinty rock, who fed you in the wilderness with manna which your fathers did not know, that he might humble you and test you, to do you good in the end. Beware lest you say in your heart, 'My power and the might of my hand have gotten me this wealth.'

(DEUTERONOMY 8: 11–17)

INDEX

Acknowledgments

The publishers wish to thank the following for the use of copyright material:

R Dardis Clarke, 17 Oscar Square, Dublin 8 for 'Burial of an Irish President' from *The Collected Poems of Austin Clarke* (Dolmen Press, 1974).

Paul Durcan, for 'She Mends an Ancient Wireless' from *Teresa's Bar* (Gallery Press, 1976).

Dennis O'Driscoll. 'The Celtic Tiger' is taken from *Dennis O'Driscoll: New and Selected Poems* published by Anvil Press Poetry, 2004.

Micheal O'Siadhail, for 'Three Charms' from *Micheal O'Siadhail, Poems 1975–1995* (Bloodaxe Books, 1999).

The publishers have made every effort to trace copyright holders, but if they have inadvertently overlooked any, they will be pleased to make the necessary arrangements at the first opportunity.

WICKED LOVELY

a Marr** has never been good at choosing just path. After finishing high school with the dubious ıonour of being voted "most likely to end up in jail", she went to college for a degree and then postgraduate research. There curiosity (and tuition bills) led her to the dual jobs of teaching and slinging drinks at a biker bar. During the daylight hours, she indulged in long literary chats; at night, she lingered with intriguing people with one word names.

Eventually, she went on to bartend at a number of other weird little bars, teach literature both live and online, and discover the joy of being under the tattoo gun. All three have been great rushes. The latter borders on addiction, but is held in check by the desire to attend the opera without flashing too many tats.

After marrying someone who shares her love of ink – on the page and on the skin – Melissa began moving around the country. In the process, she discovered how vast the Mojave really is, how many incredible museums are out there, and how hard it can be to think about settling in one place. She's continued teaching along the way, but traded beer-slinging for book writing.